WHERE ANGELS DARED TO TREAD

WHERE ANGELS DAR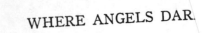

WHERE ANGELS
DARED TO TREAD

SOCIALIST & COMMUNIST UTOPIAN
COLONIES IN THE UNITED STATES

By

VICTOR FRANCIS CALVERTON

Essay Index Reprint Series

BOOKS FOR LIBRARIES PRESS
FREEPORT, NEW YORK

STANDARD BOOK NUMBER:
8369-0009-X

LIBRARY OF CONGRESS CATALOG CARD NUMBER:
68-57309

PRINTED IN THE UNITED STATES OF AMERICA

To

ERNEST SUTHERLAND BATES,

my greatest friend.

Preface

This book is concerned with an aspect of American life hitherto largely neglected, the socialist and communist utopian colonies established in so many parts of the country. Many endured a long time; none survive today. These colonies were of two varieties, religious and economic, and their social ideals were generally similar.

Both types sought to create a new way of life, a new world; and thereby gave birth to some of the most striking conditions to be found in the United States. Unlike the average frontiersman, who never cared about colonial life but went out to get as much land as possible, indifferent to the number of Indians killed in the effort, all these utopians respected both Indians and Negroes, and all other racial minorities.

Their economic aspiration was to create a new communist commonwealth—one of the most difficult things in the world to achieve. Their religious ideal was literal Christianity. If none succeeded in terms of today, it was not from lack of enthusiasm or zeal. The American environment was hostile, but they struggled on with all the power at their command.

This book describes their struggles and attempts a dynamic interpretation of their achievements.

Contents

For weeks before George (V. F. Calverton) died he frequently said to me "If anything happens to me, I'd like Alec Hammerslough to edit my book, "Where Angels Dared to Tread." Alec had already read the manuscript and offered many valuable suggestions. George would have taken this opportunity to have acknowledged Alec Hammerslough's generous help and intelligent comments on the manuscript.

In the weeks that followed George's death Alec worked tirelessly preparing the completed manuscript for the publishers, reading proof, and cooperating in the myriad ways that were necessary because of George's absence.

I wish to thank Alec Hammerslough in George's name and my own for all he has done to prepare this book for publication. I could not have done it without him.

NINA MELVILLE CALVERTON

WHERE ANGELS DARED TO TREAD

CHAPTER I

The Better Life—An American Dream

"At this very day the poor people are forced to work for 4 d. and corn is dear. And the tithing-priest stops their mouth and tells them that 'inward satisfaction of mind' was meant by the declaration, 'the poor shall inherit the earth.' I tell you the scripture is to be really and materially fulfilled. . . . You jeer at the name Leveller. I tell you Jesus Christ was the Head Leveller. . . . The day of judgment is begun . . . the poor people you oppress shall be the saviors of the land . . . and break to pieces the bands of property."

WINSTANLEY

"We are all a little wild here with numberless projects of social reform. Not a reading man but has a draft of a new community in his waistcoat pocket."

RALPH WALDO EMERSON

From every civilized part of the earth men have come to America in search of a better life. For centuries life promised more in the new world than in the old. If ofttimes that promise was not fulfilled, it was fulfilled often enough to convert it into a belief, a vital legend. Legends are not spun out of mist; they are not the inventions of poets, but the outgrowths of experience congealed in symbolic form.

Multitudes came to America, lived here, and found it livable. Many failed, but also many succeeded. And more and more came through the years, the generations, and the centuries. They came from every nation, costumed in every garb, speak-

13

ing many tongues, worshiping different gods, but all clinging to the same aspiration.

They were, in the main, members of the persecuted and hungry classes. Whether, as in the beginning, they were English Roundheads or Shortheads, Palatinian Germans, Dutch Evangelicals, gold-seeking Spaniards or madcap Portuguese, Scotch-Irish Dissenters, Huguenot or Catholic French, or, as later, pig-tailed Chinese, blunt-nosed Japanese, dark-faced Egyptians and Turks, or lonely Armenians, they were driven mainly by the same hope. They all wanted a better world— and there was no better world in their eyes than the new world: America.

North America has proved for several centuries to be the most habitable and happy environment for white men. (It would be unfair and untrue to say that it ultimately proved as much for the red men who were exterminated by white endeavor.) White men thrived in America. They found a place where it was possible to work, build, achieve, create.

Although most white men came to America for the same reason, to better the way they lived in the old world, they had different theories about how that betterment could be accomplished. Some of them thought of it in terms of religion, others as a means of escape from political oppression, and still others as a refuge from imprisonment. Whatever the terms, America was a way out, a paradise to be attained. All shared the same dream: escape.

Escape from an old world to a new!

Utopian Seekers

Among the multiplying masses of people who descended upon this country from every land, there were many who came for purely idealistic reasons. Little has been said about them. They were seekers not only after the new world, but also after new worlds of their own creation. Unlike the Pilgrims and the Puritans, who were spiritually idealistic but economically materialistic, these utopian groups strove to harmonize their social life with their religious concepts. They were utopians who believed it possible for man to live differently, organize his existence after a different economic and social pattern.

The earliest were "primitive" Christians who had believed in the apostolic way of life of Christ and his disciples, which was that of communism practiced on a simple but comprehensive scale. Later came the economic utopians who were interested in communism more as a social than as a religious doctrine, and who constructed their colonies upon what they considered a scientific rather than a spiritual foundation. After them, utopianism died—or at least the utopian approach in which they had believed. The energies which had gone into this creation were redirected into class channels, with socialism, communism, anarchism, and syndicalism as their philosophic embodiments.

New World Favors New Ideas

These ideas born in the old world were applied in the new. It was impossible to practice utopian ideals in the old world. When attempted by the Waldenses and Albigenses, the Cathari and the Taborites, resulting in communities and even cities being converted into communist centers, they met with persecution, attack, and annihilation. The old world was against them. The new world, on the other hand, afforded them an opportunity for expression and expansion.

In fact, the new world was truly new not only because it was newly discovered, but also because it provided a shelter for the new dreams which had been suppressed in the old. Space gave that newness infinite possibilities. Men could escape the heavy hand of old-world authority, translate principles into practice, beliefs into realities, initiate enterprises, inaugurate plans and projects, which would have been inconceivable in the old world. Longitude and latitude favored the hopes and dreams of those who came to realize their fulfillment. Unoccupied territory, untracked wilderness, made everything possible. Never before had men discovered such a rare and rich opportunity to test their hopes, explore their potentialities, realize their aspirations.

Only a new land, uncharted, unclaimed, and unowned by white men, made that practicable.

It was not difficult for the new colonists to adjust themselves to the individualistic way of life encouraged by the environment. They had been accustomed to it in Europe and had a far greater opportunity to extend it in America. What was difficult was to cultivate in an environment conducive to individualism a way of life that was communistic—and that was what the early utopians attempted to do in this land.

The communism these early utopians practiced was not the kind prevalent today in the Soviet Union, which is only putatively a communist state. In Soviet Russia, which is still an agrarian country striving to become industrial, communism is an ideal but not a reality. No more equality exists there today than in the United States. Differences in income remain, differences in social station continue, differences in ways of living, dress, travel, possessions persist. The old methods of competition are encouraged under different guises. Wage differentials are almost as marked there as with us.

COMMUNISM IN PRACTICE

Among the American utopian colonies no such differences were tolerated. They were truly communistic in every sense of the word. They not only believed in communism but also believed in practicing it. Any individual who failed to practice it was excommunicated and exiled. They had no laws except unwritten ones which were more sacred than written ones. They had no prisons because they had no reason for them. There was nothing to steal since no one possessed more than anyone else; there was no reason to kill since no one could find a reason for homicide. Everything was shared; no one was destitute. Whatever economic and sexual deprivation existed among some of the groups was socially imposed and no individual was forced to belong to any, if they were antagonistic to his personal philosophy.

These utopians were zealots, fanatics, visionaries, but at the same time they knew what they wanted and knew how to get it. American history is replete with the records of groups, companies, organizations, and even colonies who sought many things, fought with governors, proprietors, and kings in order to attain them; but their fights were all for greater advantages, greater opportunities to exploit the land in which they had settled. Such fights never occurred among the early utopian colonies. They were not interested in governors, proprietors, or kings. They disdained them. They were interested only in the Lord, in Jesus the Redeemer, and in the preservation and perpetuation of their lives in such a way as would lead them into the vineyards of eternity. They believed in the Bible, believed in it as a holy thing, believed in it and its doctrines as something to be lived up to, observed, practiced.

Part of the American Dream

These groups dreamed of an America in which men might be able to carve out the contours of a new society—a society which should be co-operative and not competitive, communal and not individualistic. They were not all of America, but they were an important part of it and their philosophy represents as much of the American dream as the competitive philosophy of the rest of the country.

America cannot be understood without understanding their role in its making, for it very well may be that ultimately, before this century is ended, it will be their philosophy, and not the individualistic one, which shall triumph.

CHAPTER II

The Labadists: Utopia in Torso

"So great was the fame of this Society [Labadists] that there was scarce any place in these countries where there was not talk about these Teachers and Workers so that in foreign Countries there was scarce anywhere, unless it were among such People who have no regard to what is done abroad, who had not heard something of them."

GERARD CROESE, 1696

"He, Jacob I. Van Beber, was formerly a Mennonite, but [in order to become a Labadist] he desires to depart with his whole house, to acknowledge and abandon the follies, scandals, shortcomings, and stains of his former religion."

PENNSYLVANIA MAGAZINE, XI, 440

Seventeenth-century Europe was filled with groups, sects, denominations, inspired with the high idealism of co-operative enterprise and socialist endeavor. They were sprinkled over various parts of the European and American landscape, diverse and devious as the Chinese alphabet. Each was unique in itself, pristinely singular, passionately religious. They belonged to that eternal struggle waged by man to reconcile his aspirations with realities.

Their founders were men of dreams, men dedicated to a Christian, not a Churchian, concept of life, men who wanted to make the earth paradisaical before the sons of Adam reached paradise. They believed in men and not in things, in ideals and not in possessions. Man could become good, they were convinced, if he lived in the way Christ commanded, humbly, simply, everyone sharing with everyone else, as Christ did with the multitude by the sea.

Among those who inspired such ideals were great preachers whose voices roared like the lion of Judah up and down the highways and byways of post-medieval Europe, invaded the homes of people, summoned them forth, and spurred them to battle. They were the dream-intoxicated prophets of the new era. There had been John Ball, the communist cleric, almost three centuries earlier, who awakened the English countryside, and who was far more important than any others of his time in disseminating doctrines of apostasy; there was the Anabaptist, Thomas Münzer, who, in the early sixteenth century, gave revolutionary meaning to the fight against the forces of Martin Luther, but Luther finally had Münzer decapitated; earlier still, there had been Johann Huss, a spiritual descendant of Wyclif, who had died at the stake, but whose ideas and ideals had given birth to new organizations of life in many parts of Europe.

Among them was the simple priest, Jean Labadie, whose theories terrified the Catholic oligarchy, provoked attacks upon the Labadists, and resulted in the foundation of Labadist colonies in Holland and later in America. It is with this new-world experiment that we are mainly concerned. Although not so great as Wyclif or Huss, or so internationally renowned as Luther, Jean Labadie was more advanced in his economic outlook than any of them. Returning to the apostolic ideal, he insisted upon the equality of all men, and urged the necessity of a communist system of society.

The Protestant leaders were born of the upsurge of spirit which grew out of the peasant revolts of the sixteenth century. They were representative of an economic conflict of which many of them were unaware. The puristic nature of their Christianity inevitably allied them with the peasants rather than with the proprietors.

Upon numerous occasions during the Middle Ages the

Church as well as the aristocracy had been driven to violence
to suppress various expressions of recalcitrancy on the part
of the peasants. At St. Valery, for instance, the mob burned
down the door of the church and destroyed the images and the
altars, in protest against ecclesiastical exploitation. Toward
the end of the fifteenth century such protests became part of a
tremendous mass movement. The peasant revolt in Holland
in 1491, followed by those in upper Suabia and Frisia, broke
the ground for the spread of other larger movements, the
Union Shoe, and the *Poor Konrad*, which culminated in
the Peasants' War.

THE BEGGAR KINGS

The *Union Shoe*, whose name was derived from the peasant
shoe as a revolutionary symbol, survived every form of attack
and suppression for over twenty years, and under the
leadership of Joss Fritz, who engineered its secret organization and directed the "beggar kings" who promoted its operations, it made a direct threat against state power, and was defeated only after years of continuous combat and persecution.
The conspiracy which passed under the name of *Poor Konrad*
was scarcely less menacing to the ruling class. In the peasant
revolt which sprang up in Hungary, during the crusade against
the Turks, and which was led by Dozsa, all the sadistic ferocity
of the aristocracy and *bourgeoisie* revealed itself in the ampu-
tation of noses and ears and the general disemboweling and
impaling of thousands of peasants who were captured in battle.
It was from this widespread mass unrest that the momentum
of the *Reformation* was derived. On the one side raged the
strife between the Civil State and the Papacy, and on the other
the struggle of the peasants against both clergy and nobility
flamed forth, challenging the whole economic system, with
its ecclesiastical as well as civil rulers, and threatening to
uproot it in order to create a new and more just one. The
peasant revolts, like the Peasants' War, revolved about the right

of the peasants to a resurrected communistic Christianity. Their economic opposition to the ruling class, aristocratic as well as ecclesiastic, gathered its dynamic, emotional hostility from their hatred for the debased and distorted form of Christianity practiced by the wealthier classes.

JEAN DE JESUS CHRIST LABADIE
BORN 1610; DIED 1674

Jean Labadie, who in his later years called himself Jean de Jesus Christ Labadie, was one of the most interesting and galvanic leaders of the epoch. He was a simple man, with mystic leanings and profound vision. Reared a Catholic, and dedicated by his French family to an ecclesiastical career, he early became a priest, and within a short time made his influence felt throughout the Catholic world. Enrolled as a youth into the Jesuit order, it was against the Jesuits that he rebelled when he left the Roman Catholic Church. He was never excommunicated, however. It was on the ground of ill health that he achieved his emancipation from the order.[1]

His eloquence was reminiscent of Savonarola and in his diatribes much of the challenge and fury of the Italian ecclesiastic reverberated. Ineluctably he belonged to the tradition of the reformers. In the beginning his reformism was moral rather than creedal, but as his battle against the Catholic oligarchs continued, it soon developed into a theological conflict. It was not long before the Catholic theocrats, who had threatened him for years, attempted to suppress and imprison him; he escaped their almost ubiquitous clutches and fled from place to place where, under the protection of Cardinal Richelieu, who was friendly to his ideas, he found it possible to avoid arrest. Until the latter's death he and his followers were unmolested; afterward, however, he was forced to make other

[1] John L. Mosheim: *An Ecclesiastical History: Ancient and Modern, from the Birth of Christ to the Beginning of the 18th Century*, 1819. Editor's notes, pp. 511-513.

hegiras. Mazarin, the dictatorial diplomat, persecuted him as determinedly as Richelieu had defended him.

For a while he retired to the Carmelites and there tried to rediscover himself, dig into his deeper impulses, excavate his soul. He was a strange man. Like many others of his time, he derived his main strength from intuitive sources, visions, inspirations, compulsive dreams, voices heard in remote places, spiritual chimeras, elusive portents, vague powers.[1] He did not have to fling inkwells at the Devil as Luther did because he was more interested in God than in the Devil, and was more concerned with man's virtues than with his vices. He believed in man so much that he wanted too much of him. He believed man could, if he willed and wished, live the co-operative life of a communist. He believed that man could prepare himself for eternity by scaling the battlements of evil erected by Satan. Those battlements were arrogance and cupidity and they could be conquered by the spiritual artillery of Christian sacrifice. Like Rousseau, who was to follow him, he believed that man was potentially good, not evil, and that what was necessary was to evoke the good in man in order to cure the evil. As Christ had lived, so he wanted all Christians to live—not worrying about the morrow, confident that God would protect them, and that all the men of God would spring to the aid of those in need of it.

Labadie was a good man and those who listened to him were impressed by his goodness, his overwhelming and compelling sincerity. He made converts by the multitude; men and women were stirred, uplifted by his vision and willing to dedicate themselves to its achievement. They were swayed by his eloquence, consecrated to his dream.

Among those influenced by Labadie's vision of man unfettered by human envy and greed was Gottschalck Van Schurman, who first heard Labadie speak at Geneva. In frequent

[1] Mosheim: *op. cit.*, Vol. V. Quoted from Hannah Adams: *A View of Religions*, 1791, p. 117.

letters to his sister he praised the wonder-working eloquence
of the man, his simplicity, his sincerity, his humility. His sister
Anna, moved by her brother's letters, immediately began a correspondence with Labadie. The letters were fertile in suggestion, intimation, emotional *rapport*. Very soon the sister grew
as close to Labadie as her brother [1] and within a short time her
influence became a most constructive one. After her brother's
premature death, she carried on his work in most admirable
fashion. She was determined to disseminate Labadie's gospel
abroad. It was mainly through her efforts that Labadie came
to Zeeland from Utrecht, where he had been a conquering
prophet. In an earlier century he would have been a Wyclif,
a Huss, a Zwingli, and greater than them all, in that his social
vision was more penetrating and profound.

Anna Van Schurman realized that she was dealing with a
man not only close to God, but also close to the things of earth
by which men could release themselves from the incubus of
sin. Labadie became her god. He was, to quote her own
words, a great man because "he heard the call of the heavenly
Shepherd." [2] Labadie was not only a great speaker, he was
a speaker who inspired great things. Like Christ, he inspired
rich people to give up their riches and poor people to surrender
their souls. His words thundered through the Europe of his
day like the detonations of the old prophets, challenging the
ancient citadels of convention and artifice. He was a prophet,
not a preacher; a seer, not a theologian. He loved men because he was certain he could change and reform them. Therein
lay his power.

So forthright had Labadie been in the proclamation of his
faith he soon found it impossible to remain a Catholic. Born
the son of a military governor who was religious as well as
martial, he was first placed in a Jesuit college, and despite
his father's objections, he chose the Jesuits as the order he pre-

[1] Una Birch: *Anna Van Schurman*, 1909, pp. 114-115.
[2] *Ibid.*, p. 116.

ferred. Later, his disillusionment with the order caused him to desert the faith. The Catholics persecuted him, hounded him, threatened his life. But still he held on, unswerving in his belief in his mission. He was called a Huguenot, an Arminian, and the most furious and flagrant of heretics. Worse still, he was accused by the Catholic clergy of having corrupted and seduced nuns who had come to him for confession. Nothing was too extreme to be utilized in the attacks made upon him by the clergy. On the other hand, anti-Catholics and non-Catholics sympathized with him. The poet Milton wrote an appealing letter to Labadie, urging him to come to England, where he might propagate his doctrines without persecution or attack. But Labadie decided against the English offer.

Removed from Catholic influence, Labadie was a dangerous man to the Catholic hierarchy. He could move crowds, sway masses, stir emotion in the hearts of the frigid, awaken the lethargic, dynamite men in high places, change faiths, reverse convictions, alter ideals. His influence was magnetic.

LABADIE: THE MAN

The curious thing is that Labadie's influence was not physical at all. He was unattractive in that respect. He was short, weak of body, frenetic, feverish. His aquiline nose made him unprepossessing, his carriage was not graceful—in fact, there was little about him, except his magical voice and the poems of paradise which emanated from him, to arrest and compel people. But that was enough. No one who listened to him could listen to anyone else. He was a religion, a world, in himself. He never needed notes for his sermons, never needed suggestions, reminders, recollections, to infuse what he said with the power and the wisdom of great prophecy. The peripheries of his vision were infinite.

When Labadie left Utrecht for Middelburg, Anna Van

Schurman found life unendurable, and before long she and a handful of friends followed after him. For years, even after she returned to Utrecht, Anna was able to live only because Labadie lived. He was life to her, as he was to myriads. Labadie was unconcerned with rites and rituals; his concern was with the heart, the mind, the inner self, the *sine qua non* of the soul. He sought, like an ardent Methodist, to bring men and women to God, because they had God living in their hearts and not because there was a Church waiting for their contributions. He was not interested in the Church, or in churches, but in salvation, redemption, eternity.

Labadie began his reformistic, Protestant career as a Calvinist, but there was nothing of Calvin's rigid doctrine of predestination living in his heart. He was an anti-Calvinist in every intellectual corpuscle. His poems as well as his acts are the best testimony to that fact. He believed in the infinite reformation and exaltation of men. Nothing was impossible in his eyes. He did not believe that God stopped his operations after the Garden of Eden episode, but that he continued his watchfulness, and that he had given his holy-begotten Son, Jesus, to redeem the race.

Jesus, therefore, was more important in Labadie's eyes than in those of the Catholic ecclesiastics. It was to Jesus that Labadie constantly returned, because he believed that Jesus was greater than churches or creeds or all the concoctions of the ages invented by the race. In this sense he was a forerunner of Wesley, and of all those Dissenters who placed their faith in the individual rather than in ecclesiastical organizations. Even in Holland he had not been unopposed. Dutch clergymen had attacked him for failing to repeat the regular forms of prayer, for disregarding the customary liturgy and ritual, and for dismissing all the semblances of orthodoxy then extant. But they had not succeeded in curbing or defeating him. He went on, like a turbulent tide, irrepressibly vigorous and violent.

After various conflicts, Labadie finally succeeded in setting up his establishment in Amsterdam, to which Anna Van Schurman and her friend, Anna de Veer, expeditiously fled. Labadie's enemies condemned him for running a religious brothel, but neither he, Anna Van Schurman, nor Anna de Veer, cared about what others said. These women loved Labadie, in a spiritual way, and had no desire to conceal it. Antoinette de Bourignon, another reformer and a rival of Labadie, tried to persuade Anna Van Schurman to desert the Labadist faith and join hers, but to no avail. Antoinette was no less consecrated to holy things than Labadie; she prayed endlessly, sacrificed her energies for those who needed her, slept at night in a coffin, scourged her body, and scarred and scissored her flesh, all in an attempt to purify her soul of the evil which Adam had inflicted upon it. But Anna remained adamant. She belonged to Labadie and to no one else. He was her mission, her god, herself.

New-World Ventures

Labadie and the Labadists never thought of the movement as being confined by spatial contours. It was a movement of the spirit which comprehended not only the universe but heaven, too. It belonged to the infinite. Its purpose was to conquer the world. Persecution and attack inspired rather than discouraged convictions. They became martyrs in the name of the Lord. The more they were harassed in Holland the more convinced they became that they had to spread their doctrines over the world. Their doctrine, as Labadie said, was not national, not European; it was inter-racial, inter-continental, international. Mission societies, later known as foreign missions, were organized to spread Labadie's ideas in the strange, new spheres of the universe, the new world of America which was the newest thing in the world of that day. So two colonies were sent out, one to the Surinam, strangest

jungle country in the world, where rum was more exalted
than reverence, and where people wanted to realize paradise
before they died rather than after they were dead; the other
was sent to America, where it might be possible to convert the
heathen to Labadie's way of life, there endowing it with a
significance reminiscent of the life of its founder.

Labadie's disciples supported these foreign-mission projects,
dedicated their money and their souls to their success, but in
the end they were defeated. Labadism, independent as it was
of all other churches, and advanced as it was as economic
doctrine, could not combat an environment violently antagonistic to it. In the Surinam, in South America, the colony
had only an episodic brevity, largely due to the murder of its
leader, Van Sommelsdyk. Two groups of Labadists came to
the Surinam before the colony was finally abandoned. The
second group, which was attacked by pirates on its trip over,
found the houses infested with snakes, the soil over-run with
mosquitoes, and the climate molten and morbific.[1] Sommelsdyk's assassination by recalcitrant soldiers was the final blow;
it discouraged the colonists so much they all soon hastened
back to the old world. This failure proved most tragic. The
Labadists believed that the success of their doctrine depended
not only on their ability to convert the people they knew, but
even more upon their genius in converting primitive peoples.
They wanted to save the world, and especially that part of
the world which had not heard of the gospel of the true Christ
which Labadie preached.

The Maryland Experiment

In North America, however, it was hoped their colonial
experiment would be more successful—and it was. Two leading Labadists, Danckaerts and Sluyter, were sent to New York,
toward the middle of the seventeenth century, with instruc-

[1] Bartlett B. James: *Introduction to Journal of Jasper Danckaerts.*

tions to found a colony there. Their New York venture was discouragingly short-lived. They found themselves opposed on the one hand by Governor Andros, who was a Catholic, and on the other by the Dutch clergy, in particular by Rev. Henry Selyns, who accused them of "blustering" and attacked the Labadist "head and teacher," Tellenaer, as "impudent" because he was so forward as "to disturb public divine service" by rushing up to the pulpit and challenging the congregation, declaring that he was the true ambassador of God. Tellenaer was seized by the neck and flung out of the church. From the church Tellenaer went to the schoolhouse, where he continued his exhortations.[1] The Rev. Rudolphus Varich shared the attitude of Rev. Selyns toward the Labadists.[2] In New Castle, almost midway between New York and Maryland, Danckaerts and Sluyter tried to get the famous Labadist preacher, Jacobus Coelman, to become minister.

Shortly before, Coelman, who had been minister of the church at Sluys in Vlaenderen, had been condemned as a Labadist iconoclast. He had introduced into church procedure innovations which evoked the condemnation of even the liberal Dutch clergy. Two sermons of his, published in book form, advocated volitional and optional prayer instead of regular morning and evening prayers—which was enough to stir the official ecclesiastics to demand his expulsion from the land. Coelman, however, was not quelled easily. He carried on his work, like all the ardent Labadists, in private gatherings, in vacant churches, in woodlands, on the summits of obscure hills.[3] Unfortunately, by the time Coelman got the "call" from Danckaerts and Sluyter, he had already renounced Labadism and attacked it in a book called, *An Historical Account of the Labadists.*[4]

[1] *Ecclesiastical Records of the State of New York*, pp. 906-907.
[2] *Ibid.*, p. 1053.
[3] *Ibid.*, pp. 656, 657, 724, 2263, 2289.
[4] *Ibid.*, p. 876.

Augustine Herrman: The Bohemian Adventurer

While in New York Danckaerts and Sluyter met Ephraim Herrman [1] and converted him to the Labadist credo. Ephraim Herrman was the son of Augustine Herrman, the Bohemian surveyor who achieved renown and a vast manor for drawing a map of Maryland and Virginia, which Lord Baltimore declared the best map in existence in the word.[2] Lord Baltimore thereupon made Herrman the "first person not a subject of the English Crown to enjoy the rights of a freeman in Maryland." [3] The elder Herrman had originally settled in New York, whence he had been sent by Governor Peter Stuyvesant on a diplomatic mission to Maryland, to request the return of debtors and servants who had fled to the Baltimore colony.[4]

When Augustine Herrman saw how completely converted his son was to Labadist doctrines, he offered to give the Labadists part of his Bohemia Manor, 3,750 acres, to be precise, where they could found their colony.[5] The place he gave them was very near where the city of Elkton, Maryland, the Gretna Green of the new world, stands today. Later, the elder Herrman changed his mind and when the Labadists came to settle upon his manor, he refused to allow them to occupy it. Only after an extended lawsuit were the Labadists able to compel him to give them the promised grant of land.

Augustine Herrman, son of a Councilman of Prague, was a very different man from his son, Ephraim, although they resembled each other in their proclivity to extremes.[6] Augustine

---

[1] The name is spelled in divers ways: Herrman, Hermans, Hermann, Hermen. I have chosen the Herrman spelling because it seems most frequent.

[2] P. Lee Phillips: *The Rare Map of Virginia and Maryland by Augustine Herrman*, 1911.

[3] *Narratives of Early Maryland,* edited by Clayton Colman Hall, 1910. Editor's notes.

[4] Hazard: *Annals of Pennsylvania*, p. 268. ..

[5] *Maryland Historical Society Fund Publications*, No. 30, p. 17.

[6] *Maryland Historical Magazine*, Vol. 15, 1930, p. 395.

was an adventurer who had come to the new world as an agent
of the West India Company. He loved the ways of life of
the aristocracy; he liked fine horses, liveried menials, gay
women, rich wine; he was enthusiastic about hunting and fish-
ing and all exciting sports; he kept a gala establishment and
spent his life in various forms of distraction and dissipation.
The original Labadists, especially Danckaerts, loathed him
because he was waited upon not by Christians, but by Negroes.
Ephraim, on the other hand, was an ascetic, who was severely
critical of his father's attitudes and actions. So firmly did he
believe in the truth of Labadism, one of the first things he did
when he joined the movement was to separate from his wife,
and like many other Labadists, cleanse himself of all trace
of sexuality.

His father really considered him insane but, being certain that given time his son would recover from his affliction,
he tolerated his eccentricity and did not disinherit him. In the
end Labadism proved too much for the old man, and his scorn
for his son revealed itself in his will, wherein he authorized
several of his neighbors instead of his son Ephraim to admin-
ister his estate.

Ephraim Herrman was not the only Labadist in this country
to separate from his wife and follow singly in the footsteps
of the Lord. Although Labadie had not insisted upon celibacy,
he had stressed the necessity of all his followers divorcing or
separating from wives or husbands not members of the order.
Labadism was to be endogamous. One either had to marry
a Labadist or convert the marital partner to Labadism; otherwise the marriage was unsanctified. Ephraim Herrman's wife
Elizabeth, described by her friends as the gentlest and sweetest
woman in the new world, was not a Labadist; and therefore,
as has already been noted, he had to leave her, tear-stricken
though he was at having to do so. Petrus Bayard, a hatter,
forsook his wife for the same reason.

Labadie's Attitude Toward Sex

Labadie's whole attitude toward sex was pathologic. Like many reformers, Oriental as well as Occidental, he believed that it was the highest duty of man to conquer sexual lust. He was willing that men should put on haircloth shirts, sleep in nail-pointed beds, torture their fingers and toes, resort to any extreme in order to subdue their carnal impulses. All Labadists were convinced that sex was sinful, an evil to be fought day and night, unintermittently.[1] Even married couples were urged to live as if they were not married. Succumbing to the appetencies of the flesh was like surrendering to the powers of the Devil.

It was this sexual madness on the part of the Labadists which made Augustine Herrman so fiercely opposed to them. He swore that his son could not endure such discipline and would die within two years. Ephraim rejoined his wife later but, tortured by the memory of what he had done, he went insane and died within less than the two years prophesied by his father.

Peter Dittleback, a Labadist who later revolted against Labadism, describes in his unforgettable exposé, *Vernal en Val der Labadisten*, something of the severity of sexual discipline imposed upon the colony by Peter Sluyter and his wife, both of whom strove devoutly to carry out the sexual regulations of the group, but strove undevoutly not to observe the economic:

"A friend of mine arriving from Sluyter's community has made revelations to me with regard to their doctrine of marriage. . . . He went there with a full surrender of himself, family, goods and effects. His penitence, Sluyter wrote, was unusual and the letter was read to us at Weiward and we rejoiced exceedingly over his conversion; but now since he has left them, they charge and blacken him with sin. He was compelled not only to submit to

[1] George Johnston: *History of Cecil County*, 1881, p. 98.

the mortifications imposed by Sluyter, but also to submit
to those of Sluyter's wife, who had shortly previous arrived from Weiward and took a hand in mortifying.
What they thought of at night had to be done somehow
during the day. Indeed they made it so sharp that a
brother who had been sent over from Weiward would
remain with them no longer, but returned to Weiward,
where also he was humiliated. This abasing cannot continue a long time among these people. My friend's wife
had five small children whom she brought with her to this
new cloister discipline. When she kissed them she was
rebuked for showing so naturally her fleshly cleavings. . . .
I could tolerate Weiward in some degree that there should
be no fire in the cells, although it is cold there in the winter,
because turf is dear, and so many families could not be
supplied unless at great expense, but this friend told me
Sluyter would not allow them to have any fire in order
to harden the body while there was so much wood there
that they were obliged to burn it in the fields to get it out
of the way; but Sluyter had his own hearth well provided
night and day. My friend has never suffered more cold
and hardship than among these people, and he frequently
made a fire in the woods in order to warm himself. His
wife had no mind to remain in this cloister under such an
abbess who censured her at the time she had a child nursing at her breast, because she drank too much at the table,
and when afterwards she drank less, because she left off
too soon. As they saw these things did not please his
wife they began to talk to him more plainly and freely
concerning marriage, arguing *hell was full of ordinary
marriages*, saying, among other things, these abominable
words: It was for God to judge whether he cohabited
with a harlot or with his wife. The wife, fearful lest
they should take her husband away from her, of which
there had been at that place more than one instance,
sought very affectionately to speak to her husband privately, and to exhort him to steadfastness, as she had
come away with him from Amsterdam and was there
in a strange land with her little children. They had
succeeded, however, with him so far that he began to
keep himself away from her and his wife being very

angry at it, the Abbess jeeringly asked her if she could not be one night without her husband. The husband finally began to attack their doctrine about marriage out of the Scriptures, showing that the apostles had not taught it so. He asked Sluyter what marriage *he* came of. Whether his parents were not married in the ordinary way. They began to wonder at this man's opposing them out of the Scriptures, until finally he told them soundly that all connection between him and them was at an end." [1]

SOCIAL LIFE OF THE COLONY

Sluyter had been one of the early Labadists but he lacked the moral and spiritual courage to live up to his religion. He came to America because he preferred being a dictator there to being a follower in Weiward. Neither he nor his wife knew how to handle people or manage a community. Both represented that worst of all combinations: religious fanaticism compounded with economic materialism. Once Sluyter acquired control of the colony, he perverted its purpose, and exploited it for his own personal benefit. All the Labadists were opposed to tobacco on principle—smoking was a heinous crime—but Sluyter lost no time in introducing tobacco culture and pocketing large profits from it. In the beginning, Sluyter had supported the Labadist hostility to both tobacco and slavery. In fact, when he first arrived in the new world, he was opposed to white slavery as much as to black, and condemned the whole system of indentured service as degrading to human dignity.[2] The lure of profits, however, undermined his idealism and soon converted him into a slave-driver, and few slave-owners treated their slaves worse than he.

The Labadists went on record when they arrived in Maryland as being opposed to slavery, and for that reason are often credited with being the first group in America to have de-

[1] Peter Dittleback: *Verval en Val der Labadisten,* 1692, Letter III.
[2] Matthew Page Andrews: *The Founding of Maryland,* 1929, p. 303.

nounced slavery as an institution. The trouble was they did
not put their theory into practice. They were misled by Sluyter, who convinced them that they could not survive without
slavery, and, remembering the unhappy fate of the Surinam
colony, they compromised with their convictions in order to
avoid a similar fiasco.

Sluyter was so clever in his machinations and maneuvers
that he died a rich man—rich from the profits derived from
a poor communist colony. He was, in other words, one of the
first of the radical racketeers. In 1698 he succeeded in convincing the colonists that they should divide up their land
and return to private ownership. Sluyter himself died in 1722.
By 1727 the colony was extinct.

How They Lived

It was before Sluyter got his iron grip on the colony that
it achieved its spiritual triumph. For years it was the only
community in the new world[1] which converted communism
into a living reality. Communism with the early Labadists was
a way of life, a vital principle. To live otherwise would have
been to live in sin. To take was evil, to give was good; such
was their ideal until Sluyter vitiated it.

One of the best pictures of how the Labadists lived is to be
found in Samuel Bownas' *Account* of his experiences among
them:

"After we had dined, we took our leave, and a friend,
my guide, went with me to a people called Labadies,
where we were civily entertained in their way. When
supper came in, it was placed upon a long table in a large
room, where, when all things were ready, came in, at a

[1] There was, of course, the famous communist colony initiated by the
Jesuits in Paraguay, which existed longer than the Bohemia Manor experiment, but its organization was more monastic than civil, and the concern of this volume is with civil rather than monastic ventures, and with
North American, especially United States ventures rather than with those
in the lower Americas. Many of the early Catholic orders were communistic, but they did not try to run civil communities, as the Labadists did.

call, about 20 men or upwards but no woman: We all sat
down they placing me and my companion near the head
of the table, and having paused a short space, one pulled
off his hat but not the rest till a short space after and then
one after another they pulled all their hats off, and in
that uncovered posture sat silent (uttering no words that
we could hear) near half a quarter of an hour, and as
they did not uncover at once, so neither did they cover
themselves again at once; but as they put on their hats and
fell to eating not regarding those who were still uncovered, so that it might be about two minutes time or
more between the first or last putting on or off their hats.
I afterward querried their conducts, and he gave this for
answer, that they held it unlawful to pray till they felt
some inward motion for the same; and that secret prayer
was more acceptable than to utter words; and that it was
most proper for every one to pray, as moved thereto by
the spirit in their own minds.

"I likewise querried if they had no women amongst
them. He told me they had, but the women eat by themselves, and the men by themselves, having all things in
common, respecting their household affairs, so that none
could claim any more rights than another to any part of
their flock, whether in trade or husbandry; and if any
had a mind to join with them, whether rich or poor, they
must put what they had in the common stock, and if they
had a mind to leave the society, they must likewise leave
what they brought, and go out empty handed.

"They frequently expounded the Scriptures among
themselves, and being a very large family, in all upwards
of a hundred men, women and children, carried on something of the manufactory of linen, and had a very large
plantation of corn, tobacco, flax and hemp together with
cattle of several kinds. But at my last going there, these
people were all scattered and gone, and nothing of them
remaining of a religious community in that shape." [1]

In short, these were simple people, people who believed in
the better virtues of life, who were intent upon living differently from the way other people lived. Their attitudes toward

---

[1] Samuel Bownas: *Account of Life, Travels and Christ*, 1705, pp. 95-96.

sex and economics were individual, even eccentric, but they were not nearly so peculiar or queer then as they seem to be now. People in those centuries believed in religion in a way that they have ceased to do now. It was an inspiration to repression on the sexual side, but a tocsin of revolt on the economic. They were opposed to Sluyter's jurisdiction and domination, but were helpless in the face of it. They were communists, but Sluyter forced them to become individualists.[1]

As in Weiward and in Friesland, old-world Labadist centers, these new-world Labadists attempted to practice the communist, apostolic way of life of Christ.[2] They wanted everyone to live alike. They began their meals with chanting and ended them with prayer. Labor was divided equally among all. Some were in charge of the kitchen, others of the furnace, others of ablutionary activities, and still others of divers functions; attending the ill and incapacitated, or occupied with sartorial repair, dyeing, laundry work, religious instruction, printing, and different hand manufactures.

Their lives in the beginning, before Sluyter came to dominate them, were rigidly administered. A record was kept of how many pieces of bread and how many slices of butter were taken by each person, of what dresses were used, what coats worn, and a check was kept upon all personal activities, extending to the most microscopic details. Liberty for the individual was outlawed. The individual was part of the group, indivisibly, inextricably. His life was not his own; it was part of the group, of the colony. No one possessed any more than any other. All wealth, therefore, was common. And it remained so until Sluyter forsook the communist ideal of Labadie and introduced private property into the colony, divided up the land and initiated the profit motive.

Although the women ate separately and performed different

---

[1] James: *op. cit.*
[2] William Hand Browne: *Maryland, the History of a Palatinate,* 1884, p. 133.

functions from the men, there was no sense of inequality between the sexes. The women were considered as important as the men and possessed equal rights and privileges. In all conferences and assemblies the women participated; both sexes shared equally in decisions made by the group. At meals, as Bownas has related, the Labadists did not pray in common, but only when the spirit stirred them. Their prayers were always silent ones, because they believed that God preferred that type of intimate, secret prayer to the vocal supplications of other sects. This was a way of curbing the conceit and arrogance of the "worldly spirit." In silence, within their own souls, all men were equal. No one could claim superiority since no one knew how the other had prayed.

The Quakers and the Labadists

Like the Quakers, they did not believe in the exaltation of ritual, but in the dynamics of inspiration. For a time the Labadists were confused in various parts of Europe with Quakers, and when they left Amsterdam for Hereford they were denounced en route as Quakers and stoned. In self-defense the Labadists attacked the Quakers, and published a book entitled *An Examination of the Confusion of the Quakers*, which purported to show wherein the two sects were dissimilar in religious and social outlook. Danckaerts and Sluyter distrusted the hysteria of the Quakers. Their description of their experience with a Quaker prophetess is more revealing than ever today:

"In the evening there also arrived three Quakers, one of whom was the greatest prophetess, who travelled through the whole country in order to *quake*. She lives in Maryland and forsakes husband and children, a plantation and all, and goes off for this purpose. She has been to Boston and was there arrested by the authorities on account of her quakery. This worthy personage came here in the house where we were, although Ephraim

avoided her. They sat by the fire and drank a dram of
rum with each other, and in a short time afterward began
to shake and groan so that we did not know what had
happened and supposed they were going to preach, but
nothing came of it. I could not stand them and went out
of doors. [The next day the journalist continues.] The
dinner being ready I was placed at the table next to the
before named prophetess, who while they all sat at
the table began to groan and quake gradually until at
length the whole . . . shook, then rising up she began
to pray, shrieking so that she could be heard as far as the
river." [1]

Upon another occasion Danckaerts and Sluyter, who were
more puritanic than the most perfervid of the Dissenters, railed
against the Quakers because the latter were so worldly as to
have in one of their houses, "lying upon the window a copy
of 'Virgil,' as if it were a common handbook."

ENTER WILLIAM PENN

Back in Holland, in Anna Van Schurman's days, she claimed
that the Labadists had gained 60,000 converts. Facts do not
confirm her contention. However, life among the European
Labadists those days was far more joyful than it was among
the American group. There was singing, dancing, and other
gala activities among them then, and when they moved to the
Hereford estate of the Princess Elizabeth of the Palatinate,
they were far from a suffering and suppressed sect. William
Penn, hopeful of converting them to Quakerism, visited them
in 1671, and in the journal of his *Travails*, wrote thus about
them:

"I was moved to Visit this Man and his Company (at
Herford) six years ago, and did see him and his two great
disciples, but they would not suffer me to see the People
which I laboured for. In that day I saw the airiness and

[1] Extract from Danckaerts' *Journal*, quoted from B. B. James: *The
Labadist Colony in Maryland*, p. 33.

unstableness of the man's spirit, and that a sect-master was his name.   And it was upon me, both by word of mouth and writing, to let them know that the enemy would prevail against them to draw them into inconvenient things, if they came not to be stayed in the light of Jesus Christ, and to know the holy silence; and that at last they would come to fall out one with another, and moulder away; which is in some measure come to pass as I feared.   For I clearly perceived that though they had received some divine touches, there was a danger they would run out with them, and spend them like prodigals; not knowing then where to stay their minds for daily bread.   Yea, though they were something angelical and like to the celestial bodies, yet if they kept not their station, they would prove fallen stars.   They moved not in the motion of Him who visited them, but were filled with gross mixtures, and thereby brought forth mixed births, that is to say, things not natural but monstrous.   In fine, they were shy of us, they knew us not; yet I believed well of some of the people, for a good thing was stirring in them." [1]

Penn was a young man then, but he recognized at once the similarity between the spiritual doctrines of the Labadists and the Quakers.   He was not, to be sure, willing to subscribe to the economic doctrines of the Labadists with their communist imperatives.   After all, Penn was a rich man, and no matter how much he might agree with a religious group he could see no justifiable reason why he should surrender his wealth.   He was no Gautama, no St. Francis, no Kropotkin.

But Penn never succeeded in converting the Labadists to Quakerism in America or Europe.   They were made of stubborn, unconvertible religious coin.   They were willing to listen to Penn but not to be persuaded by him.

Though his own life did not correspond with theirs, Penn could not but admire their simple ways.   In Weiward as in

[1] Quoted from William I. Hull: *William Penn and the Dutch Quaker Migration to Pennsylvania*, 1935, p. 7.

Bohemia Manor, they eschewed the gaudy and the glamorous in attire and interior decoration; their clothes were homespun, crude, but durable, and the buildings and rooms they lived in were as severe in their bareness as their food was in its tastelessness. Any dish which excited or delighted the palate was forbidden. Gold and silver trinkets, gewgaws, or jewels, and all other varieties of ornament were excluded from the colony, including pictures, drapes, curtains, hangings, vases, rugs, carpets, or anything suggestive of comfort or sensuous charm. Anyone hoarding a jewel was rushed to confession and forced to do penance in public for his sin. Anyone daring to admit that he disliked any particular food was obligated, for the sake of his conscience, to eat that food repeatedly for an indefinite period, depending on the profundity of his repentance.[1]

Not only William Penn, but other humanitarian leaders were influenced by the Labadist way of life. George Keith, the Quaker firebrand, and Barclay, the religious sage, were among those inspired by Labadist ideas. Most conspicuous also was Conrad Beissel, spiritual shepherd of the Ephrata colony, which was founded upon similar principles. Beissel's visit to Bohemia Manor left a decisive and indelible impression upon him. There he not only conversed with the leading Labadists and learned their philosophy from their own lips, but he also read their literature in manuscript as well as published form.[2] He was so influenced and moved by it that he revised the organization of his Ephrata colony, divided the sexes in Labadist style, and introduced a number of innovations suggested by the Labadist philosophy.

Many Mennonites heard of the Labadist experiment and it was not long before a number of them began their trek from Pennsylvania to Maryland to join the communist venture. The picture of them in their staid, old-world attire, bare

[1] Murphy, *op. cit.*, p. 43.
[2] J. F. Sachse: *German Sectarians of Pennsylvania*, p. 58.

of color or frill, the men in their dark, wide-brimmed hats, the women with their prim little bonnets, walking through a strange country to an even stranger province, is dramatic, indeed. They found Bohemia Manor the best spiritual haven in the new world. They wanted to reconcile and unite their other-worldly belief with their this-worldly life, and Bohemia Manor afforded them that opportunity. As Johann Gottfried Seelig wrote, describing the decision of Jacob I. Van Beber:

> "He was formerly a Mennonite, but (in order to be-come a Labadist) he desires to depart with his whole house, to acknowledge and abandon the follies, scandals, shortcomings, and stains of his former religion." [1]

The Labadist colony supplied a need which was imperative in that day. Men with idealism burning in their hearts, and with a masochistic craving for sacrifice, could best realize their aspiration in the land of the Labadists, who thrived upon such physical and psychological immolation.

The Labadist experiment did not fail because of economic insufficiency. From that point of view it was a marked success. The Labadists not only lived well, but better, on the whole, than their individualistic neighbors. The food they ate, despite its ordinariness, the clothes they wore, despite their plainness, and the houses they lived in, despite their simplicity of structure, were equal if not superior to those of the rest of the colonists in the province.

It was not their communist way of life which proved a failure, but the non-communist way of life introduced by Peter Sluyter. It was Sluyter's avarice which destroyed the colony. Sluyter, inspired by the magnitude and magnificence of the land, became more interested in private profit than in social prosperity. As we have already seen, this led him to the cultivation of a private-profit regime, with himself as the dominant force in the community. After becoming the main

---

[1] *Pennsylvania Magazine*, Vol. XI, p. 440.

proprietor, he divided the property among the various members of the colony, retaining the best lands for himself.[1] In Weiward, home of the Mother Church, a similar dissolution occurred, Henry Van Deventer functioning there as Sluyter did in Bohemia Manor. Within a few years nothing was left of either group—nothing except memories and a few fragmentary records, vague and obscure souvenirs of what once had been radiant with the glory of a new life.

[1] Charles Payson Mallery: *Historical Society of Delaware,* 1888, p. 33.

CHAPTER III

The Woman in the Wilderness

"Or painful Kelpius from his hermit den
By Wissahickon, maddest of good men,
Dreamed o'er the Chiliast dreams of Petersen."
JOHN GREENLEAF WHITTIER.

Stranger far than the Labadists were the god-intoxicated followers of Kelpius, founder of the *Woman in the Wilderness* colony in Pennsylvania. Kelpius was a spiritual inebriate, an humble man who identified himself with the creative spirit of the universe. Like many other preachers, prophets, and seers, he believed his mission was divine.

Kelpius was a queer, eccentric figure, scissored out of the clairvoyant pattern. He had a melodramatic genius for visions, portents, and prophecies. He considered himself more than a Pietist; he was a Rosicrucian, holier than the holiest in spirit and dream. He was a man of the Lord who walked in the way of goodness and light all the days of his life. He lived only thirty-five years, but he crowded into his life as much of virtue and wisdom and holy sacrifice as any man of his day.

THE ARRIVAL

Kelpius and his forty followers came over on the good ship *Sara Maria* (the full name was *Sarah Mariabonae spei*), and arrived several years after the Labadists had settled in Maryland.[1] The original leader of the group was the ex-Lutheran

---

[1] J. F. Sachse: *The German Pietists of Provincial Pennsylvania,* p. 4.

pastor, Zimmerman, whose published works were as multitudinous as they were sulphurous. He denounced the Lutheran Church, denounced all churchmen, and went to live among the lonely isolated hermits and millennialists, and soon decided that the only way to escape the Babylon of Europe was to retreat to the wilderness of the new world.[1] On the very day before he and his group were to embark for America, Zimmerman died, and Kelpius succeeded him as leader.

A few days after their arrival, Kelpius and his disciples walked from Philadelphia to Germantown, and ultimately established their colony on the shores of the Wissahickon,[2] which is now close to the confines of Philadelphia's celebrated Fairmont Park. Like the Labadists and practically all other religious utopians in the seventeenth century, they were millennialists, convinced of Christ's early return to earth. Kelpius himself believed in this dream and was sure that he would not die until Christ had made his second appearance in this world. As it was, he died long before most of his followers, a victim of tuberculosis, which he contracted as a result of the privations and hardships he had to endure because of his faith.

A Society of Students

Kelpius, a small, slight man with a paralyzed eyelid, was only twenty-one when he left for the new world. He and many of his votaries, the best known of whom were Kosher, Biderman, and Seelig, had been students in German universities where they had absorbed a vast part of the esoteric learning of the day.[3] Kelpius himself knew five languages and many of his followers were equally gifted. Their intellectuality, though mystical and culpably impractical, was most rare among the colonists of that century.

Kelpius had early fallen under the influence of the writings

[1] Lucy Forney Bittinger: *The Germans in Colonial Times*, p. 42.
[2] Sanford H. Cobb: *The Story of the Palatines*, p. 268.
[3] Francis Howard Williams: *The New World*, 1894, p. 218.

of the great mystic, Jacob Boehme, who had sprung from shoemaker to seer; later he had been so moved by the eloquence
of Rev. Philip Jacob Spener, founder of the Pietists,[1] that he
became one of his followers. In England later he met Jane
Leade, the leader of the Philadelphists, from whom he imbibed
further mystic wisdom and a deeper understanding of the
significance of Boehme. In addition, Kelpius was deeply read
in the theologians, Tertullian, Chrysostom, Ambrose, was
familiar with the works of the Greeks, and was a great admirer
of Thales, one of the earliest of the Greek philosophers.

Kelpius' colony became known as the *Society of the Woman
in the Wilderness*, although neither Kelpius himself nor any
of his acolytes ever called it by that name. They had no name
for their colony, but spoke of it simply as a colony of the
"Contented of the God-loving Soul." Nevertheless, the name
Woman in the Wilderness clung to it, and it is by that name
that it will always be known. The name was derived from
the chapter in the Book of Revelation which relates how the
woman emerged from the wilderness to deliver the true church.[2]
Her emergence was to be concomitant with the arrival of the
millennium. She was to advance from the wilderness, leaning
upon the arm of her Beloved; the disciples of Kelpius went
into the wilderness, therefore, to be close to her; they sought
to be the "Beloved in the Wilderness," preparing themselves
for the final revelation. With their telescopes they read the
skies, and with their subtle alchemy they probed the stuffs and
substances of the earth, in an attempt to discover harbingers
and portents of the advent of Christ. They believed that only
in the infinite solitude of the wilderness could one equip oneself
to step into the presence of the Lord. Zimmerman, their
original leader, had figured out by astronomical calculations
of a most minute order, that the world would come to an end

[1] *National Society of Colonial Dames*, Vol. I, p. 7.
[2] Sydney George Fisher: *The Making of Pennsylvania* (8th Edition).
It was the Collegia Pietatis that Spener founded. (Oscar Kuhns: *The
German and Swiss Settlements of Colonial Pennsylvania*, p. 159.)

and Christ return in the fall of 1694, for which reason he was most eager to gather a group to go to America and await the advent of Christ in the wilderness of the virgin country.

Pursuant to the practices of ancient German mythology, the group celebrated the rites of St. John's Eve, burning the bushes and trees, dispersing them down the hills, and shouting hallelujahs as they watched them descend and be consumed. Strange incantations and conjurations of heavenly spirits accompanied the ceremony, weird symbols were erected and necromantic powers evoked, to endow it with ultimate sanctity.

Like most millennialist colonies, the *Woman in the Wilderness* was founded upon communist principles, with celibacy as a moral ideal. Carnal desire had no place in a colony which did not believe in the perpetuation of the species, but only in the perpetuation of the soul. Everything was organized to subdue the senses and exalt the spirit.

A log house, forty feet square, was early erected, with an iron Rosicrucian cross fronting it as its challenging symbol. It was called the Tabernacle, and therein religious and musical services took place; within it a schoolroom was also set apart, and an observatory built for the telescopes and other astronomical instruments in which the whole group was so consumingly interested. Its interest in the skies, to be sure, was more astrological than astronomical, more theosophical than scientific—but such were the interests of everyone else then. Even the great astronomer, Kepler, whose aunt was burned as a witch and whose mother almost suffered the same fate, believed in spirits and their operations and housed the heavens with supernatural forces.

There were in the colony separate cells for all the brethren. Like all the German groups of that day, Kelpius and his friends were musical and devoted considerable time to the cultivation of the art. Kelpius himself composed many musical scores and published a book of hymns which was the first musical volume to appear in the new world. In addition, there is good reason to believe that it was the Kelpius band which brought over the first organ played in Pennsylvania; they also carried with them a virginal, the first to be seen or heard on these shores. Unlike the English Dissenters who viewed most music as a diabolical art, these German Pietists encouraged and advanced it. Music was for them a voice of the soul. In fact, they insisted that music inspired the higher impulses, evoked the finer instincts in man.

Kelpian Outlook Versus the Puritan

In that regard, as well as in many others, the *Woman in the Wilderness* group was superior to the Massachusetts Bay one. Both contained many learned men, a number of whom were university graduates, but their outlooks were dissimilar. German universities of that day were interested in metaphysical problems, investigations into esoteric and mystical realms, and German theologians reflected that concern in their approach to Christianity. Kelpius was an exemplar of it.[1]   He wanted

[1] In this connection, Sachse gives an excellent description of Kelpius:
"Kelpius, educated in one of the most distinguished universities of Europe, and having had advantage of the best resources for the acquirement of knowledge, was calculated to edify and enlighten those who resorted to him for information. He had particularly made great progress in the study of ancient lore, and was quite proficient in theology. He was intimately acquainted with the principal works of the Rabbins, the Heathen and Stoic philosophers, the Fathers of the Christian Church, and the Reformers. He was conversant with the writings of Tertullian, St. Jerome, St. Augustine, St. Cyprian, Chrysostom, Ambrose, Tauler, Eck, Myconius, Carlstadt, Hedio, Faber, Osiander, Luther, Zwingli, and others, whose opinions he would frequently analyze and expound with much animation. He was also a strict disciplinarian, and kept attention constantly directed inwards upon self. To know self, he contended, is the first and most essential of all knowledge. Thales, the Milesian, he maintained, was the author of the precept 'Know thyself,' which was adopted by Chilo the Lacedemonian, and is one of the three inscriptions which, according to Pliny, was consecrated at Delphos by golden letters, and acquired the authority of a divine oracle; it was supposed to have been given by Apollo, of which opinion Cicero has left a record. He directed a sedulous watchfulness over the temper, inclinations and passions, and applauded very much the counsel of Marcus Aurelius: 'Look within; for within is the fountain of good.'"

people to emulate the apostles, search the avenues and streets of life for hidden mysteries, live like communists, study the skies with telescopes for heavenly signs, probe into the nature of strange substances and stuffs, compound spiritual elixirs, achieve an enraptured oneness with God. Without question, occultism, as it is familiarly known, was important to them. The mystic signet, upon which were inscribed various astrological abracadabra, was considered most precious, and was used not only to stamp papers, but even upon the bodies of humans and animals. Horoscopic prophecies and portents were viewed with awe, as if spoken by God.

John Greenleaf Whittier's poem about Kelpius reveals much of the man aspiring toward God in his simple reclusiveness:

> "Or painful Kelpius from his hermit den
> By Wissahickon, maddest of good men,
> Dreamed o'er the Chiliast dreams of Petersen.

> "Deep in the woods, where the small river slid
> Snake-like in shade, the Helmstadt Mystic hid,
> Weird as a lizard over arts forbid,
> Reading the books of Daniel and of John,
> And Boehme's Morning-Redness, through the Stone
> Of Wisdom, vouchsafed to his eyes alone,
> Whereby he read what man ne'er read before,
> And saw the visions man shall see no more,
> Till the great angel, striding sea and shore,

> "Shall bid all flesh await, on land or ships,
> The warning trump of the Apocalypse,
> Shattering the heavens before the dread eclipse."

The Mathers and Cottons, on the other hand, lacked such metaphysical and mystical interests. Like all Englishmen, they were concerned with more practical things, things immediate, tangible, negotiable. They despised the mystical extravagances of the Germans and had no sympathy with their millennialist faith and communist conceptions. They believed in a theocracy, but it was divided into classes and its way of life was individualistic and not communistic. In other words, they were modern, capitalistic Christians, and not primitive, apostolic ones. They seated people in their churches according to their rank and wealth; they believed in the right to acquire, hold, and defend private property; they organized courts, selected juries, built prisons; they fought any semblance of communism in their community.

Kelpius loathed the Puritan outlook as much as the Puritans scorned his. They belonged to different intellectual species: the one mystical, the other rationalistic.

He believed in transcendental instead of realistic values. He was not interested in wealth; the Puritans were. He was not concerned with the organization of a successful community; the Puritans were. This difference was based mainly upon their contrasting conceptions of the duration of the world; Kelpius believed the world was ephemeral, and was bound to end in an imminent millennium, whereas the Puritans believed it would continue for indefinite centuries, with no promise of the millennium visible upon the horizon. Kelpius believed in "that glorious Primitive Church of Christ Jesus," of apostolic derivation.[1] Kelpius cared only about preparing himself for eternity; the Puritans cared about preparing themselves for tomorrow or the day after, which was enough for them.

Because Kelpius was an intellectual equal of the Mathers, and many of his disciples were intellectual equals of the leaders of the Massachusetts Bay settlement, he and his colony deserve conspicuous consideration in American historical annals. About him clung a mystery, a romantic enigma, in which his whole career was wrapped. No one really knew him. It is doubtful if he ever knew himself, he so subdued his deepest impulses and appetencies in his frenetic search after God. He

---

[1] Proceedings of the Pennsylvania German Society: *Diary of Kelpius*, p. 15.

and his followers were always subject to the command of the populace; at the slightest behest they ventured out into remote regions, dangerous impasses, difficult woods, to pray with the sick, succor the dying, spread light in dark places, bring God to the godless. They were the greatest humanitarians of their day. Their good efforts did not stop with the whites; like Roger Williams, who embodied something of their vision, they were interested also in the Indians and lent to them their best energies in the way of conversion—and they were not without effect. One of their main concerns was whether the Indians were descendants of the ten lost tribes of Israel, and they carried on extensive investigations in hopes of proving that they were. Never once did Kelpius or any of his disciples, all of whom were true communists, ask or accept a penny for their services. They were messengers of the Lord and with the Lord's hosts money was an insult, a proof of man's sin and failure.

Kelpius Versus William Penn

When Kelpius was urged to become a Quaker, he refused, but made his reasons clear in his characteristically temperate but unequivocal manner. "I love them [the Quakers] from my inmost soul," he wrote to Dr. Fabricius, the head of the Helmstadt University, "even as I do all other sects that approach and call themselves Christ's, the Papists even not excluded," but then went on to add that he believed in distributing property and not in acquiring and holding onto it. His condemnation of William Penn in that regard was most forthright. He denounced Penn for not believing in Christ's doctrine of sacrificing one's own wealth for the sake of the poor. In Kelpius' eyes one could not be a landed proprietor and also a Christian. "For you [Penn] have now made your own the land we held in common amongst ourselves and our friends," Kelpius wrote. "You now take heed, night and day, how you may keep it, so that no one may take it from you. Indeed, you are anxious even beyond your span of life, to divide it among your children."

The death of Kelpius was a bodkin which put an end to the colony. Other members of the community tried to take over his leadership, but all of them failed. Seelig, the favorite disciple, was the first choice, and reluctantly he accepted the office. Without Kelpius, however, he felt bewildered, lost, and it was not long before he begged to be relieved of his function; he did not want to be a leader. He felt unequipped, unqualified, for all that it demanded.[1]

Within a short time he forsook the office, pleading that it was impossible for him to fulfill it, and went off alone, away from the colony, into the wilderness, into his microscopical cell, where he could be alone with himself and God. Seelig was a great apostle, but not a leader. After Seelig came another hermit, Conrad Matthai, a zealot from Switzerland, who strove to pull the community together, give it new life. Already most of its members had become recluses, each living within his own sunless cell. They had removed from their existence all traces, however vague, of the outside world, with its suggestions and promises of perpetuity. To think of this world as anything but ephemeral was sinful in their eyes. They wanted this world over as soon as possible. Their concern was with the eternal world which would begin with the millennium.

Matthai failed in his purpose because the hermits in the community by this time had become hopelessly and incorrigibly isolated and insulated. They were concerned only with themselves, their heavenly futures. Like Kelpius, however, Matthai attracted people to him, and among those who visited him was Zinzendorf, who had led the Moravians to their American haven. Matthai eventually joined with Zinzendorf in an attempt to unite all the divers sects in Pennsylvania,

[1] Lucy Forney Bittinger: *op. cit.,* p. 49.

with Philadelphia as the center of their organization, but that, too, proved futile.

With due humility, Matthai requested that he be buried at the feet of Kelpius instead of at his side—no one, in his opinion, deserved the honor of lying at the side of so great an apostle of Christ. Matthai's burial was a noteworthy event, with all the brethren in their long-flowing robes and starved, emaciated faces, genuflecting before the bier. For hours they stood there, bowing and crossing themselves, speechlessly reverent, as at the passing from the earth of a new son of God. People came from many places, far and near, bearing flowers, gifts, tributes.

Still the colony did not die. Like a moribund octogenarian it wriggled on, struggling somehow, some way, vaguely, fumblingly, to survive. Its last important descendant was Dr. Witt, who, blind, deaf, and hopelessly senile, still maintained its traditions. Since his death, whatever remained of the colony has been dispersed and today is undiscoverable.

The memory of it, however, has not died; instead it has grown with the years. It has been ivied with mystery and enchantment, with wonder clinging to its spiritual cerements. Its high towers of imagination, with its telescopes shoveling into the skies, have grown taller in retrospect, blotting out the rest of the countryside. People have come and searched for the remains of the colony; historians have worried their fingers turning the pages of old books in quest of its records; antiquarians have hunted for its relics, prowled about to find its cells, the dishes the hermits used, the clothes they wore.

But there is nothing left of it today except its memory. That memory belongs among the holy things. It is a memory of men so devoted to an ideal they were willing to sacrifice anything and everything for it. It dissolved of itself, but it did not disintegrate like the Labadist colony. No Sluyter invaded it or corrupted its high resolve. It did not change from a communist to a capitalist society, but remained co-operative to the end. Economics had nothing to do with its demise. If, after the death of Kelpius, a number of the brethren forsook the faith, married women, and joined organized churches,[1] the leaders of the group did not, and to the day of their death they lived as cenobitic communists, awaiting the return to earth of the Lord.

[1] Brother Lamech: *Chronicon Ephratense,* p. 14.

CHAPTER IV

Ephrata: Colony of Paradise-Seekers

"The Christian's A.B.C.
Is: suffer, bear and hope;
If you have mastered that,
Then you have reached the scope."

Ephrata was the spiritual child of Kelpius. The founders of Ephrata,[1] Conrad Beissel, Heinrich van Bebber, Jacob Stuntz, George Steifel, did not plan to organize a new colony in the new world. They intended joining the *Woman in the Wilderness* group, reports of which had spread throughout the religious world of Europe. Kelpius' fame was not confined by boundary, frontier, or nation. It had overleaped all such contours, penetrated all physical pales and borders.

These admirers of Kelpius started out for America in 1720, expecting to discover a flourishing colony on the Wissahickon. They were haunted by the dream of Kelpius, of a wilderness retreat wherein they could meet the Lord face to face, as the Bible had promised, in a Tabernacle removed from the haunts of unconsecrated men. When they reached the place, however, they found abundant wilderness, but no *Woman in the Wilderness* colony. Kelpius was dead, and his followers were dispersed; the few that remained were already too scattered to constitute even the fragment or fraction of a community. The famous Tabernacle was in collapse when they arrived. They hunted among the remains for a haven for their weary bodies, exhausted with the agonies of horrendous seas.

[1] The name Ephrata derives from the Bible, wherein it seems Ephratah meant fertile or fecund. (Sachse: *op. cit.*, p. 259.)

54

Beissel and his followers were at a loss what to do, or in what direction to turn. Pennsylvania was Quakerland, but they were not Quakers. They wanted to be free of every group, every association; they wanted to be by themselves, alone with God. After reflection, they decided to wander on, and from the Wissahickon they ventured in the direction of the Cocalico,[1] where they founded the colony of Ephrata, which is today practically halfway between Reading and Lancaster, Pennsylvania. There they strove to relight the torch of Kelpius.

Before arriving at what later became Ephrata, Beissel stopped at Conestoga, where the Dunkards had organized a community and established a church. Beissel was made assistant to Peter Baker, a disciple of Alexander Mack, the founder of the Dunkard faith. There he was baptized in 1724 in Pequea Creek, a branch of the swift-flowing Susquehanna; before long, however, he found himself in conflict with the congregation over the question of which day was the Sabbath. Beissel, a Seventh-Day Baptist, could not convince the Dunkards to accept his day of worship, and after being outvoted on the issue, he and his faithful followers departed to found the colony of Ephrata.[2]

Ephrata became so long-lived a colony it was known in time as the colony that would never, could never, die. Indeed, it became one of the longest-lived communist colonies in the world, certainly one of the longest-lived in the new world.[3]

[1] Cocalico derives from "koch-hale-kung," meaning a cave of serpents. (Oswald W. Seidensticker: "A Colonial Monastery," *Century Magazine,* December 1881, p. 216.
[2] Kuhns: *op. cit.,* pp. 179, 181.
[3] So well known did it become, it was included in Voltaire's famous dictionary: *Dictionnaire Philosophique,* Amsterdam, 1789, Vol. IV, p. 81. It sprouted up in various places, with divers disciples functioning as the Moses of the group, each seeking sight of Canaan. The best known of these groups was that led by an Englishman, Israel Seymour, who founded an extension of Ephrata in South Carolina. By 1783 it had forty members. (John E. Jacoby: *Two Mystic Communities in America,* Paris, 1931, pp. 49, 50.)

Like the Labadists and the *Woman in the Wilderness* group, they believed that it would not be long before Christ would return to earth, crowned in glory, sheathed in the mantle of the Lord. Like millennialists, they were convinced that the days of our world were numbered, limited by a heavenly horoscope, destined to a quick end. Life, in their eyes, was something to be gauged in terms of the future, the incalculable paradisaical spans wherein time and space were blurred, blotted out.

In this way Beissel carried on the tradition of Kelpius, who was a most ardent and fanatic millennialist. Following the example of his master, Beissel founded an *Order of the Solitary*, and it was the very nature of this conception which antagonized the Dunkards, who were a most canny and practical sect.

The Dunkards were really willing enough to prepare themselves to meet the Lord, but they were not overwhelmingly convinced of his early return. In Ephrata, where Beissel was free of the Dunkards, he was able to work out his experiment unmolested. He infused it with vision and song. To this day his mode of singing and the hymns he composed are remembered, though vaguely, by the people who still inhabit the territory adjacent to Ephrata. Beissel not only became America's first distinguished hymnologist, but he also became the author of the first book of German poetry published in the new world. The volume, entitled *Göttliche Liebes und Lobesgethöne* (*Godly Chants of Love and Praise*), was printed by Benjamin Franklin in 1730.

Beissel's achievements became so numerous that it was not long before he began to believe he had been selected by God as a special ambassador to earth, and when Count Zinzendorf, the noted Moravian, asked to see him, he replied that it was Zinzendorf's duty to come to see him and not his duty to see Zinzendorf. The result was the men never met.

Colony of Religious Savants

Like Seelig, Matchai, and Kelpius, the founders of Ephrata were men of learning and wisdom. Many of them were students of German universities, some graduates with *cum laude* distinction. Beissel himself was of most humble origin. He was the son of a dipsomaniacal baker; he early identified himself with the Bakers' Guild, fought the church authorities, learned in America to be a weaver,[1] visited the Labadists in Maryland, and, after his unfortunate stay with the Dunkards, wrote his famous *Ninety-nine Mystical Sentences*, which was also printed by Benjamin Franklin. It was the first book to be published by the Ephrata colony, which was later to prove prolific in such literary activity.

Beissel was deeply influenced by his experiences among the Labadists and also among the last remaining members of the *Woman in the Wilderness* colony. He immediately modeled his own group upon their pattern. To begin with, he insisted upon celibacy not only as an ideal, but as a necessity, and tried to make Ephrata into a monastic community.

Beissel Attacked as a Sexual Demon

His struggle in this regard was not an easy one. It came about that he was charged by his enemies with "whoremongering," and being the father of an illegitimate child. Brother Lamech's account, dealing with the struggle in the Pennsylvania courts, is most interesting:

"In the year 1730 the Tempter first began openly to raise an outcry of whoremongering against the Superintendent; for reports of the celibate life now began to spread abroad in the land, and many persons were displeased with it, since one already saw here and there

[1] Phebe Earle Gibbons: *Pennsylvania Dutch and Other Essays*, 1882, p. 138.

solitary ones of both sexes who had renounced the world,
living alone in the wilderness.   Then a rumor became
current among people that the Superintendent had sinned
with one of his spiritual daughters, and that she had actually brought into the world a bastard.   A justice of the
peace, by the name of Samuel Jones, became exercised
about it, and had them both summoned before him on a
King's Warrant.   To the question, Whether they were
guilty? the Superintendent demanded the witnesses, and
they not being forthcoming, administered a sharp reproof
to the justice, and went his way; for he had interfered
with his office and it was the Sabbath. . . . Then the
misunderstanding was disclosed; for this one had said it
concerning a sister after the flesh of the accused sister,
who had a husband; it had been understood, however, of
the latter, who was single.   The Justice hereupon begged
pardon of the accused sister and let her go in peace.
Afterwards, nevertheless, he levied upon her household
goods sufficient to pay the costs of the hea·ing." [1]

Beissel was acquitted, but it took a long time before the
scandal lost its force.   People in the surrounding territory
perpetuated the story, attacked Beissel as a "rapist," a demon,
taking advantage of the simple devotions of his feminine followers, polluting their purity.   They terrified their children
by threatening them with similar disasters.   This opposition
on the part of the inhabitants became so violent that they attempted to burn the houses of the colony and extinguish
it.   The plot failed, however, and the Ephrata brethren went
on building, erected more houses, and in time had a colony
which became growing and progressive.

[1] To give the other side of the case we must quote Brother Lamech:
op. cit., p. 57.   Of course, it is by no means impossible to believe that
Beissel was guilty.   That he held "love feasts" was undoubtedly true, and
it is also equally well established that he spent a suspiciously large part
of his time in the Sisters' Convent.   One of his Brethren, Conrad Weiser,
even threatened to condemn him in public if he persisted in revealing such
intense and continuous concern for the salvation of the Spiritual Virgins.
He was, it is true, attacked by a jealous husband, and when he retreated
into the woods with two of the Sisters as well as with a number of the
Brothers, the attacks multiplied.

In their house, Kehar, where they held sacred watches every night, everyone was silent. The Brethren were not idle men, impractical ecclesiastics. They were men who knew life, knew that to live men had to be carpenters, bricklayers, masons, farmers. The women could knit, spin, sew, and even manufacture paper and toys. But such work did not interfere with their religious exercises. Each member of the colony wrote every week a paper, confessing his sins, and these papers were read aloud by the Leader, known in their community as the Superintendent. They were discussed in detail, scalpeled apart, scissored into fragments, but always viewed in a mood of spiritual exaltation.

Beissel, who also had a stripe of Rosicrucianism in his mental texture, was not the only inspiring member of the group. In fact, their I.Q. was just as high as that of the *Woman in the Wilderness* colony. Peter Miller, who joined the Beisselites after the religious awakening at Tulpehocken, was a Heidelberg graduate, a distinguished linguist, and an internationally known theologian. Conrad Weiser, who became the magistrate of the colony, and attacked Beissel for his inordinate concern for the salvation of the Spiritual Virgins, was equally learned, and was best known for his intimacy with Indian dialects and the habits and customs of the Indians themselves. Later he became an interpreter for the government.

In those early days of Ephrata, poverty predominated. Everything money symbolized was evil in their eyes. Not only did they condemn man's proclivity to sin as evil, but they also condemned inanimate objects as sources of spiritual destruction. They considered iron, for example, a "wicked, sinister" metal, and refused to allow its use among them.[1]

When the Brethren were hustled into the courts because they refused to pay the "single-man's tax," they were outraged

[1] Wm. Chauncy Langdon: *Everyday Things in American Life* (1607-1776), p. 75.

at the presumption of the state. Six of them stayed in jail for almost a fortnight, each one of them determined not to succumb to the institutions that were Caesar's. They also refused to worship on the state-established Sabbath. Their Sabbath was, like that of the Jews, on Saturday, as specified in the Bible. Like the Puritans, they preferred the Old Testament to the New and lived according to its rigid regulations. They even calculated time in the ancient Jewish style; six o'clock with other communities was one o'clock with them. Besides, they read the Jewish prophets far more than the New Testament apostles.

Like Thoreau, whose recalcitrance they anticipated by almost a century, they did not believe in the right of the state to dictate to them in any way. Thoreau refused to pay the poll-tax and, unlike Emerson, would not compromise on the issue. The Ephratist Brethren refused to pay the single-man's tax for a not dissimilar reason. They were concerned with higher values. Finally they consented to pay a group tax which did no violence to their consciences as individuals or to their belief in personal freedom.

Germs Become Animals

The Ephratians were sticklers for everything in which they believed, so when a skin disease began to ravage the community they were at a loss how to attack it, since their religious ideal precluded the use of medicines. To combat this "itch," which was the characteristic symptom of the disease, they held a solemn conference, and decided after prolonged discussion and debate that it was not a disease at all, but an invasion on the part of "a noxious animal which they might innocently destroy." [1] The decision once made, they destroyed the "animal" with extraordinary expedition, and both the bodies and the souls of the community were preserved from blemish.

[1] J. F. Sachse: *German Sectarians of Pennsylvania,* p. 107.

In Scotland in the same century, men had been arrested for squeezing a boil, because it represented an attempt to frustrate God's will. If the Scotch had acquired the genius of the Ephratians, they might have discovered also that boils were the product of "a noxious animal," and not of God's design.

Ephrata did not long remain an impoverished, cenobitic community. In a short while people who were not hermits, and who sought to improve its economic life, crowded into it. Their influence was decisive. Industries were established, as also were bakeries, grist mills, oil mills, saw mills, flour mills, tanneries, bookbinderies; and it was not long before they all became prosperous enterprises. Various arts were cultivated. Weaving, quilting, embroidery, basket-making, and pottery became popular pursuits and some of the products were among the best of their time.

Following the command of Jesus that the rich should give up their fortunes and follow after Him, many wealthy people joined the colony, surrendered their possessions, and adopted the humble way of life of the rest of the community. Benedict Yuchly built a convent for the Sisters; Sigmund Landert furnished the funds to construct several buildings and then brought his daughters to live in them. No member was ever able to withdraw any of the funds he contributed to the colony. Such donations belonged to God and could not be touched again by man. Henry Bone, a quaint specter of a man, with eyes that darted at you like those in an El Greco portrait, was, alas, loath to accept that conclusion, and when the colony refused to return his possessions, he committed suicide.

MIDNIGHT MEETINGS TO WATCH FOR THE LORD

Night after night, following the vigilant practice of Kelpius, these eternity-seeking Ephratians scanned the skies for sight of the comet forecasting the advent of the Lord. They held midnight meetings, watching the heavens, certain that one night they would hear the Judgment blast and see the firmaments split wide with the Light and Presence of the Saviour. The discovery of the comet first seen by Klinkenberg in September, 1743, convinced them that this was the heavenly orb described in the Zohar, the appearance of which was supposed to warn the inhabitants of the earth of the return of Christ and the approaching inauguration of God's reign in this world. Crouched over their astronomical instruments, these monkish zealots, believing that their Mount Zion would prove to be the site of the new Jerusalem, must have resembled the disciples of Paracelsus and Cagliostro, slaving in their laboratories in quest of an elixir of life.

Most interesting in that connection is an article (February 16, 1744), of Christopher Sauer, the community printer:

> "Since the first night of Christmastide a comet has appeared with ample opportunity to view it. Such as saw the comet Anno 80 (1680) say: that the present one is greater and hath a longer brush. Following the former came a long weary war, for which the star was evidently not at fault, but rather the wickedness of mankind. What will follow this one, the future alone can disclose unto us. From certain indications we expect much sickness and death, but little conversion and betterment.
>
> "In mornings, one hour before day, another such comet is visible, whereof more in the future."

MASTERING THE METALS

The appearance of Jacob Martin upon the Ephrata scene extended this mystical approach. Martin was esteemed as a genius at chemicals; he was praised as having discovered at last the technique of transmuting metals, inferior ones into superior ones, lead into gold. Martin claimed to have found a mystic formula in harmony with the "hermetic philosophy," which was his contribution to the future transformations of all stuffs, substances, and eventually personalities.

MUFFLING THE BODY

The Ephratians were a strange group in attire and custom. To the ordinary Anglo-Saxon they seemed like a delegation from some weird medieval clan. They dressed like Capuchins, with a surplice extending to the feet, an apron in front and a veil behind, entirely indistinguishable as to sex. The men were tonsured, Beissel himself scissoring and shaving out the circular symbol; the women had their hair severely shortened and their faces rendered as plain and unprepossessing as possible. The men wore their beards to their ears, in imitation of Adam, whose fine-flowing ebony whiskers were their constant inspiration. They also admired the Jewish patriarchs, whose beards would have made Nestor envious. They swore by their beards as did the ancient Jews, and grasped them as today one would seize a hand in cordial salutation.

What Beissel aimed at in this stress upon simplicity of dress and unattractiveness of appearance was pathetically obvious. He aimed to eliminate every possible form of sexual attraction, remove as far as possible every display of the human body. Like the ancient monastics, he believed that the human body was seductive and that the best way to eliminate its enamoring and inveigling qualities was by ecclesiastical decree. He insisted, in keeping with many of the older monastic orders, that the main thing to do was to conceal the body, its lines, its contours, its seductions; and this is mainly why priests, sisters, and nuns wear such dress today.

"It was resolved to muffle the mortal body [it must not be forgotten that the Ephrata group believed in the new arrival of Christ, which was the conception of all Adventists] in such a style and in such a garment as would fit it for its immediate transportation to the skies and the eternal hereafter." [1] More

[1] Brother Lamech: *op. cit.*, p. 88. The *Chronicon Ephratense* deserves more extended mention. Brother Agrippa, as well as Brother Lamech, was responsible for its substance. It is, perhaps, the most valuable document concerning Ephrata still extant. It purported to be the life of

than that, they insisted upon discomfort as a virtue. They exposed themselves to tortures in order to prove their religious zeal. Never would they sleep upon a mattressed bed, but only upon a hard one, a bench if necessary, and always without a pillow; a comfort they considered a symbol of sin. They washed one another's feet as a sacred ritual, a vestige of ancient Judaic practice, and adopted such astringent and abstemious diets that many of them looked appallingly emaciated. For most of their meals they had little more than "pearled barley boiled in milk, with bread broken into it; another course was pumpkin mush, with slices of small crusted bread on a plate. . . . During the meal not a word was spoken; at the close another chapter was read out of the Bible." They lived in diminutive cells, wore coarse clothes, and ate constantly off wooden tables with wooden utensils.[1]

The sight of them as they "drew their carts themselves, and were their own horses" must have been striking enough, but even more startling must have been a glimpse of them at twilight "when they travelled . . . heavily laden like camels . . . the whole Brotherhood . . . trooping down the hill of Zion." They were, indeed, a fantastic band.

THE DEFEAT OF THE ECKERLINS

The coming of the Eckerlin brothers, an unforgettable if not an ideal trio, gave the colony an organizational pattern, a business aspect, an efficiency which it had lacked before. All three, but especially Onesimus, the cleverest of the brothers, fostered the economic life of the group, and soon developed it into a flourishing enterprise, an industrial establishment the like of which had not been witnessed in the land before. In fact, they might readily have created a colony which would have

Beissel, but it is far more than a biography. Its complete title should be recorded: *Father in Christ, Peaceful Godright (Friedsam Gottrecht), late founder and "Vorsteher" of the Spiritual Order of the Solitary in Ephrata, collected by Brothers Lamech and Agrippa.*

[1] Israel Acrelius: *A History of New Sweden,* 1874, p. 382.

surpassed all others on the continent, gloriously successful in every detail, had it not been for the predominating monastic influence which made it possible for Beissel and his followers to expel them in 1745.

Before the expulsion of Prior Onesimus, Ephrata had become as much an economic as a spiritual venture. The colonists became concerned with investments, property, usury; and even marriage, forbidden by Beissel, became an issue. Finally the 'Brethren rose up on the side of Beissel, burned Onesimus' writings, and drove two of the brothers from the community. The pair later settled in the wild wastes of Mississippi. The third Eckerlin brother remained for a while, but found that anyone bearing his name could never be happy in Ephrata.

After the departure of the Eckerlins, many of the mills were shut down and most of the industry of the community ceased. Ephrata became, as it originally had been, an agrarian colony, interested in production for use but not for profit.

Their Rhythm of Life

Busy as the colony was with its agrarian and industrial tasks, it never lacked time to devote to reading, writing, and study. Its whole life was routinized in such a fashion that it was impossible to waste time. The members worked all day long, with the exception of the time consumed in eating, and then from seven to nine at night they read, wrote, or studied; from nine to twelve they slept; they arose at midnight, spent an hour at song service, or matin, as they called it (they detested the word *mass*), slept again, woke once more at five, celebrated another matin, and then went to work afterward until nine in the morning, when breakfast was served. Such was the life of these simple, solemn folk, who believed that Christ was a communist and that to be Christians they had to be communists, too.

Israel Acrelius, who visited the colony while Beissel was still alive, gives a vivid picture of an Ephratian service and of

the antics to which the "Vorsteher" (also known as Father
Friedsam) resorted to gain his effects:

"On Saturday morning, at six o'clock, the cook came to
waken me, and said that Divine Service would begin in
half an hour. This was a black-bearded old man, very
serviceable; but I did not know why he should have such
a long coat of black cloth, when all the others wore white,
unless it was that the pot-black might be better concealed
in this way. . . .
"The church was not large, and could be filled by some
hundred persons. When they were assembled they sat for
some moments perfectly still. In the meantime Father
Friedsam was seen to be preparing himself; he held his
hands upon both his sides, threw his head up and down,
his eyes hither and thither; pulled at his mouth, his nose,
his neck, and finally sang in a low and fine tone. Thereupon the sisters in the gallery began to sing, the Cloister
brothers joined in with them, and all those who were
together united in a delightful hymn. . . .
"Father Friedsam then recommenced his former movements, and appeared rather ridiculous than devotional.
Finally, he arose with his hands clasped together, with
his eyes turned upwards, and began to speak of the natural
darkness of man's understanding, and prayed for enlight-
enment and a blessing. . . .
"When the service closed it was eight o'clock. . . .
The women went out of the church first, in such manner
that those from the benches nearest to the door first
marched off one after another, then those that were next,
and so the whole of the women's side of the church. . . ." [1]

EPHRATIAN MUSIC

Survivors of the Ephrata Community are living yet, and
their music is preserved by votaries in Snow Hill, who still
believe it the most beautiful music ever composed.[2] Although
it is obviously inferior to the Catholic masses, or the masses of
Bach, it retains a quality unique, subtle, and sublime. The

[1] Acrelius: *op. cit.*, pp. 387-390.
[2] Rev. S. G. Zerfass: *Ephrata Cloister. Souvenir Book*, 1921, p. 16.

Ephratians composed over seven hundred hymns, of which Beissel was the author of four hundred. Something undoubtedly lived in the Ephrata people that was rare, communicative in the higher and finer sense of the word, and that has lived on, like an echo that cannot be forgotten, in the lives of those people who eventually took over their land and occupied what was once the original colony. A great fire which destroyed their best farms and industries played havoc with their plans and reduced their aspirations to a nullity.

Ephratian music, however, did not die. It is not sung today, to be sure, as it had been in the original, by the simple, homespun folk, votaries of an other-worldly ideal, and it never will be sung that way again. But the notes remain.

Christopher Sauer, who battled with Beissel over the type as well as the content of hymnology, was most instrumental in preserving its substance if not its spirit. An early book published in German in America was Sauer's *Zionitischer Weyrauch's Hügel oder Myrrhen Berg, &c.*, Germantown, 1739.[1] Sauer was also the person who printed the first Bible in German in this country; he got it out in quarto size, partly because he wanted it to appear in large type so that old people as well as young would be able to read it. In Bradford's *Weekly Mercury*, April 1, 1742, he declared that he wanted everyone to be able to read, not only old as well as young, but poor as well as rich, servants as well as masters. Sauer advertised the book in the *Pennsylvania Gazette*, and it soon commanded a popular appeal.

Peter Miller the Extraordinary

Peter Miller, born in the Palatinate, proved to be one of the most intellectually distinguished figures in Ephrata. He was described as a profound philosopher, a man of portentous vision, who, in addition, spoke Latin as well as German. Miller

[1] Samuel W. Pennypacker: *Pennsylvania in American History*, 1910, p. 327.

joined with the original cenobites and soon became a profound influence in the colony. He translated the *History of the Persecutions of the Anabaptists* from Dutch into German, and translated the Declaration of Independence into seven languages. His letters form part of the finest remains of the group.

In a letter which Peter Miller wrote to Benjamin Franklin, he explains, in simple, succinct language, what happened to the Ephratists, namely, that "the Genius of the Americans [was] bound another way." Peter Miller lamented that fact beyond words. It broke up his life because he believed in a different ideal. His ideal was a cenobitic one, in which the individual sacrificed himself, his family, and everyone, no matter how precious, in behalf of Christian communism, which he considered the glorified gateway to the future life.

Despite its failure, noted by Miller, the Ephratian community achieved far more in the way of felicity for its followers than did any of the adjacent settlements, all of which envied the success of the Ephratians. Ephrata, or at least a remnant of it, remains for scholars and tourists, but little of it remains in the essential sense of the word. At no time did it possess more than three hundred followers. Those who go to it as on a pilgrimage, find little to convey the original spirit of the place. Nevertheless, as one of the most long-lived communist colonies in the new world, it will always be remembered by those who cherish a co-operative way of life as superior to a competitive one.

CHAPTER V

The Rappite and Zoarite Ventures

"Whereas, by the favor of Divine Providence an Association or Community has been formed by George Rapp and many others, upon the basis of Christian fellowship, the principles of which, being faithfully derived from the sacred Scriptures, include the government of the patriarchal age, united to the Community of property, adopted in the days of the apostles, and wherein the simple object sought is to approximate, so far as human imperfections may allow, to the fulfillment of the will of God, by the exercise of those affections and the practice of those virtues which are essential to the happiness of man in time and throughout eternity."

THE HARMONY SOCIETY

"Of the more than two hundred communistic societies that have sprung up in the United States, the Harmony Society was by far the most successful."

DICTIONARY OF AMERICAN BIOGRAPHY

From Ephrata we move to Harmony, where other souls consecrated to the life of Christ gathered and organized a colony. This group, headed by George Rapp, a strapping six-footer with flashing blue eyes and Nordic fairness of skin, first established a settlement in Pennsylvania in the winter of 1805, about twenty-five miles north of Pittsburgh. The group came over in three ships: the *Aurora*, which landed on July 4, 1804, the *Atlantic*, which landed two months afterward, and the *Margaretta*, which came still later. Most of the group on the *Margaretta* settled ultimately in Lycoming

County, Pennsylvania, under the leadership of Haller, a friend of Rapp.[1]

After spending ten profitable years near Pittsburgh, the Rappites, as they were often called, became dissatisfied with the lack of a water outlet and the fact that they found the soil unconducive to vine cultivation. They sold their land for the remarkable price of $100,000 and migrated to the banks of the Wabash in Indiana, where their new purchase of 30,000 acres promised a more fertile setting. But the nine years they spent there proved the waters of the Wabash to be mischievous and malaria-laden,[2] and they were compelled to move once more, this time to the kindlier shores of the Ohio, where they founded the town of Economy, the site of their greatest fruition.

The original Harmonyites, or Rappites, belonged to the old apostolic tradition. They were more concerned with religious than with economic matters. Like the Labadists and Ephratists, they sought to establish the Kingdom of Christ on earth, in preparation for that final kingdom in heaven in which all the redeemed would enjoy eternal life.

All the members of the community gave over their goods and all other forms of wealth to the central authority of the group. Thus they lost their individual identification and became part of the social being of the colony. They changed from "I's" to "we's," became socialists instead of individualists. Like Christ, they wanted nothing for themselves, but everything for others, nothing for today, but everything for tomorrow, for eternity. They were born of the same tradition as the Labadists, the Kelpiusians, the Ephratists. They wanted to plant God's kingdom upon earth as an inspiring prelude to Christ's return.

Rapp was a conservative utopian, paradoxical as that may sound, and never believed in contradicting or conflicting with

[1] *German American Annals*, 1904, Vol. 2, p. 406.
[2] Nordhoff: *op. cit.*, p. 76.

civil powers. His domain was religious and he wanted to
confine his power to that realm. Many of his followers in
Europe could not tolerate that limitation, and it was not long
before certain of them, led by the aggressive and challenging
Bimeler, threatened to divorce themselves from the community
if it succumbed to such influence. The Bimelerites, as they
were known, condemned everything extant, civil and religious,
and insisted that the individual was supreme, and that any
surrender to the state meant capitulation to the Caesars.
Bimeler denounced church and state as vestiges of that "Great
Babylon" of ancient origin.[1] Rapp disapproved of such extremes and urged the group to avoid them.

THE ZOARITES

The Bimelerite group, which came over in 1817, eventually
settled in the town of Zoar,[2] (from which name they became
known as Zoarites) and there they practiced the simple communist ideals advocated by Rapp. As in the other communist
colonies, the Zoarites began their venture as a celibate one, but
after the settlement prospered they established it upon a marital
basis, and Bimeler himself was one of the first to choose a wife.
The children, however, as in other groups of this type, were
reared in a public nursery from the age of three to twenty-one.[3]
In fifty years the colony acquired so much property that it was
estimated as being worth more than a million dollars.[4]

As in most of the other communist colonies, one man became the leader, and when he died the group disintegrated and
decayed. Bimeler was the leader, and during his life his
personality dominated the project. His genius was practical

[1] Aaron Williams: *The Harmony Society,* Pittsburgh, 1866, p. 19.
[2] Zoar in Biblical days was the city to which Lot fled when the cities
of the plain were destroyed.
[3] George B. Landis: *The Separatists of Zoar.* Annual Report of the
American Historical Association, 1898, p. 176.
[4] George Browning Lockwood: *The New Harmony Communities,*
Marion, Indiana, 1902, p. 19.

as well as spiritual and, under his aegis, mills and factories were opened and prosperity flowed into the community like milk and honey from Canaan.

In terms of their respective groups, Bimeler was no less influential than Rapp. Both men possessed an eloquence which was hypnotic. Neither of them was handsome; their power resided in their voices and the mystical wonder of their insights and intuitions. Bimeler was lame, with a bulging eye which often distracted the attention of his listeners; when his voice began to soar, however, he became magical as a prophet. What he had to say was never premeditated; it was always spontaneous, inspired by the immediacy of the occasion. As he himself said, "I generally come empty, without knowing whereof I am going to speak . . . As soon as I commence to speak an infinite field of ideas opens before me so I can choose where and what I like and what seems to me the most necessary." [1] One of his disciples copied down his "Discourses"—Bimeler hated clergymen so much he would never allow his addresses to be called sermons—and after Bimeler's death, which occurred in 1853, one of his "Discourses" was read every week and no preacher was ever allowed in the colony. No other ceremony—if this be called a ceremony— was ever tolerated by the Zoarites. Ceremony and ritual were anathema to them.

During the Civil War all the old Zoarites refused to fight, their opposition to military service being so intense; some of their sons, however, succumbed to the lure of the fife and drum, and before the war was over more than a dozen of them enlisted in the Northern Army.

It was not long before the economic carrion birds descended and devoured Bimeler's spiritual remains. Many of the members of the group began to maintain that private ownership was superior to communal ownership—the schoolteacher in the colony even printed a paper, "Nugitna," in which he argued

[1] E. O. Randall: *History of the Zoar Society*, 1904, p. 17.

that it was imperative "to educate the members of the society to see that our by-laws need revision; to bring them to look upon communism as not consistent with modern civilization," [1]—and on March 10, 1898, the communist experiment was abandoned, the property divided among individual members, and, surprising as it may seem to many, from that time on Zoar lost its economic stability and soon became an obscure and desolate place.

The Rappites

Even at their apogee, the Zoarites never achieved the success or influence of the Rappites, by which name the colony founded by George Rapp became familiarly known. Both groups believed in the same religious and economic philosophy. Like the followers of Kelpius and Beissel, they were millennialists and based their conceptions on New Testament revelations. Rich and poor shared alike in the wealth of the community; they dressed alike and lived alike, without finery or ostentation. The tailor, as Nordhoff describes, kept "his eye upon the people's coats and trousers, and the shoemaker upon their shoes, and so on, each counting it a matter of honor or pride that the brethren shall be decently and comfortably clad." After they learned the culture of silk and how to spin it, the dress of the community improved. The men as well as the women wore silk attire, and they were a handsome spectacle marching to church on Sunday, their garments shimmering in the sun.

The economic activities of the Harmony Society were conducted with remarkable efficiency. The foremen, appointed by the group, were so expert that it was not long before the town of Harmony became a thriving center. As Frederick Rapp, the adopted son of George Rapp, wrote to William Young, the colony "by constant application converted the wilderness into pleasant gardens and extensive fields." No

[1] Landis: *op. cit.,* p. 197.

other community surpassed it in mechanical skill or economic genius. Because of its superior organization and more prosperous achievement, it was hated by its individualistic neighbors. [1]

RAPP'S STRANGE CONCEPTIONS

George Rapp, an humble peasant, a vine-dresser and farmer by vocation, was a German puritan, which meant a Pietist. He was born in Württemberg in 1770, and until the time he died, in 1847, he headed the colony which he had founded. His simple upbringing gave added intensity to his convictions. Like the cobblers, the plumbers, the candlestickmakers, he believed in God because he was sure he had met him face to face, heard him in the whispers of the wind, talked with him in quiet valleys, been with him in obscure, dark places. Like other religious sans-culottes, Rapp was scorned, persecuted, and attacked. He housed within his brain eccentric ideas, and defended them with an eloquence impressively Miltonian. One of the strangest of his ideas was his belief that Adam contained within himself both sexes, and that if it had not been for Eve's sin, he would have been able to give birth to children. Because of the sin in the Garden of Eden, men and women were made separate, endowed with only one sex, uncreative within themselves as single individuals. Rapp believed, however, by consecration, it was possible for both men and women to become as they had been before the Garden of Eden catastrophe. Then each would be able, within himself and herself, to bear children and continue to do so until paradise was won, whereafter future generations would be unneeded, for all would be inherent in the loins of the Lord.

At first, it must be said in his defense, Rapp did not demand celibacy of his followers, though he always exalted it as the highest ideal. Later, however, when his group felt as he did on the issue, he insisted upon it as a categorical imperative.

[1] John Archibald Bole: *The Harmony Society,* p. 45.

He believed that in time men and women would both possess the qualities and powers of the opposite sex and that celibacy was only an interval, a stopping point, necessary before they re-acquired that genius.

Rapp claimed to be in such intimate connection with God that he could work miracles. Whether his miracles were the products of a morbid mind afflicted with hallucinations, or whether they were fraudulent inventions, as his enemies alleged, will never be known. The sincerity of the man, however, leads one to believe that the former conclusion was the more likely. He ofttimes informed his followers that God had spoken to him, as centuries before He had to Moses, and that signs had appeared in the heavens blessing their communion. There is still to be seen the stone, known as Gabriel's Rock, upon which the angel Gabriel is supposed to have left his imprint. It was the unanimous belief of the Rappites that Gabriel had descended to earth in order to give them his special blessing.

Rapp also liked to cultivate the mysterious. He had tunnels, trapdoors, sliding walls, and elusive passages built, and upon frequent occasions would spring suddenly from one of them as if he had been conjured out of air. Undoubtedly this form of legerdemain impressed the more credulous. He even had a special tunnel constructed, extending from his house to the church, and he would emerge from that in a rush of glory, his face shining, his shaggy hair blown like a wild thing about his head. In the eyes of his acolytes he must have looked, with his bushy eyebrows and piercing bright eyes, like a holy creation sprung from the infinite.

THE MILLENNIALIST DREAM

Like Kelpius and all the other millennialists, in whom the European and American worlds were abundantly fertile in those days, he believed that he would not die until he had seen the Saviour with his own eyes, talked to him, touched his hand.

He was convinced that he would live to lead his followers into the paths and lanes of the Lord, sheltered by trees of divine umbrage and caressed by sward of incredible softness and sweetness, like eiderdown found in heavenly hands. Rapp's dream was not unique. All millennialists shared it. God in those days belonged to everyone; he was not the monopoly of the ecclesiastics; he was the product, the invention of Everyman, of everyone who sought, pleaded, begged, for eternal life.

RAPPITES NOT PROSELYTIZERS

Unlike the Labadists, the Rappites evinced no desire to convert others to their cause. They established no outposts, despatched no vanguards into the wilderness, had no concern with proselytizing the natives. They were friendly with the Indians, as they were also with the white settlers, but they did not seek to change their lives or convictions. The Rappites were content to let their community stand as proof of the superiority of their religious and economic way of life. They were always willing to help others; they sought, as Frederick Rapp declared, "to be useful to mankind," but they did not seek to persuade mankind to follow them. In fact, they were so exclusive in attitude and philosophy that at times they seemed like celestial snobs; they felt they had a monopoly on heaven and were loath to share their advantage with other earthly groups. They rejected most of the individuals who applied for membership in the colony. Typical of their attitude is the following letter of Frederick Rapp to Chester Chadwick, who wanted to join the group:

"Your letter of the 15th ult. came to hand, in which we discover your desire to be admitted into our Society with your Family, in order to get rid of the trouble and care which is requisite to support and procure an honest living for yourself and family; which is a good meaning so far, yet we doubt very much whether you could submit to our regulations and manner of living, for no person here possesses anything as his own, nor can anybody act or do according to his own will, every member of the community must be obedient to the ordained superintendents, which is very hard for people who have not the kingdom of God for their chief object. For the fundamental principles, whereupon our community is established, are altogether religious. The religion of Jesus is practised here, in fact, no unrighteous man can abide here, far less a daring sinner, who lives yet in vices; therefore one has to bethink himself better before joining our Society than you perhaps are aware of. We advise you not to do it. We have not admitted any person this long time, having been so often deceived by people who lived here one or two years, and finding the path to follow Jesus too narrow, they break off and calumniate us, then all our trouble spent to make them do better was lost. The German language is also the only one spoken here, which you do not understand, and in consequence could derive no benefit from church or school.

"Content yourself for a while yet, the best way you can, a greater plan will develop itself perhaps before long, when all the honest and upright which are now scattered here and there through the world may be relieved from their burden.

"Your well wisher,
"FREDERICK RAPP."

Next to George Rapp, Frederick Rapp was the most important member of the colony. He lacked the weird, mystical genius of his adopted parent; he was more practical and prosaic, but he was not without vision. Tall, good-looking man that he was, quondam stone-cutter and architect, he strove to keep the colony on a sound economic footing, and it was largely due to his business acumen that it proved to be such a successful economic enterprise. Rapp had cultural interests, however, as well as economic; he was interested in science, literature, and music, and was himself a talented musician. In short, he was a rare man to be discovered in the hinterland of America in his day.

Communism in Practice

The elder Rapp's communism is best expressed in his own words or, to be more precise, in those of his colony, in which his philosophy is most definite and demonstrative:

"Unless the human mind be pure and enlightened, the principles of a Fraternity can neither be understood nor appreciated. . . . O, presumptuous man! You view the treasures of Heaven as a common stock; why not consider then the treasures of Earth in the same light? It is reasonable to suppose that he who cannot learn to share with his brother in this life will not easily do so in the World to Come and that no one need expect to find happiness in a heavenly society of men unless he first learn and practice the social virtues here among his fellow creatures.

"Here are no sects, nor parties, no partialities nor prejudices, nor is anyone excluded from or preferred to any others." [1]

So successful was Rapp's group that before long it became the envy of the whole vicinity. People came from near and far to witness the miracle of the colony. Simple hunters with fresh-shot meat, humble farmers with new-cut grain, sophisticated travelers with an eye to the curious, paused when they saw it—paused to wonder. Here was a community which lived as unselfishly as the Christian apostles and which thrived better than those groups and settlements which were dominated by individual greed for gain. Even the dogs propelling the treadmill seemed co-operative. This explains, to a large extent, why the outside groups and settlements felt so hostile to the Harmonyites—and to all the other communal groups, and later to the Mormons.

"This singular community of Germans," wrote George Flower, a sturdy trail-blazer, who visited Harmony in 1819,

[1] *Thoughts on the Destiny of Man.* The Harmony Society, 1824, pp. 84, 88.

"had little or no communication with the outside world, except through the miller, the storekeeper, the tavernkeeper, and Mr. Rapp. All who went to Harmony with surprise observed with what facility the necessaries of life were acquired and enjoyed by every member of Rapp's community." In 1823 Frederick Rapp wrote to Samuel Patterson that "we live in peace and unity, which gradually binds us faster and faster into one body, whereof one member renders to another the necessary assistance, which facilitates the toils of life in great measure." From the famous *Treatise* of the colony we learn that:

"One cannot expect to commune with God who can not get on with his fellow men. Only in social life can mankind attain its destiny. Only in such a society is life truly free. There political and religious institutions are united. There is no fear of slavish laws and penalties; for the good man is also the truly free man, for he obeys the law of nature, as well as of truth, from a sense of love. When he recognizes what is true, good and useful, he does it without compulsion, entirely because it is good and true. This freedom prevails in the Harmony Society.

"In the common household of this brotherhood, the greatest order, skill and diligence are observed in the most minute as well as the most extensive transactions. Here wealth is possessed in abundance, and all cares for sustenance are removed and forgotten. No sluggard can live in this amicable confederation, for permission is never given to any one to eat his bread in sinful indolence. Male and female, old and young, are usefully employed according to their powers of mind and body; all contribute to the welfare of the whole, and from the common stock all are supplied with all the necessaries of life.

"The various branches of this economic commonwealth, regularly conducted and united, form one great machine, the principal wheel of which, when in motion, puts all the rest in motion for the interest of the whole. In their mutual enjoyments all the members are contented and happy; none is rich or poor; the causes of distress and clamor in the world are not experienced or even known here. How could it be otherwise? In eating, drinking and clothing, everything is plain and simple, like nature herself in her household, which we necessarily take as an example for imitation in our economical regulations for the restoration of a happier age. Here are possessed sufficient means for convenience, and a competent knowledge for their application to the rational and useful purposes of life. Where so many useful, active persons are harmoniously united, there must be, and evidently is, a true kingdom of God.

"Those who choose such a life are such as are conscious of their imperfections and dissatisfied with themselves and have not perverted their moral faculties.

"In this manner the whole human race will eventually be ameliorated."

Life on the Outside

Life among the individual settlers in the outlying territories seldom achieved such comfort and security. There was a rough co-operation among them when it came to building cabins, husking corn, breaking trails, clearing roads, constructing forts and churches, fighting Indians, but there it stopped. Aside from such functions they worked as individuals, concerned with their own immediate personal and family interests. Their outlook was more competitive than co-operative; they wanted to get all they could for themselves as individuals, to acquire the best land, develop the best farms, accumulate the greatest wealth. The result was that a few acquired great wealth, more acquired small wealth, but most acquired very little wealth at all.

The Great Contrast

In the Rappite community, on the other hand, no one acquired any wealth, and yet everyone shared in the total wealth of the group, which meant that the community as a whole was

far wealthier than any of the surrounding communities.   In
1810 there were only one hundred and forty families in the
community; later the number grew rapidly.   In the eighteen
seventies they were at the apogee of their career.   "The town,"
the Rev. William A. Passavant wrote in 1840, "is divided into
regular squares by three streets running due north and south,
which are again intersected by five others lying east and west.
Of these the principal one, being the one on which the house
of Rapp and all the public buildings are placed, is situated in the
centre of the place.

"It is really a pleasure to walk over this immense plantation
and see the perfection to which farming is carried.   If the
land is too steep for the plough, it is covered with rows of
white mulberry trees to supply the silk worms with leaves.
Should the ground prove too harsh for the purposes of agri-
culture, it is planted with a species of osiers for the manufacture of baskets.

"Much attention is paid to the raising of fruit trees, and
in the fall of the year every variety of apple, pear, plum, peach,
quince, etc., may be had for the asking." [1]   The people lived
better, enjoyed better food, wore more substantial clothes,
possessed better dwellings, had better industries, manufactured
better goods than those in the individualistic communities in
the same territory.   Even their brewery and distillery produced
better beer and alcohol than those of the other settlements.
Their whisky was praised for miles around as the best in the
new country.   More than that, their cutlery shop, one of the
largest in the world, was internationally renowned for the excellence of its wares.   But most important of all, they were
among the first in the new world to purchase a steam engine
and utilize steam power as a productive force.   Oddly enough,
George Rapp, fearless in every other respect, was afraid to

[1] Rev. William A. Passavant: "A Visit to Economy in the Spring of
1840," *Western Pennsylvania Historical Magazine,* 1921, Vol. IV, pp. 145,
148, 149.

operate a steam engine.[1] The colony built a steamboat in
1824, which was their greatest pride. Before that, they had
relied on flatboats to deliver their cargoes, some of which went
as far south as New Orleans.

Their rhythm of life, like that in all communist communities,
was regular and precise. They arose at dawn, breakfasted,
then ate again at nine, had an afternoon lunch at three, and a
simple supper at seven. There was music when they worked,
a band playing German hymns from the hillside, and again at
night, as they dined, and afterward as they sat upon their
porches, gathered about the church, or conversed on the road-
sides, the band filled the air with lighter and gayer tunes.
Until curfew time, which was at nine, the band played, so that
everyone would go to bed with music in his heart.

Rapp was so concerned with the spiritual felicity of his followers that he wanted them to feel pure as they went to sleep
every night, because there was no telling when God might come
with His Son, bursting asunder the clouds and bestriding the
land. Each night transgressors had to come to him and confess their sins, and secure forgiveness before they retired.
Forgiven, they could face the Lord and all His hosts with
confidence and courage. These confessions were in addition
to the nocturnal prayers, to which the whole colony resorted
just before the curfew tolled it to rest.

The Count Leon Episode

In 1829 the Harmony Society was considerably concerned,
and not a little elated, about a letter which Rapp received from
an aristocrat, Count Leon, who introduced himself in his epistle
as a convert to the Harmony ideal. As was later proved,
Count Leon was none other than a German adventurer by the
name of Bernard Müller. The Rappites might not strive to
convert people, but they were not averse to concerning them-

selves with people who, by their own impulse, were converted
to the cause. Two years elapsed before Count Leon and his
entourage of servants and followers arrived upon the scene,
and began their strut across the new-world stage. Economy
had looked forward with almost childlike eagerness to their
coming, but it was not long before they began to regret the
fact that they had invited them.[1] Count Leon came with
banners flying, like a conqueror to a conquered city; before
him he had sent his fuglemen, fast and furious, to herald his
coming; when he approached the town, caparisoned like a
cavalryman of the gods, the Harmonyites stared and wept.
They were unaccustomed to such a spectacle; more, they
loathed it.

From that time on, after Leon settled in the community,
the relations between the Rappites and the Leonites sped from
bad to worse, with every day adding new irritations and exas-
perations to their conflict. Leon was a military man and
accoutred himself with the weapons befitting that vocation;
the Rappites were pacifists and hated the sight of anything
suggesting war or any other form of bellicosity. Leon was in
favor of matrimony; the Rappites were opposed to it. Leon
held wild parties at night; the Rappites wanted to sleep, happy
in the arms of the Lord. Leon promised much; the Rappites
promised little. But the little which the Rappites promised
was much since eternal life was included in it. Leon was
interested in everyday life, not in life beyond the grave, and
he made that plain in demonstrative form. He insisted that
all the bills of the colony be turned over to him; he would pay
them out of his own pocket, unhesitatingly and immediately.
This tactic was recognized by the Rappites as a way of acquiring financial control of the colony, and they opposed it
with unflagging vigor. Before long the Rappites realized that
for the sake of their own peace and felicity they had to rid

[1] Agnes M. H. Gormly: "Economy, A Unique Community," *Western
Pennsylvania Historical Magazine,* July, 1918, Vol. 1, No. 3, p. 120.

themselves of the Leonites, and after paying off the latter with adequate sums they succeeded in disencumbering themselves of their presence, at the same time losing to the Leonite cause a number of their own vacillating adherents. After the separation took place, however, conflict did not cease. The Leonites settled in Phillipsburg and built their own colony in that vicinity. It was not markedly successful, and protests grew and multiplied. At that point, to save his own face, Count Leon denounced the Economy community and urged his band to demand sufficient sustenance for their felicity. On April 2, 1833, a mob, inspired by the Leonites, attacked Economy, wrecked the place, and created havoc for miles around. The Harmonyites refused their demands. Most of the colony stayed in their homes, and scorned the invaders. They would have nothing to do with them. Finally they took courage and, marching to the strains of the "Rogue's March," they attacked the Leonites, drove them from the town, and shipped them to Alexandria, in Louisiana, where Leon himself died shortly after.

The best philosophy of the Rappites, which explains why they were one of the most successful of the utopian colonies, is condensed in their manifesto, from which the following excerpts are chosen:

"In America nothing hinders the Society from practising its belief. It is a special providence that this land became a free republic.

"The golden treasure of this world is friendship. This heavenly virtue, the first principle of which is implanted in the nature of man, begins to spread around us its genial influence, and to flourish in a brotherly society of harmonious members. If all mankind were to live in thousands of such brotherly communities, their happiness would be greatly promoted. The experience of twenty years shows the superior advantages of a united religious community, based on the principles of brotherly unity established and practised by Christ and His apostles.

"It is decreed that the whole human race shall become united by the sacred bond of mutual interest and brotherly affection. The two chief obstacles to this union are the sensual propensities and the ignorance of men.

"The proper education of the youth is of the greatest importance to the prosperity of any plan for the amelioration of mankind. That kind of learning and those fashionable accomplishments which are useless and only calculated for show should be entirely abolished, and in their stead those true principles and habits of life should be established and confirmed, which most strongly tend to unite the hearts, minds and fortunes of the rising generation, and arouse their sleeping faculties for the performance of all that is truly good and great.

"*It is ardently hoped and believed that this sublime, predestined system of Brotherly Union and Social Harmony will ere long be universally established for the restoration of the golden age, the dignity of human character, and the happiness of man.*"

CHAPTER VI

Bethel and Aurora

1844-1877. Keil died 1877. Colony dissolved 1881.

*"For there in the East they dream the dream of the
things they hope to do,
But here in the West, the crimson West, the dreams
of the East come true."*

It is revealing to note that all the religious communist colonies founded in the new world were dominated by individual leaders toward whom the members constantly looked for inspiration and guidance. The Labadists were votaries of Labadie, the *Woman in the Wilderness* group were devotees of Kelpius, the Ephratists acolytes of Beissel, the Rappites disciples of Rapp. The leader-psychology prevailed among them all.

In the Bethel and Aurora colonies, Dr. Keil, originally a merchant tailor, was the avatar of authority. He early disposed of his business and became a reformer. He resorted to the same technique that the other leaders did: had visions, discerned signs, acquired insights, developed intuitions, conjured up prophecies and divinations. Originally he had been a disciple of Jacob Boehme, as had been most of the German idealists and utopians who had settled upon these shores, and for a considerable time he adhered to that philosophy. After a while, however, he became more mystical than Boehme, and, influenced by Paracelsus and Cagliostro, he began to seek for a "Universal-medizin" which should prove to be the panacea of the ages. This *medicine* should not only cure disease, but it should also provide eternal life.

DER HEXENDOKTER

Although far from an educated man, as his letters attest, Keil plunged into the study of medicine, botany, and physics in his quest for this elixir. He finally claimed to have discovered the magic fluid and in his drugstore in Pittsburgh he sold it in infinitesimal quantities to those who desired and needed it.[1] He effected a number of cures, employing hypnotic procedure when his *medicine* did not work; in other cases he resorted to the simple mental-healing technique later to be made so popular by Mrs. Eddy, and in this art he likewise achieved marked success. As his cures multiplied, he soon became known among the ignorant populace as *Der Hexendokter.*

Keil was an arresting personality who dominated everyone who came under his influence.[2] His strong-set face, with his high forehead and forthright chin, was a compelling asset in his field. People believed him before he opened his lips to speak. And there was just enough of the suggestion of the charlatan about him to make him excite the interest and whet the curiosity of the credulous.

Strangely enough, Keil had been interested originally in becoming an actor, and vestiges of his interest in the theatrical clung to his personality long after he gave up the stage as a potential vocation. He translated his love of the drama into his speech, his gestures, his actions. Few preachers of his time were more finished actors than he. He strutted as he spoke, orated as he preached, vociferated as he prayed. Nothing he attempted was without some tinge of melodrama.

[1] Wm. Godfrey Bek: "A German Communistic Society in Missouri," *Missouri Historical Review,* 1908-1909, Vol. III, p. 55.
[2] John A. Roebling, the designer of the Brooklyn Bridge, learned to his regret how powerful Keil's influence was over the feminine members of his flock. Roebling fell in love with the exquisite Helena Giesy, became engaged to her, but discovered that she would not marry him unless he joined Keil and accepted him as a spiritual leader. He refused and she remained unmarried to the end of her life.

Even after he was converted from mysticism to Methodism, it was as another act in a play. He was overcome with ecstasy at a revivalist meeting conducted by the vibrant Dr. Nast, founder of German Methodism, and in the swirl of words, prayers, songs, and hallelujahs, he succumbed and joined the Methodist Church. Nast's influence upon him, however, was ephemeral. It was the minister, J. Martin Hartmann, who changed the career of Keil's life, and led to the foundation of the Bethel colony, in the sparsely settled territory of Shelby County, Missouri. The colony was reasonably elastic in all respects save in its devotion to its communist ideal. There was even a Jewish family enrolled in it. There were no restrictions of dress, no circumscriptions of diet, no severe regulations of conduct. All the money in the community was shared equally, at the inclination or urgency of any or of all. There were no records taken, no bookkeeping kept up, no punch-clock reports, no economic check-ups.

Everyone had all that he needed in the way of shoes, clothes, food, shelter. No one ever suffered from insufficiency. Everyone thrived.

Keil had arrived in America in 1835, been converted to Methodism in 1838, and licensed as a Methodist preacher in 1839. Hartmann instructed him in the ideas of communism, and convinced him that true Christians had to live as communists. From that time on, Keil knew his mission, namely, to found a communist society dedicated to the way of the Lord.

The Book Written in Blood

Keil's old habits, however, soon came into conflict with his new, and it was not long before he deserted Methodism, and declared that he would call himself nothing other than "Christian." All creeds had limitations which he would not abide, could not tolerate. When he was first converted to

Methodism, he had burned his mystic book, containing the hieroglyphic symbols and magic formulae for eternal cures, and condemned it as an opus of Satan. Amid the conflagration ceremony, to which many had gathered, Keil denounced himself for having worked the miracles he did, and blamed his powers upon Lucifer; all the assembled prayed en masse, their voices soaring with every chant, interspersed frequently with hysterical hallelujahs and amens. It was a wild, weird scene, with Keil, the protagonist, more wild than all the rest of the crowd.

After Keil left the Methodists, he never returned to his snake-oil elixir, never repeated his charlatan cures. Instead he became a communist, and directed his energies toward the creation of a Christian community based upon apostolic ideals. He took his entire congregation with him, and it constituted the original membership of the Bethel community. He instructed the young in his new philosophy, and soon had disciples spreading his gospel throughout the new land, in Ohio, West Virginia, Indiana, Kentucky, and Iowa.[1] Keil ordained these disciples as ministers whose sole function was to spread the gospel of the true Christ as espoused by the Twelve Disciples. They refused to adopt any specific creed, were scornful of all denominations, and went up and down the countryside, in hamlet, village, and town, disseminating their revolutionary doctrine.

What made them seem so revolutionary to the settlers of that time was not so much the communism they preached— and lived—but their opposition to all denominations, and their refusal to accept a cent of money for their ministerial services. Naturally, the clergy of all denominations loathed them, encouraged their followers to eschew them, and, if need be, stone them from the vicinity. But no such attacks could discourage their fierce and fanatic ardor.

[1] Bek: *op. cit.,* p. 58.

"Thou Art Christ"

Keil himself, as the Bethel colony grew more and more successful, cultivated what Hitler today has made popular as the Fuehrer-concept. He not only developed the clairvoyant propensities previously noted, but he actually went so far as to declare himself the *Centralsonne* (Central Sun), and his leading followers as *Lichtfuersten* and *Lichtfuerstinnen.* Women in the colony, swayed and overcome by the magic of his words, would often scream out, "Thou art Christ," and it seems that Keil was not loath to don the robes of the Master.[1] In fact, Keil even went so far as to announce that he was to die on a certain day as a sacrifice to God; he mentioned the day, and a mob ventured forth to witness the event. God, however, did not fulfill his promise, and Keil thereupon avowed that it was only because there was a greater work for him still to fulfill upon earth. At times, he declared himself omniscient and assumed to himself preternatural, if not supernatural, powers.[2]

Keil's influence over his followers was similar to that of Rapp. Both were self-made men, with a dominant power drive which they canalized in a religious direction. Neither would tolerate interference with his plans or criticism of his actions. Both resorted to kindred techniques in fortifying their control over their groups. Keil even introduced a confessional not unlike that of Rapp, wherein he challenged his people to be good by threatening to inflict severe penalties upon all who deviated from the moral law. Morality with both men was paramount. It was the final test of salvation. Neither had any tolerance for the sinner converted on his deathbed, hoping thereby to be ushered into the presence of the Lord. One had to be good throughout his life to merit such a reward. Salvation had to be through good works as well as faith.

[1] Bek: *op. cit.,* p. 59.
[2] John E. Simon: "William Keil and Communistic Colonies," *Oregon Historical Quarterly,* 1935, Vol. XXXVI, p. 146.

At no time in the history of the colony was Keil's authority disputed or challenged. There was no Count Leon episode to disturb the serenity of its career. In fact, Keil was often called "King Keil," so complete was his authority.[1] Keil promised everyone work, food, and shelter, and a short cut to God's kingdom, and none of his followers asked more. He never insisted upon the complete communism of some of the other apostolic groups, but what private possessions the members possessed were microscopical. All told, its communism was wiser than that of the other groups, because it allowed for that slight but interesting interplay of private possession which helped rather than harmed the communist ideal.

Dancing and Festivals

As in the other communist colonies, the buildings, their interiors, the food served, the dress adopted, were of the simplest and most unalluring kind. Simplicity and sacrifice went hand in hand in the struggle for salvation. But Keil was not so severe and ascetic as Rapp and Labadie; in his colony dancing prevailed, as did many of the old gala customs of the Germans, in all their pagan abandon. Many festivals were held, sometimes several a month, and everyone participated in them with enthusiasm and gaiety. People from the surrounding territory came to join in these celebrations, and the food and drink provided for all, made a feast which the individualistic frontiersmen had every right to envy. Competitive production was not able to keep up with communal. The communal groups produced more, provided far better conditions of life, afforded greater social advantages, achieved more security.

When Bethel became surrounded by individualistic settlers who threatened to encroach upon its domains, Keil was the first

[1] Robert J. Hendricks: *Bethel and Aurora*, 1933, p. 137.

to declare that the colony should move its location, and find one where it could be alone, removed from all the predatory aspects of competitive civilization. His followers agreed with him, consented to send out a delegation into the Oregon territory, and, after receiving favorable reports, undertook their trek to it.

THE HEARSE-LED TREK

Just before the Bethelites set forth on their extended journey, Keil's son Willie died, at the age of nineteen, and for a brief period the venture was delayed. It did not take Keil long, however, to decide what he was going to do. To begin with, he was determined not to allow his son's body to remain behind, buried in forgotten soil. Besides, he had promised to take him west, and that he would do at all costs. Utilizing his chemical knowledge, he purchased sufficient alcohol to serve as a preservative, poured it into the casket, which was lined with lead, sealed it, and proceeded to carry the body of his dead son across countless miles of hills, gullies, rivers, mountains, deserts, to the Pacific coast, where he could be buried near his family.

It was a weird, macabre spectacle, this troop of settlers hazarding the West, a coffined body leading them, like some ghost from the world beyond. Such reverence was seldom shown to the dead by the rest of the citizenry. For miles around, people who had heard about this strange bier watched for its passing and listened to the deep, guttural hymns sung by the mourners. It was like something which had stolen its way out of the grave and, wraith-like, was worming its way across the continent. Even the Indians, witnessing this fantastic caravan, with the special wagon of singers accompanying the corpse, were awed into immobility as they watched. This was Keil's hope. He had outriders to apprize him of the approach of Indians, and when these messengers came riding back with an ominous warning, Keil would cry, "Sing; everybody sing."

The group did not arrive in Willapa, where the original delegates had decided to settle the colony, until six months later, November 1, 1855. Willie Keil was not buried until after Christmas, at which time the whole colony joined in the obsequies, every moment of which was tense with emotion and drama. The singing, the wailing, the prayers, rising like the wild lamentations of an ancient people, were ineffably weird, against the woodland background.

AURORA

The group struggled hard and vainly in the Willapa territory to make it fertile. After six months, the colonists moved to a more happy location, called Aurora after the name of Keil's favorite daughter.[1] There they were closer to the enterprises of the day, the land was more yielding, and the forests more penetrable. By the spring of 1857 the venture was in full swing, houses built, stores opened, businesses established— but all upon a communal basis. No money was permitted within the colony. Everyone obtained from the various stores and businesses whatever he needed, without price, without any stipulation. All he had to do, as in Bethel, was to work with the rest of the community to produce the goods which were necessary for its survival.

Life in Aurora was a continuation of life in Bethel. There were supervisors, foremen, managers of the various enterprises, but none of them had the authority to demand more work from an individual than he wished to contribute. Such liberty was too sacred to be violated. In fact, the colony was far more interested in leisure than in work, and they spent more of their time devising celebrations and festivities than they did in organizing their work. Everyone had to learn

[1] Hendricks: *op. cit.*, p. 107.

to play some instrument, and great stress was laid upon the need for melodic beauty in all musical performances.

As in a number of the other colonies, the men and women were separated, men entering the church by one doorway, women by another, and they sat in different sections of the church, which was beautified by the handiwork of the colonists themselves. There was no antagonism between the sexes, yet they believed that the more separate they remained, the better able they would be to face God and win his sanction. After all, men and women who were interested in sex could not be profoundly interested in God.[1] God was sexless. God was eternal within himself. Ordinary men and women sought perpetuity in the flesh, in carnal relationships, in children; those dedicated to God sought it in something higher, more spiritual, more removed. The latter wanted to live as the Lord lived, as simple communists; their interests were not ephemeral but eternal.

THE SECOND CARAVAN

After Keil's successful trek to Oregon, Professor Christopher W. Wolff led another group from Bethel to Aurora. Wolff's wagon train did not reach Aurora until 1863, eight years after Keil's arrival. Wolff and his followers added much to the new community. Wolff himself was a graduate of the University of Göttingen, and a sophisticate in the dominant political and economic philosophies; undoubtedly he influenced Keil to a great degree in his thinking and helped him formulate the details of his social program.

Wolff had no hearse before him to overawe the Indians when he led his caravan of the faithful from Missouri to Ore-

[1]Keil urged celibacy so strongly at different intervals of the colony's existence that few of the members had the courage to marry, and Aurora became familiarly known as "Bachelor Town." (John E. Simon: *op. cit.,* Vol. I, XXXVI, p. 147.)

gon. But he was more concerned with his books than with the natives and the other perils of the environment. Day after day he pursued his study of Cabet, Babeuf, Fourier, Proudhon, and even Marx. Ideas formed a great festival of inspiration in his life. His cohorts would look at him in amazement, bewilderment, and incredulity, as he sat there, incessantly reading his books, ignoring the country through which he was passing, ignoring everything but the written word.

The wagons, however, reached their destination, and it was not long after their arrival that the colony entered the most prosperous phase of its career. The members numbered more than a thousand. The land they owned exceeded 23,000 acres, and the value of it was over $1,000,000. Their homes were surrounded with flowers and filled with music, and there can be little question but that Aurora was the gayest and most joyous of all the religious communist colonies in the new world. Their restrictions upon conduct were far less severe than in most of the other religious groups. They could smoke, drink beer, sing, dance, and be almost as human as the colonists in the non-communist settlements.[1]

THE END OF THE EXPERIMENT

Aurora dissolved, as did most of the co-operative colonies, when its author and leader died. Although all these colonies were communist in economic philosophy, they were held together by the individualistic energies and powers of a forceful leader. When the leadership of the Labadist colony became corrupted, the colony dispersed. When Kelpius died, the *Woman in the Wilderness* group lost its identity. After Beissel's death, Ephrata was never the same. After Rapp's death, Economy became a lonely, uninspired retreat. And after Keil's death, Aurora died. The members agreed to

---

[1] William Alfred Hines: *American Communities,* 1878, p. 46.

divide the property, share the assets of the community, and begin their lives anew, not as members of a co-operative community, but as individual settlers in competitive communities.

This would have broken Keil's heart, but Keil was dead, and, alas, his good works did not live after him.

CHAPTER VII

The Shakers and the Woman Christ

"Yet once, it is a little while, and I will shake *the heavens, and the earth, and the sea, and the dry land; and I will* shake *all nations, and the desire of all nations shall come."*
HAGGAI: ii: 6, 7

"No man can come fully into this kingdom (Christ's Kingdom on earth), keeping back a part of his possessions. . . . This drives into exile the unrighteous Mammon and all his seed."

One of the oldest of the religious communist sects to settle in this country was that of the Shakers. They were different from other groups in derivation, outlook, and behavior. Their origin can be traced to France, to those fierce, hectic days following the Revocation of the Edict of Nantes (1685) when the lives of all heretics were unsafe and men of the Protestant faith had to hide in the tenebrous retreats of the religious underworld to escape arrest and execution.

Such persecution increased rather than decreased the religious resistance of the Protestants, and before long new sects sprang up in numerous places, published new manifestoes and credos, organized different groups, developed unique convictions. Among them were the Camisards, founded and led by a baker, Jean Cavalier, whose eloquence won the hearts of all who heard him; very soon he built up a group so large that he became a terror to the nation. He and his followers strode up and down the land, prophesying the end of the world and the coming of the millennium. Their enthusiasm

97

was so intense that it burst out into various forms of hysterical acrobatics, windings and twinings of the body, contortions of hands and feet, twisted trunks, gnarled mouths, climaxing in strange cries and screams and songs wordless and weird.

So extreme did their antics grow, they soon became known as Shakers, which name clung to them through the years in the new world as well as the old.

Persecution of the Camisards

The wild, abandoned enthusiasm of the sect appealed to the multitudes; it presently became a mass movement.[1] The French Government was so alarmed it determined to annihilate every living Camisard. It executed most of the leaders, burned several at the stake, broke others on the wheel, strappadoed a number, splintered the spines of still others, gouged out eyes, severed ears and tongues, snapped arms and legs, and when such measures failed, resorted to wholesale massacres.[2]

Although the Camisard movement was exterminated in France, Jean Cavalier and several of his confreres adopted various disguises, hid in huts, snatched food wherever they could find it, and finally discovered a boat whereby they managed to get to England. Cavalier's success in England was scarcely less phenomenal than in France. His following increased so rapidly that a number of Quakers, in particular James and Jane Wardley, joined him, and from that time on the movement became a sound and lasting success.

The Woman Christ

Among the many peculiar ideas entertained by the Wardleys, one was outstanding: the belief that the Christ ideal would be embodied this time in the form of a woman instead of a man.

[1] Clara Endicott Sears: *Gleanings from Old Shaker Journals*, 1916, p. 5.
[2] *Ibid.*, p. 6.

The woman whom they believed to be God's ambassador was Ann Lee, and it was largely through the efforts of the Wardleys that she became one of the most influential religious figures of her time.

Ann Lee herself was a simple person, of proletarian background; her father was a blacksmith who worked hard and long to eke out a living, and who had to send his daughter to work in a cotton factory at an early age. She had a Joan of Arc complex, suffered from visions in childhood, contemplated herself as a divine spirit, an angel in human guise, watched her shoulders for signs of wings, stared into mirrors to detect her own transformation into a supernatural being. Throughout the later years of her life she was certain that she was in intimate contact with God, that she had been created as His Daughter, sister of Jesus, and would never die.

Instead of feeling ashamed of her illiteracy, she boasted of it. She would have none of man's learning; she wanted only God's. There were times when she doubted whether she was her mother's child; she was the child of the Lord, conjured from the loins of the firmament. Life was a blurred thing in her eyes; she always saw beyond it. Even her marriage, her four children, all of whom died, seemed unreal to her, and in time they were blotted out like light in a tunnel and had no existence at all. She could scarcely remember their names.

Ann Lee gloried in punishment, persecution, and sacrifice. When mobs attacked her she rejoiced because she knew she was suffering for the Lord; when she was flung into jail, she sang with happiness because she knew that God had wished it so in order to test her courage. Whenever life became dark and fearsome, visions sprang before her and she saw God's feet upon the horizon, and heard his voice amid the spheres. At night she saw his sidereal hosts push up the moon, light the stars, and lock up all the cracks and crevices of the day. At dawn she saw another shift of heavenly minions at work, folding back the parchment of the night, releasing the sun from his bondage, and speeding him forth on his daily course. Night after night and day after day, in prison and out, Ann Lee would sit and see this dramatic spectacle enacted before her eyes, just as Blake did in his vision of Jerusalem. It became a ritual with her.

In America, where she had come after a vision urging her to undertake the journey, and after due deliberation and debate with God had convinced her of the wisdom of her course, she established Shakerism upon a sound and enduring basis. She and her closest followers had come over on a boat called the *Marish;* it arrived in New York in the middle of the year 1774, but conditions were not favorable for the immediate organization of a colony, and for several years the movement was forced to disperse and gather strength from centrifugal sources. Mother Ann, as Ann Lee became familiarly known, spent several years slaving at various menial jobs in New York City before she found it possible to realize her mission as a creative force in the new world. As Shaker literature has shown, she had been "by a direct revelation instructed to repair to America," to save the souls of her group and the soul of the new world. When she and her followers finally acquired enough means to undertake a settlement of their own, they ventured forth into the northern part of the state, not far from Albany, where they established a center in Watervliet. It was there that Mother Ann died in 1784.[1]

Origin of the Name

Although the name Shakers was at first resented by the group—it had originally been applied to them in a derogatory sense—they soon not only became accustomed to it, but cherished it. Like all the other religious communist sects,

[1] Nordhoff: *op. cit.,* p. 128.

they went back to the Bible for their defense. In the book of Haggai they found words which gave to the meaning of the word Shaker an inspired significance: "Yet once, it is a little while, and I will shake the heavens, and the earth, and the sea, and the dry land; and I will shake all nations, and the desire of all nations shall come."

From that time on they became proud of the name, and wherever they founded communities, the name Shaker was unanimously adopted. Great as Mother Ann's influence was, Shakerism did not perish with her demise. In this respect the Shakers proved superior to the other religious colonies. Their survival was not dependent upon that of the individual. *The Woman in the Wilderness* group disintegrated after the death of Kelpius; Harmony gave up its ghost when Rapp died, but Shakerism, born though it was of the spiritual meditations and machinations of Mother Ann, persisted long after its author had made her exit. It had a vitality which for generations seemed undying.

Mother Ann's Spirit Goes Marching On

Almost all religious prophets of that day believed that they would live to see the end of the world, witness the opening of the skies and the coming of the Lord; few of them, however, were presumptuous or arrogant enough to believe that they were ectoplasmic extensions of divinity. Mother Ann was one of the few who did, and her followers were indubitably convinced of it. She was God's Daughter on earth, and as such could never die. Her body might be buried, her flesh disintegrate, but her soul would live forever, close always to those who believed in her godliness. In that sense Mother Ann, though dead, lived on as the other founders of religious colonies did not.

After her death, testimonies in her favor increased, and her apostles worshiped her with no less devotion than the

Twelve Disciples adored Christ. There was wonder in her name, magic in its sound, beauty in its suggestion. Her followers felt that, in Mother Ann, something was born which was not only divine, as was Christ, but also something which was profoundly human, housing within itself an element of the cosmos that was different from both gods and men. Her personality was *sui generis,* singular as prophecy, yet simple as breath. She was tender as a mother, yet awesome as a god. "I really loved and feared her more than any person I ever saw," wrote Rachel Spencer,[1] one of the Sisters of the Society, and in those words she epitomized the feeling shared by all the members of the group. John Farrington, one of the Brothers, told how he loved her, but at the same time stood in awe of her strange, clairvoyant powers. After confessing his sins to Mother Ann, he was amazed when she told him that there was still much more for him to confess. "She then told me," Farrington writes, "of a number of secret sins which I had committed, which I had not recollected, and which I well knew were unknown to any living mortal but myself; and I was fully convinced that she could not have known these things but by the revelation of God." [2]   Ann Lee almost always had that effect upon people. Many who came to scoff remained to pray. Eliab Harlow related his own experience, which was illustrative of that reaction. Speaking of the first time he attended a Shaker meeting, he wrote:

> "I did not go with the expectation of getting or hearing anything good, but merely to gratify my curiosity, as I had heard that they were exercised with singular and strange operations. But when I came to see the people and their worship and heard their testimony and observed the remarkable operations which attended them, my mind was struck with the fear of God and I was fully con-

[1] *Testimonies Concerning the Character and Ministry of Mother Ann Lee,* given by some of the aged Brethren and Sisters of the Society, 1827, p. 26.
[2] *Ibid.,* p. 12.

vinced that the power of God was there. Mother Ann's appearance seemed truly beauteous and heavenly while walking the floor under the . . . operations of the power of God; such Godly fear and heavenly love I never beheld in any person before." [1]

Like Kelpius, Beissel, and Rapp, Ann Lee believed in the millennium, and expected to live to see the Son of God disperse the clouds, fold up the firmament, and greet her as His Divine Sister. When her group was attacked and once more she and her followers were flung into jail, she was surer than ever that God was preparing her for his heavenly mission. She wanted to be crucified like Christ; the pain, the torture of having nails driven into her hands and feet, her body exposed to the cruel invasions of nature, her face mutilated by the minions of Lucifer she contemplated with joy and ecstasy. If she was to be killed she insisted that she had to be crucified. But no one wanted to kill her. All the authorities wanted to do was to silence her, but to do that was impossible. It would have been easier to murder her.

ORGANIZATION OF THE SHAKER COMMUNES

Mother Ann had always been most precise in her plans for the organization of her community, and after her death that precision persisted. The Shakers were divided into families, or communes, most of them consisting of from thirty to ninety people; [2] they lived in a single house, large enough to accommodate them all, the men separated from the women, in order, as Mother Ann declared, to prevent any carnal feelings arising between them. The commune was impeccably celibate. Even the shops and manufacturing establishments were operated upon a monastic basis. There were Brothers'

---

[1] *Ibid.*, p. 19.
[2] Nordhoff: *op. cit.*, p. 136.

shops and Sisters' shops, in each of which work befitting the respective sexes was undertaken. The women had as much to say in the organization and management of the community as the men, and in this respect Shaker communities were far more advanced than those of the Labadists, the *Woman in the Wilderness* group, the Ephratians, the Rappites.

In fact, the Shakers can be said, in more senses than one, to have been the forerunners of the feminist movement in America, the original suffragettes; in the first place, their leader was a woman, and more than that, the Daughter of God; in the second, women were exalted by them and treated, economically as well as spiritually, as complete equals of men. The government of Shaker communes was vested in both sexes, the same number of women being in authority as men. Even the family organization was based upon the same pattern. Two elders, one a man and the other a woman, controlled the destinies of each family. In addition, there were deacons and deaconesses who aided the family in its various pursuits, and lent spiritual aid to it whenever it was needed. There was no favoritism shown in the manner of work; women might undertake less arduous, but not less tedious, tasks. Everyone regardless of sex was forced to labor with his hands, work at unattractive and unhappy tasks and do so without hesitation or reluctance. That was part of the natural discipline and ritual.

THE MOTHER COMPLEX

There can be little doubt but that one of the strongest attractions and compulsions of the movement was its mother concept. In the history of the race the mother-affinity is older than the father one, and till this day the mother remains in emotional ascendancy in the family picture. The members of all the Shaker groups, no matter where they spread, always spoke of Ann Lee as their mother, which explains why she was able to exercise such incredible power over her followers. She became the substitute mother for them all. They felt for her what they had once, as children, felt for their own mothers.

Ann Lee's looks, the way she talked, prayed, sang, lent uncanny strength to that illusion. No one could doubt her function. In the eyes of her followers she was not only their mother, but the mother of the universe, subordinate not even to the Virgin Mary. She had sprung from God as naturally as Jesus. In many ways they felt her to be even superior to Jesus, since she was not only the Daughter of God, but also the mother of the race. For that reason, the Shakers never expected the Resurrection, in which the other millennialist groups believed, because, as Ann Lee said, Christ is a spirit, not a body, and whatever resurrection there ever was to be had already occurred in the hearts and minds of men. One should not wait to *see* Christ return, but *experience* his return within one's soul.

Every Shaker believed that the Shaker groups or kingdoms, wherever founded, were a manifestation of Christ's second appearance, except that this time He appeared in feminine guise, as a woman, Ann Lee, the Daughter instead of the Son of God. Shaker communities, therefore, were organized upon a theocratic basis, because no one but God's representatives should govern the behaviors of men. Their theocracy was different from that of Salem, in that women as well as men were included among the theocrats, both in equal proportion, with Ann Lee at the top of the spiritual pyramid. In every Shaker community, woman's place and privilege were equal to man's.

ABSENCE OF RACIAL DISCRIMINATION

The Shakers believed their communities were embodiments of the "Kingdom of Christ," other-worldly instead of this-worldly affairs; they therefore refused to allow themselves to become mixed up with political or economic matters, and above all, abstained from voting, which was the nadir of this-worldliness. The result was that all this-worldly distinctions and discriminations between people exercised no influence over their philosophy. They cared nothing about what men thought about other men; they cared only about what God thought about men. All men and women were equal in themselves, regardless of race, color, or political conviction. All they needed to do was to come to God with a clean heart, pray, and be forgiven for their past sins.

Among many of the Shaker groups, for instance, were to be found Negroes and Jews, and if opportunity had offered, there would have been, no doubt, Chinese and Japanese, too. Only Roman Catholics were excluded from membership. Jews and Negroes were treated with the same cordiality as everyone else. Many Jews found Shakerism a great retreat, an escape from the tortures and desolations of the orthodox Christian communities and colonies. Negroes who could find a haven among the Shakers were among the lucky of their race; the Shakers protected and supported them, and gave them peace, which is what they never found in the other settlements, Northern as well as Southern.

Few if any of the other communist groups ever afforded a haven for Jews, and fewer still for Negroes. The Shakers lived up to their word, their belief in the equality of man before the Lord on this earth which belonged to the Lord, and not to the ravenous propensities of man. Ann Lee wept copiously over the fate of the Jews and Negroes, begged them to join with her followers, and enjoy life in the vineyards of the Master.

Few people were better Christians than Ann Lee. She wanted little for herself and took less. The stories about her inebriety and immorality are based upon exceedingly dubious evidence derived in the main from people hostile to her and her sect.[1] She may have been mad, mad with a holy vision, a Joan of Arc of the Americas, a hallucinatory zealot, but she was not a sot or a nymphomaniac, as her enemies alleged.

PROSPERITY OF THE COMMUNITY

Despite the other-worldliness of the Shaker groups, they all prospered. They grew richer than the non-communist groups, and if their followers yearned for the fleshpots they might have indulged themselves with impunity. They had enough resources to enjoy life to the full, but their conception of enjoying life was a Christian and not a pagan one. Life to them had meaning only insofar as it was eternal, born of the fluid of creation, of God himself.

Their communes were mainly agricultural and as long as they continued as such they were successful; when they tried to expand them, however, and convert them into industrial communities, they failed. Agrarian communism is always easier to plan and organize than industrial communism, where a multitude of contradictory elements invade the picture.

NO STOCKS, NO PILLORIES, NO PRISONS

None of these religious communist groups would have succeeded, had they not been originally dedicated to the apostolic ideal. The Shakers, like all the other groups, got up early, prayed devoutly, labored eagerly and joyfully, and believed

---

[1] Typical of such attacks was that of James Smith, who visited the Shaker group in Kentucky, where he said that they "whip their laborers or underlings severely and also their children or young people if they refuse to kneel or dance or confess their sins," that they actually had sex relations despite their protestations to the contrary, and that they lived from day to day in a constant state of terror. (James Smith: *Remarkable Occurrences Lately Discovered among the People Called Shakers, of a Treacherous and Barbarous Nature*, 1810, pp. 3-21.) So much other evidence contradicts Smith's that it is not hard to believe that prejudice marred his vision. Other critics were even more extreme. Josiah Watson, for example, stated that the Shakers "live in whoredoms," and adds that he knew of one case of a Shaker woman being delivered of a child.

in the idealistic principles of their leader. Unlike the non-communist groups and colonies, they never erected stocks, pillories, or prisons. There was no need for such punitive techniques and contraptions. There was no law among them, because there were no lawless people in their colonies. Anyone who would violate another's rights could never be a Shaker.

In that regard no settlements were so free from crime, and from those spectacles of sinners in the stocks, women branded for adultery, witches tormented and burned, as the communist colonies which were never harassed by such troubles. Punishment did not belong within the category of their experience. If a person committed a sin, he punished himself; the community never had to worry itself with the matter.

People who believe in an ideal do not believe in violating it. They do not need threats, punishments, or incarcerations in order to "keep them good"; they are good because they cannot be bad. They could be bad only if they lost their belief in goodness, and when they lost that they would leave the group or colony, and wend their way to different parts. Goodness with these simple people was simple, too simple often. They wanted little and they got it. They were interested in little, so they missed little. In education, in which they were most defective, they were concerned with celestial and not mundane things. They would tolerate no books, for example, except the Bible and literature cognate to it. Other books were *verboten*.

More than that, they would allow no picture of anything to appear in their rooms because God had ordered it so. Clocks were also forbidden. In fact, anything decorative or even suggestive of ornamentation was prohibited.[1] Severity of discipline prevailed thus in their outer as well as their inner lives. But they rejoiced in it. They were even happy about their

[1] Hervey Elkins: *Fifteen Years in the Senior Order of the Shakers,* 1858, p. 25.

celibacy. They maintained that it prolonged life and gave it new power. Christ believed not in generation, but in regeneration, and his angels, sistered by the Daughter of God, Ann Lee herself, were dedicated to paradise.[1]

Mother Ann's personal exaltation of celibacy was undoubtedly an outgrowth of her unhappy marriage and the memory of her four dead children. At all events, she viewed procreation with horror, and would have no one near her who did not share her reaction. In her youth she was a decidedly normal woman, with natural sex urges, but as she entered upon her religious role she discouraged her physical impulses and encouraged her spiritual, and in the eyes of one of her followers she became "as free from carnal desires as a newborn infant." [2]

But with all this discipline and morbid terror of sex, the Shakers were not an unhappy people. Their dances were gay and spirited, and they flung themselves into them with pagan abandon. No modern dance hall, with its tempestuous exhibitionism, its pigeonhips, snakehips, shags, and boogie-woogies, is any more electrified than was a Shaker dance-fest. The Shakers did not earn their name without exertion.[3] According to Martha Stanley, an outside observer, they would whirl like our Holy Rollers of today, "until they would fall as though lifeless and talk with a lingo which they called

[1] Avery: *op. cit.*, p. 30.

[2] *Testimonies Concerning the Character and Ministry of Mother Ann Lee*, p. 22.

[3] One of Mother Ann's former apostles, D. Rothbun, who later turned against her, declared that the Shakers always got drunk before they danced. Rothbun's animosity was bitter, and his description is no doubt much exaggerated. Unquestionably, some of the Shakers "liked their liquor," but there was no law against their imbibing it. At all events, Rothbun's account is vivid enough to deserve quoting: "Mother Ann was riotous and unruly; she . . . drank hard, sang and danced all night—strip naked, pushing, hunching, pulling, biting and spitting . . . this in the most venomous manner, calling it fighting the devil. Those who were opposed to such conduct the Mother would judge and condemn to hell with awful oaths and curses." (Mary M. Dyer: *Portraiture of Shakerism*, 1822, p. 55).

the unknown tongue." [1] As another Shaker wrote, "It is surely no convent life with its rigid laws and penances; no dark vaults or gloomy cells, no high walls or grated windows. Strong, willing hearts are here, bearing a firm but gentle rule." [2]

Altogether, the Shakers, who are best known today for the furniture they produced and the handiwork to which they lent their genius, were in the eighteenth and early half of the nineteenth century so exciting and challenging as a religious group that their name became known throughout the length and breadth of the land. Shakers might be looked upon as strange people but not as unhappy or unsuccessful people. They were among the most vibrant and vital people in the new world.

The number of communities they established is hard to calculate, but they were all similar in rule and pattern. Those that linger today, in Kentucky and New York, have lost the drive of the earlier ones. An industrial age has made such agrarian communities anachronistic.

[1] Dyer: *op. cit.* p. 125.
[2] *Correspondence between Mary F. C. and the Shaker Sister, Sarah L.* Edited by R. W. Pelham, Union Village, Ohio, 1869, p. 4.

CHAPTER VIII

Amana

Amana was a colony whose communism derived from the new world instead of the old. Unlike most of the other communist colonies, the founders of Amana had no interest in communism until they arrived in America. It was the American environment which drove them to the communist way of life. They adopted it because they believed that it would provide the best means for their economic survival.

Amana is one of the few colonies which still exists today, although its original economic program has been considerably modified. It was so successful during the heyday of its existence that it excited the admiration and envy of adjacent settlements. It was looked upon as a miracle-place, something conjured up by magicians out of the blurred horizon of nowhere, an unreal thing that nevertheless existed and persisted and which could not be ignored.

Since individualistic frontiersmen could not understand the Amanites, they regarded them as evil.

Under the leadership of Herr Metz, Amana was founded in New York State between the years 1842 and 1843. Metz himself and four of his followers arrived in New York in September, 1842, bought five thousand acres of an old Seneca reservation, and set to work making it into a prosperous community. Their first settlement near Buffalo, where they remained until 1855, was not nearly so successful as their second one in Iowa, where they have stayed ever since.

Within a year close to four hundred people came over,[1] and

[1] Nordhoff: *op. cit.*, p. 28.

it was not long before the total number grew to a thousand. They called their colony Amana after a Biblical reference in the Song of Solomon:

> "Come with me from Lebanon, my spouse, with me from Lebanon: look from the top of Amana, from the top of Shenir and Hermon, from the lions' dens, from the mountains of the leopards."

Like the other religious communists, they believed in living economically, humbly; their food was of the plainest kind; their dress was severely simple and unadorned. They forbade anything insinuating the exquisite in their houses or on their persons. Women were not allowed to prettify themselves; to wear an attractive garment was regarded as sinful; even to wear the hair in a loose flowing fashion was condemned. They were as anti-intellectual as the Shakers, as anti-ecclesiastical, as anti-progressive. In fact, in their attitude toward women they were far more backward than the Shakers. Women had no important position in the community; they were not permitted to vote on the governing council or voice their sentiments upon any issue of significance. They were forced to eat separately from the men and to stay by themselves upon many occasions. Marriage was allowed, though it was not extolled. The marital ceremony among the Amanites was as gloomy as a funeral service. It inspired terror rather than joy in the hearts of the participants.

Although the Amanites, unlike the Shakers, did not turn to dancing for emotional and spiritual release, they were given to similar fits and orgies of weird inspiration. Metz, for example, was known to "shake" for hours at a time, then swoon, rise again, fling his arms toward the skies, mutter strange sounds, more animal than human, foam at the mouth, writhe, gesticulate, and faint once more, with Christ's name written in letters of fire across his mouth. Metz was a queer little fellow, a contorted goat-man, fantastic, with the marks of the menagerie stamped upon his countenance. He lived, a spiritual schizophrenic, in a world of his own, in which he and God were intimately allied. Every day he sought God, wandered off into one of his trances, snatched a slice of eternity, and then came back to divide it with his followers. He was an American Bunyan, racing footloose toward the celestial city.

His followers worshiped him, watched him with awe as "inspiration" rushed through him, electrifying him like a meteor burst into sudden flame. When he prayed, when he preached, he became another person, his body flowing into another form, transfigured. His eloquence was no less wondrous than that of Ann Lee, Kelpius, Beissel, or Rapp. Even after he died, his followers continued to read his words as if they were gospel, spoken from the lips of the Lord. The memory of Metz was never allowed to die.

HYMNOLOGY

The Amanites, although they did not adore music, loved hymns. They had a most impressive collection of them, most of them written by members of their group. When collected, they assumed gigantic proportions. They were combined into two volumes, both of ponderous size. *The Voice of Zion* was almost a thousand pages in content, and their other collection was far larger. These hymns meant something to them that hymns never meant to other groups and congregations. They were an integral part of their lives. They lived in their hymns as profoundly as they lived in their work. They were their work, or at least a most essential part of it. Hymns were not hymns, but things apart, divine vocalizations, imperishable records of sacred sentiments. Some of the hymns were unendurably long, but all of them afforded inspiration to those who sang them. They sang them as if they were evocations of the infinite.

No wonder that these people lived to such an impossibly old age, a number of them reaching almost a hundred, many of them into their late nineties, and a vast number into their eighties. They were a strong, sturdy people, born of stout peasant stock of German extraction, able to endure and survive the attacks of the American winters and wilds. All worlds were new worlds, heavenly worlds, to them. They were heaven itself.

Religious meetings among the Amanites were demandingly frequent: every Wednesday, Saturday, and Sunday morning devotions were held, and then every evening they were resumed. Little time was left for anything but sacred exercises.

The Amanites often called themselves the "True Inspiration Congregation," because they believed that they were direct descendants of God. Their inspiration was intimate, personal. It sprang from individual closeness with divinity, something born of higher things, unconnected with earthly sources and significances.

Their prophets were often simple, untutored people, whose only claim to leadership was that they had talked with God, walked with Him in the gardens of dream, and returned from them to disseminate His message. Barbara Heynemann, an unschooled chambermaid, was typical of that tribe. Her tiny head with its bright, shining eyes, thin, tensely pursed lips, her fingers with their long sweep of gesture, set her apart from other people, gave her a saintly aspect, and made people believe in her religious genius. She was a strange sight, in her sullen black clothes, unrelieved by ornament or design, as she stood before her followers, challenging them to attune their ears and hear God's voice through her lips. She did not come to her sainthood without a struggle. There was a time when she was accused of being attracted to men, and later a time when she succumbed to marriage, but throughout it all she retained a dignity which robbed all attacks of their sting. When Metz died she became the leader of the colony. As the Quakers, she refused to allow her followers to take oaths, doff their hats, or serve in the army. In addition, they would not allow their children to attend the public schools for fear that they would become contaminated with ideas antagonistic to the conception of life of the group. Among the hundred volumes published by the Amanites none was of a non-religious character. Religion was life to them and life was religion.

MODERN AMANA

In later years Amana changed from a communist colony into a semi-capitalist one. For seven generations it remained communistic; ever since it has been an industrial democracy with a private-profit cast.[1] It has tried to combine the virtues of both communism and capitalism, preserving enough communal control to give it stability, yet at the same time providing enough economic leeway to stimulate individual initiative.

The colony, divided into seven villages, still has over fifteen hundred members, and sixty-one separate businesses and enterprises, with corporation stores and modern emporia in which to trade. Its main occupation is still farming, although it has been successful in developing various industries, particularly those connected with woolen manufacture. The people now own their own houses, buy their own goods, pay their own debts. Automobiles have become a common sight in the community; bright, variegated clothes and even sports suits are worn by all the younger folk; even the theater and the dance hall have become popular in what was once so solemn a colony.

Women have acquired equal rights with men now, vote in the councils, decide upon policies. They have advanced schools,

---

[1] Bertha M. H. Shambaugh: "Amana in Transition," in *The Palimpsest*, State Historical Society of Iowa, May, 1936, Vol. XVII, No. 5, pp. 150-181.

free medical service, and have passed most progressive social measures to provide against the evils of poverty.

Along with this great change in the colony, which occurred in 1931, church and state were separated, and no longer were the religious authorities allowed to govern and dictate the nature of economic and social life.

CHAPTER IX

The Swedish Christ

"All authority hath been given unto me in heaven and on earth. If I so willed you should at once fall dead at my feet and go to hell."

ERIC JANSON

Among all the strange religious leaders who settled in the new world, none was more arresting or commanding than Eric Janson, the scarfaced Swede, who founded the Bishop Hill Colony, so named in honor of his birthplace, Bishopskullen.[1] Janson did not consider himself Christ's emissary on earth; he believed that he was Christ himself, the actual reincarnation of the Master. It was a curious, puzzling, and frequently unhappy sight to see this thin-faced man, with his sharp, aquiline nose, protruding teeth, and fierce, frenetic eyes, striving to look like Christ, simulate the Saviour's sweetness and gentleness of countenance. Worse still was his attempt to make his shrill, strident voice sound like that of Jesus echoing through the ages.

Like Rapp, Janson exercised a hypnotic influence over his followers, but it was more by virtue of his strangeness of appearance and weird compulsive personality than by his goodness or charm. Added to his outlandish features was his left hand minus two chopped-off fingers, the grotesqueness of which became almost terrifying when he waved the hand through the air. The sight of the stumps, always an alabastrine white, seemed to compel the attention of his listeners almost as completely as if they were shining crystals or gems. He

---

[1] Florence E. Janson: *Background of Swedish Immigration*, p. 182.

never failed to employ them to good effect, closing down his other fingers to make the stumps more conspicuous.   Many claimed that his gifts as an orator were dependent to a large extent upon the horror of his fingers, which kept his audiences fascinated and awe-stricken.

Like Beissel, Janson was accused of having illicit relations with various members of his colony; in Beissel's case the evidence is too prejudiced and insubstantial to warrant credence; in Janson's case, on the contrary, there seems to have been no doubt that he did succumb to sexual sin.   His own wife attacked him upon several occasions for infidelity.[1]   In one case he was forced to admit his guilt, pusillanimously blaming the sin upon the woman, Karin Erson, whom he accused of having used her evil charms and wiles to seduce him.   Strange as it may seem, even these deviations from moral rectitude did not destroy his influence among his followers.   It was almost as if, being a god, he had the same right as Zeus to refresh himself with the bodies of the opposite sex and with libations and other abandonments which finite man had invented.

SWEDISH BACKGROUND

Janson was born in 1808 in Sweden, grew up as a Lutheran, developed clairvoyant tendencies as a youth, recognized that he was Christ in his early twenties, and set forth to convert the world in his early thirties.   His first decision, after hearing the voice of God inform him that prayer was the secret of power, and discovering that he was the returned Christ, was to break with the Lutheran Church and establish a church of his own.   This church was to be the true Church of Christ.   Only through him and his church could redemption and salvation be attained.   He invented his own catechism and wrote his own hymns.

In Janson's defense it should be said that his fight against

[1] *Journal of the Illinois State Historical Society,* Vol. XVIII, No. 3, pp. 519-526.

the Swedish Lutheran Church was based upon more than subjective hostility. Egomaniac though Janson was, as for that matter were most of the religious enthusiasts and prophets of that day, he was fighting a battle which was more than individual; it was more than national; it was international. All Protestant reformers fought against that exaltation of outward forms and sterile rituals characteristic of Catholic orthodoxy; they wanted individual dedication, individual consecration, individual sacrifice.

Janson battled so vigorously against the Lutheran Church that he soon found himself attacked on all sides as a charlatan, arrested six times, and finally driven into hiding because a price was put upon his head.[1]

Aided by his followers, Janson succeeded in reaching the mountains and thence managed to get into Norway. Some time later he set sail for New York, with a considerable group of his followers. Shortly after, he began his migration to Illinois, where he arrived in July, 1846. There, as the returned Christ, he established his commonwealth, based upon the apostolic ideals of the early Christians. He founded his society, called the New Jerusalem, upon the basis of communism because the Scriptures commended its practice.

Eleven hundred Jansonists, divided into nine groups, set sail for America during the next two years, abandoning all they had in the old world because of the religious promise of the new. At least they could find freedom from persecution in the new world, freedom to organize their own religious community, freedom to worship as they pleased. After this hegira all traces of the Jansonists in Sweden disappeared.

Few groups suffered as much hardship in their crossing as the Jansonists. One ship was lost at sea and no record of it was ever found; two others were shipwrecked and only a few of the passengers survived; the fourth was the only one

[1] Michael A. Mikkelsen: *The Bishop Hill Colony.* Johns Hopkins University Studies, 1892, p. 24.

that ultimately arrived in New York. These Jansonists were transported to Red Oak Grove, three miles from Bishop Hill, in Illinois. Within a short time a large canvas tabernacle was erected, log cabins were built, and dugouts excavated, into which beds were placed in double and sometimes triple formation.[1] In these latter enclosures disease and death spread so rapidly as, for a time, to threaten the practical extinction of the colony.

A common practice every morning was to remove fresh corpses from these dugout contrivances. So severe did these conditions become, over two hundred followers withdrew from the community in 1848.[2] The suffering of both men and women was horrible; insufficient medical attention combined with totally inadequate supplies made life almost unendurable.

In time, however, after almost half of the community had perished, things changed. Whether the survivors acquired immunity to the prevailing diseases, or whether the improved economic conditions were more accountable, is hard to say; at all events, Bishop Hill became a relatively healthy and remarkably prosperous community. Agricultural pursuits multiplied and industries increased. The manufacture of adobe and flax, which became their main industries, provided a superior living for them.

All men and women in Bishop Hill considered themselves God's messengers, and consequently envisioned their work as a temporary exercise undertaken to busy themselves until the advent of the millennium. Janson was their leader and their God because he was like unto God Himself; what he said they believed, swore by, defended. Almost all their life was directed by Janson, who appointed overseers, foremen, supervisors, distributed jobs, devised undertakings, planned industries, scheduled programs. Their own responsibilities were

[1] Florence E. Janson: *op. cit.*, p. 183.
[2] Mikkelsen: *op. cit.*, p. 33.

microscopic. All life was organized and regimented for them. All went well with the community until the arrival of the overweening swashbuckler and adventurer, John Root. Root, a dash-as-dash-can soldier, who had fought without undue exposure in the Mexican War, made his way to Bishop Hill in the autumn of 1848. He was tired and eager for a place of refuge. Bishop Hill promised that, and when he found that Janson and his followers welcomed him with much enthusiasm, he decided to stay. Once he recovered from his weariness, however, he soon showed that he was more interested in hunting and other sports than in the simple labors of the colony. This worried the community, but when it became apparent that he was falling in love with Eric Janson's niece, everyone became happier. At least she would stabilize his life and inspire him to become more interested in the work of the colony.

Root was a shrewd as well as a swaggering fellow, and when it came to signing the marital contract, he insisted upon his right to take his wife with him if ever he left the group. At first Janson would not consent to such an outrageous demand, but, after consideration, a compromise was devised, which provided that if Root decided to leave the community, his wife should be allowed to decide for herself whether she wanted to go with him or remain with the Jansonists. All this was signed and sealed in a document of which few foresaw the future importance.

For a time things went well. Root and his wife lived happily, and Root made a valiant attempt to adapt himself to the Bishop Hill way of life. After a while, however, Root became restless, the soldier's *Wanderlust* taking hold of him, and he decided to leave for other parts. He asked his wife to go with him, but she was under the influence of the other members of the colony, and demurred. Janson himself supported his niece in her refusal to accompany Root to other territories. Root became furious, battled day and night with the colonists, and finally, unable to persuade them of the wisdom of his logic, he resorted to force, and carried his wife away as his prisoner.

This was a turning point in the entire history of the colony. Nothing like it had ever occurred before. It undermined the faith of the colonists and destroyed their belief in their own omnipotence. They had no choice. Immediately their fastest horsemen set out in pursuit of the absconder. They met on a dark crossroad; sharp words passed, threats ensued. Root tried to ride down his adversaries, but they seized his horses, surrounded his buggy, imprisoned him, and carried his wife back to the welcoming arms of the community. Later Root was freed; within a few hours he went to the nearest town, and swore out a warrant for the arrest of Janson and his cohorts for obstructing the peaceful passage of his wife and himself.

Impulsive, irrational, and reprehensively very impatient, Root would not wait for the law to act, but once again attempted to steal his wife—and this time he succeeded. He took her to Chicago, where he kept her in the home of his sister. The sister, however, betrayed him, and informed Janson where he could retrieve his niece. The Jansonists reacted immediately to the situation, sent an accoutred contingent to Chicago, recovered the wife, and sped back with her to Bishop Hill.

At that point Root became maniacally furious, gathered together a horde of hoodlums, paid them well, instructed them in what he wanted them to do, and en masse they marched to Bishop Hill and laid siege. Janson and his group refused to surrender Root's wife, whom they considered inalienably theirs, and the siege continued. Soon Root began to appeal to the near-by frontiersmen, and before long a small army was assembled and plans were laid to make a direct attack upon the place.

THE ATTACK UPON BISHOP HILL

For a considerable time Root and his men were not able to decide what would be the best manner of attack. To continue the siege they considered too protracted and costly. Finally they agreed on burning the village. In the meanwhile, however, a number of other frontiersmen, angered at this invasion of a peaceful community, came to the support of the Jansonists, and when the numbers on both sides became almost equal, Root's followers lost heart, gave up the siege, and retreated to their homes.

Janson himself was still under indictment, and his trial was scheduled to take place in May of that year, which was not far off. Root and his attorneys had gathered enough evidence to show that he was a violator of the law in his attempt to prevent a duly wedded wife from accompanying her husband to wherever the latter moved. In those days little attention was given to the wife's choice in the matter; only the husband counted.

Before Janson left for the trial he gave a Last Supper to all his followers, assured them of a future eternity, and told them, with clairvoyant genius, that he would be there, in heaven, to greet them when they arrived. They stared at his tired, careworn face, commiserated with him as they traced the thin crow's-feet beneath his eyes, watched with morbid anxiety his tremulous fingers as they strove to hold fast to the communion cup. It was a funereal spectacle—this man, carrying within him a preternatural awareness of imminent disaster, passing wafers and wine to his followers, the latter staring at him with uplifted eyes as at something incredible, divine, yet macabre.

The trial proved catastrophic. Janson went, testified, defended the right of his niece to nuptial independence, listened dull-eyed to the contrary evidence, waved his mutilated fingers in the air when he was addressed, stamped up and down, thundered disapprovals, challenged opponents, and at times turned the courtroom into a bedlam of attack and abuse. No one could control him. Judge and jury were terrified of him as he strode up and down the courtroom; they feared to stop him lest he call down some almighty power to punish them. He was like an ancient magician, holding the universe within the palm of his hand.

But all this ended abruptly. Root, still determined to have his rights, decided to kill Janson, and on the thirteenth day of May, 1850, he stole into the back of the courtroom, waited for the session to adjourn, and while Janson was standing alone before a window, contemplating the brevity of this man-contrived universe, he suddenly heard his name called out as if by some celestial messenger. He turned his head, his mind still in a daze, and there, but a few yards from him, was Root himself, revolver in hand, informing him in sharp, decisive words, that he was going to kill him.[1]

At first Janson could not believe his eyes; it was too much like a mirage, a fear which had suddenly assumed physical form. He hesitated, stammered, tried to speak; but before a word could escape his lips he was dead. Root was an excellent shot and Janson thereby escaped all suffering.

THE JANSON BURIAL

It was a melancholy journey for the men who bore the body of Janson back to Bishop Hill. For a long time they refused to believe that their leader was dead. Most of them were certain that, at almost any moment, he would rise from the dead, and, like Christ, rob death of its sting. They watched his body vigilantly, and some of them were sure at times that it palpitated, and expressed signs of returning life. At moments one of them would burst into a spasm of ecstasy, shouting, "He lives, he lives," and the others would have to quiet

---

[1] Mikkelson: *op. cit.*, p. 42.

him, each hoping, however, that he was right, that life, in some invisible, secret way, had begun to creep back into the frigid frame of their Swedish Christ.

For three days Janson's body lay, with his apostles beside it, hungrily watching for some sign of divine import. But none came. The body remained as still at the end of three days as it had been on the first. No second arisen Christ was to be discovered. There were many who wanted to hold the body a fourth day, still believing that by that time Janson would be able to break through the bonds of death, and walk again, as Jesus had three days after his crucifixion and burial. No stone was put upon Janson's grave; in fact, it was filled with fine, loose dirt in order to make it easier for him to free himself from coffin and soil and walk like a second Christ upon the earth again. For many nights his followers did not give up hope. They watched his grave, and some, at night, sat beside it, praying for his resurrection. They did not believe that their Swedish Christ could be irrevocably dead.

When all hope disappeared, and the community had to accept the inevitable—that Janson was not going to return to them in the robes of the Master, in a chariot of fire, blessing them with hands which had touched those of God—they reconciled themselves to their lot, elected Jonas Olson as their new leader, and continued their weary way toward a dreamless future.

The Olson Regime

Olson was a better businessman than Janson, and very soon he had the colony incorporated, erected a brewery and a broom factory, initiated new agricultural pursuits, planted fresh orchards. Business began to hum. The other world was for a time almost forgotten in the absorption of new activities. Bishop Hill became a thriving place; its streets were straightened, embroidered with grass and canopied with trees, its buildings repainted, its shops repaired, freshly decorated, and newly designed. Smoke wreathed in plentiful abundance from the chimneys of the bakery, the brewery, the dye-house, the weaving factory, the wagon and harness shops, the tailor and shoemaker establishments, the laundry, and the divers other places in which furnaces were busy turning out new products for the community.

This new prosperity did not change the character of life at Bishop Hill. The men and women continued to eat in separate places; fine foods were still forbidden; exquisite clothes were still anathema. The men did not cut their hair, and the women did not ornament their bodies. They still believed in the humble life of the Saviour, and tried to practice it in all its primitive simplicity.

Introduction of Celibacy

Nils Heden, one of Janson's twelve apostles, visited a number of the other communist colonies and became converted to the ideal of celibacy. Upon his return to Bishop Hill he persuaded Olson to see the wisdom of the celibate way of life, and together they attempted to proselytize the rest of the community. They met with stout opposition, found it necessary to expel a number of the group, but after an extended battle they succeeded in making celibacy a new ideal. A compromise was effected as to the sexual relations of the old members of the group; those who were married were allowed to live together, but were supposed to exercise great moral restraint in their sex practices; the younger people were forbidden to marry, and marriage itself was denounced as a sinful act.

In a few years the colony died. Celibacy helped to kill it more than anything else. The younger people would not tolerate it, and the older people became restless after the 1857 crash, which swept away most of their savings and reduced them to penury. There were quarrels and battles among the trustees, and the end of the adventure was clouded with bitterness and regret.

CHAPTER X

The Mormon Dream

"Woe unto those who are rich as to the things of this world. For, because they are rich, they despise the poor, persecute the meek, and set their hearts upon their treasure. Wherefore their treasure shall perish with them also.

"Woe unto you rich men, that will not give of your substance to the poor, for your riches will canker your souls; and this shall be your lamentation in the day of visitation, of judgment, and of indignation: The harvest is past, the summer is ended, and my soul is not saved."

JOSEPH SMITH, in THE BOOK OF MORMON
AND DOCTRINE AND COVENANTS

"Its basis was not commercial but social. . . . Joseph Smith expected to supplant in the average man the motive of love in the Christian sense for the motive of selfishness."

A SHORT HISTORY OF THE CHURCH OF
JESUS CHRIST OF LATTER DAY SAINTS

"Possession without ownership makes us stewards."
"Economic freedom becomes the nursing mother of social development."

BISHOP ALBERT CARMICHAEL

Of all the co-operative colonies founded in this country the one that is best remembered is that of the Mormons. The Mormons established more than one colony, but all their groups were impressively similar. Their tradition sprang from a common source. They were the new saints, the true horsemen of the Apocalypse.

127

Like the Labadists, the Ephratists, the Rappites, and all the other communist groups, the Mormons were a Biblical cult. Their inspiration, however, was derived as much from the Old Testament as from the New. In many ways they were more Judaic than Christian. Their adoption of polygamy, for example, was Jewish in origin. The fact that Solomon had a thousand wives and many of the Jewish patriarchs were also bountifully supplied in that respect was a determinative factor in their *mores*. They wanted to live as God's "chosen people" had lived. To live differently, they believed, was sacrilegious.

The Mormon philosophy was not a suddenly conceived thing; it grew gradually, and then matured and expanded, as new situations and new environments demanded. They wanted to reorganize small sections of the cosmos, and build them into New Jerusalems, in which all men should be equal, regardless of color or creed.

Like most of the other utopian religious groups, the Mormons. believed they were "the chosen people" to whom God had given his special blessing, and had them sent forth into the wildernesses of the new land to convert it into paradise. Joseph Smith, like Eric Janson, George Rapp, Conrad Beissel, and others, was God's emissary, a human emanation of divinity. Without claiming that he was Christ arisen, as Janson did, he swore that he had seen God's Angel face to face. It was he, Joseph Smith, who discovered the golden plates, upon which *The Book of Mormon* was supposedly written, and he who gave it to the world for all to read. Down in the dark recesses of the Hill Cumorah, close to Palmyra, New York, he swore he had found the plates, hidden there since 420 A.D., and from those plates he deciphered a message which has since rung around the world.[1]

Joseph Smith envisaged himself as a nineteenth-century prophet, a direct descendant of the tribes of Israel, as close

[1] G. W. Curran: *Who Are the Mormons?* p. 4.

to the Lord as Isaiah, Hosea, or Moses. Tall man that he was, practically a giant, he impressed people with great ease. It was not his height alone which compelled their admiration. Above all there were his piercing blue eyes, limpid as light, his blond hair challenging as that of a Viking, which disarmed them, hypnotized them at a glance. After gazing at them, most people were unable to resist him and became votaries of his cause. It was this man who led the Mormons from the bogs and swamps of superstition into the hard, fast lands of revelation. With him they fought their way through the wildernesses of the East into the New Canaan of the West.

Who Was Joseph Smith?

Like most of the other religious leaders who founded communist colonies, Smith was of obscure origin and unexalted background. Both his parents, however, claimed to possess clairvoyant genius, and without doubt their son was profoundly influenced by their eccentric powers. The father, who was best known as a well-digger, had at different times been a counterfeiter, a farmer, a hunter, a storekeeper, a cake and beer-shop merchant;[1] the mother, in ordinary life a simple *Hausfrau*, was also a fortune-teller who believed in demonology. Both had visions, teeming with supernatural insignia, crosses which glittered with emerald fire, moons that hung like baskets carrying the Christ Child from Bethlehem to Palmyra, stars that gleamed like the eyes of God. They described them as closely and intimately as if they had just seen them.

The younger Smith was born in Sharon, Vermont, in 1805, and was brought by his parents to Palmyra, New York, where he spent most of his younger years following his father about in his well-digging profession. He early became interested in the Bible and ethical dialectics, and occupied many hours

[1] Pomeroy Tucker: *Origin, Rise, and Progress of Mormonism*, p. 18.

disputing moral questions with the men and youths who hung about the grocery store. It did not take him long to discover that he had unusual gifts in that direction, and soon he began to challenge his superiors in the field: doctors, lawyers, ministers.

Originally he was a member of the Methodist Church, but a sudden vision from heaven told him to resign from the congregation, to belong to no congregation, to no church, but to wait for a message, and then to found a church of his own. The vision had been a gorgeous one, filtered through a pillar of fire, as clear and luminous as Paul's on the road to Damascus. Years passed before he had a second vision, which surpassed the first in wonder and magnificance. It led to the discovery of the golden plates, upon which *The Book of Mormon* was putatively written, and to the foundation of the Mormon Church.

Smith's description of this second vision and revelation is unforgettably vivid:

"He had on a loose robe of most exquisite whiteness. It was a whiteness beyond anything earthly I had ever seen; nor do I believe that any earthly thing could be made to appear so exceedingly white and brilliant. His hands were naked and his arms also; so also were his feet naked, as were his legs, a little above the ankles. . . .

"He called me by name and said unto me that he was a messenger sent from the presence of God to me, and that his name was Moroni. That God had a work for me to do and that my name should be had for good and evil among all nations, kindreds, and tongues; or that it should be both good and evil spoken of among all people. He said there was a book deposited, written upon gold plates, giving an account of the former inhabitants of this continent, and the source from which they sprang. He also said that the fulness of the everlasting Gospel was contained in it, as delivered by the Saviour to the ancient inhabitants. Also, that there were two stones in silver bows (and these stones, fastened to a breastplate, constituted what is called the Urim and Thummim) deposited with the plates, and the possession and use of these stones was what constituted Seers in ancient or former times, and that God had prepared them for the purpose of translating the book. . . . Again, he told me that when I got those plates of which he had spoken (for the time that they should be obtained was not yet fulfilled) I should not show them to any person, neither the breastplate with the Urim and Thummim, only to those to whom I should be commanded to show them; if I did, I should be destroyed. While he was conversing with me about the plates, the vision was opened to my mind that I could see the place where the plates were deposited, and that so clearly and distinctly, that I knew the place again when I visited it. . . .

"I left the field and went to the place where the messenger had told me the plates were deposited, and owing to the distinctness of the vision which I had concerning it, I knew the place the instant I arrived there. Convenient to the village of Manchester, Ontario County, New York, stands a hill of considerable size, and the most elevated of any in the neighborhood. On the west side of this hill, not far from the top, under a stone of considerable size, lay the plates, deposited in a stone box; this stone was thick and rounding in the middle on the upper side, and thinner towards the edges, so that the middle part of it was visible above the ground, but the edge all around was covered with earth. Having removed the earth and obtained a lever which I got fixed under the edge of the stone, and with a little exertion raised it up. I looked in, and there indeed did I behold the plates, the Urim and Thummim, and the breastplate as stated by the messenger."

That such plates ever existed is scarcely credible.[1] But our concern here is not with the dubious origins of the Mormon religion—the origins of all religions are extremely dubious—

[1] James H. Snowden in *The Truth about Mormonism* considers all the evidence relative to the possible existence of the plates, and comes to the conclusion that they were the invention of Joseph Smith's fabulous imagination—pp. 52-77.

but with how it developed, the social outlook it encouraged, the nature of the society it cultivated. To expose the contradictions, fallacies, and absurdities of any religion is an easy task. The difficult task is to explain how religion, in the face of such contradictions, fallacies, and absurdities, has managed to survive, and retain through the ages the support of countless millions.

Joseph Smith was little different from many other religious leaders; he combined elements of the saint and the sinner, the clairvoyant and the charlatan. Perhaps he was a little more crass than many of the ancient prophets, and more mundane than many of his other-worldly contemporaries. Certainly he was more practical-minded than Rapp, Beissel, or Janson, in his vision of a theocratic society, as is proved by the fact that the Mormons continue to exist today as a religious group, and practically control the life of a city, as well as of a state.

In time, Smith worked out a whole historical philosophy, explanatory of the origin and nature of the American people. The following passage is typical of his theory:

"The history of America is unfolded from its first settlement by a colony that came from the Tower of Babel at the confusion of languages, to the beginning of the 5th Century of the Christian era. We are informed by these records that America in ancient times has been inhabited by two distinct races of people. The first were called Jaredites, and came directly from the Tower of Babel. The second race came directly from the city of Jerusalem about 600 years before Christ. They were principally Israelites of the descendants of Joseph. The Jaredites were destroyed about the time that the Israelites came from Jerusalem, who succeeded them in the inhabitance of the country. The principal nation of the second race fell in battle toward the close of the fourth century. The remnant are the Indians that now inhabit this country." [1]

[1] Joseph Smith: *Times and Seasons*, March 1, 1842.

In other words, Smith, like many others before as well as after him, believed that the Indians were a "lost tribe of Israel." They were the Lamanites, descendants of Laman, one of the sons of Lehi, who accompanied his father on his ancient pilgrimage to South America. That this visionary theory is not supported by prevailing scientific evidence means no more to present-day Mormons than it would have meant to Joseph Smith. They were anti-scientific, anti-intellectual in their outlook; their approach to religion was emotional, ecstatic.[1] They were concerned with its revelation, not with its logic—or lack of it. *The Book of Mormon* was founded upon theories no more fantastic than those of the Bible; it was interspersed with the doctrines of the day, rife with paradoxes and contradictions, and shot full of irrational and incredible suppositions and conceptions.

Everything that Joseph Smith did depended upon visions and revelations. Before he could found the Mormon Church [2] he had to have a visitation from heaven. When he cured people of ills, it was because the strength of God had come into his hands and eyes, endowing him with magic power.[3] It was a spiritual messenger, no one less than John the Baptist, who commanded him and his comrade Cowdery to be baptized, and to spread the new gospel throughout the land. That marked the beginning of Mormonism as a special religion. From that time on, Smith and Cowdery became proselytizers for what they now conceived as the new church: "The Church of Christ." The movement began with a handful of members, but it spread rapidly, and today it has hundreds of thousands of members.

[1] This is not so true today. The Mormons have many sound scientists among them, especially a notable biologist, and also the inventor of television.
[2] The Mormons never liked to call their church the Mormon Church. For a long time they called it "The Church of Christ." Today it is known as "The Church of Jesus Christ of Latter Day Saints." This latter name was adopted as early as 1834. (Snowden: *op. cit.*, p. 118.)
[3] Mrs. Maria N. Ward: *Female Life among the Mormons*, 1855, p. 24.

The heavenly messenger instructed Smith to appoint twelve
apostles, to keep a careful record of all the activities of the
Church, and to call himself "a seer, a translator, a prophet,
an apostle of Jesus Christ." Like other utopian, theocratic
sects, the Mormons modeled themselves upon the credo of
primitive Christianity, believed in "the gift of tongues,
prophecy, revelation, visions, healing," and in addition they
believed "the Bible to be the word of God," but also "the Book
of Mormon to be the word of God."[1] More than that, they
believed in things strange to ordinary Christians, that "men
and Gods are one species: Gods, angels and men are all of one
species, one race, one great family, widely diffused among the
planetary systems, as colonies, kingdoms, nations." To that
they appended the dictum that man's purpose was to increase,
and from that conclusion they derived their belief that polygamy, which made the race multiply faster, was the best system for the race.

Further than that, they were convinced that "Jesus Christ
and his Father are two persons, in the same sense as John
and Peter are two persons. Each of them has an organized, individual tabernacle, embodied in material form, and composed
of material substance, in the likeness of man, and possessing
every organ, limb and physical part that man possesses.
(K. 39-40.) Jesus Christ is the son of the Adam-God: The
Father had begotten him in his own likeness. He was not
begotten by the Holy Ghost. And who is the Father? He
is the first of the human family. (Young, J. of D., 1:50.)
He was a *polygamist:* We say it was Jesus Christ who was
married (at Cana to the Marys and Martha) whereby he could
see his seed before he was crucified." (Apostle Orson Hyde,
Sermon 3.)"[2]

Polygamists, as Mormon lore later revealed, became "gods,"
sacrosanct individuals, beatific idealists. They modeled their

---

[1] Quoted from the *Articles of Faith of the Latter Day Saints.*
[2] Quoted from Snowden: *op. cit.,* pp. 129, 130.

lives upon those of the old Jewish patriarchs and prophets:
David, Solomon, Abraham. They were holy men.

BLOOD SACRIFICE

They also developed early a faith in blood purging, more
familiarly known among them as "blood atonement," by which
they believed grave sins could be washed away. Water was
too mild; only blood would suffice. After all, the Lord Jesus
had sacrificed his blood that mankind might be redeemed;
why, then, should not men be willing to spill theirs when they
had sinned? This faith in blood redemption became a mania
with them, and later when Brigham Young became their leader,
he declared:

> "All mankind love themselves: and let those principles
> be known by an individual, and he would be glad to have
> his blood shed. This would be loving ourselves even
> unto eternal exaltation. Will you love your brothers or
> sisters likewise when they have a sin that cannot be atoned
> for without the shedding of their blood? That is what
> Jesus meant. . . . I could refer you to plenty of instances
> where men have been righteously slain in order to atone
> for their sins. . . . The wickedness and ignorance of the
> nations forbid this principle being in full force, but the
> time will come when the law of God will be in full force.
> This is loving our neighbor as ourselves; if he needs help,
> help him; if he wants salvation and it is necessary to spill
> his blood on earth in order that he may be saved, spill it." [1]

The blood sacrifice has always been inalienably allied with
religious practice. Primitive, ancient, and medieval man viewed
blood as the secret of the life-force, the potency of creation.
He supped and drank it as if it were a combination of elixir
and aphrodisiac. Blood was energy, strength, omnipotence.
The gods lived upon blood, were sustained by it as mortals

---

[1] Quoted from Snowden: *op. cit.*, p. 133.

are by the sun. To drink blood was to be one with the gods. Among the natives of South Africa, the blood of a dead animal was drunk before a sacrifice was attempted.[1] In other cases, the blood of divers animals was poured over the sinner's head, and sometimes over those of relatives and friends to complete the absolution. Few religions, however obscure, have been free from the blood motive.[2] Various evangelical sects, lit with holy ardor, have ripped, stabbed, and scissored themselves with no less zeal than primitives in their passionate concern for blood absolution.

The Mormons exceeded the Christians of their time in sanguinary practices, but it must not be forgotten that their zealotry was derived from the same source. The Mormons themselves were Christians plus, who gloried in the more violent aspects of the Christian religion. Like the Jews and the various communist sects, they believed they were set apart by God, saved from annihilation, and that the future of the world depended upon their destiny. If they perished, everyone else would. If they survived and succeeded, everyone might be saved, because they were sure that eventually they would be the true guardians of salvation.

One of the most unhappy forms in which this blood-concept manifested itself was in the punishment for adultery. The Mormons viewed adultery as an uncondonable sin. It could be erased only by blood, the blood of the guilty one. If an adulterer or adulteress failed to give blood, which meant life, they would never find peace in the next world, but would suffer in constant torment through eternity. Salvation for sinners was founded upon blood atonement. The books of Matthew, Hebrews, Leviticus all proclaimed it. For a number of years Mormon husbands, in pursuit of this belief, killed their adulterous wives to save their souls.

[1] Paul Radin: *Primitive Religion*, p. 179.
[2] Harry Elmer Barnes: *Twilight of Christianity*, p. 117. See also B. Z. Goldberg: *The Sacred Fire*, pp. 67, 68.

THE WESTWARD MOVEMENT

Undoubtedly the Mormons moved westward mainly because they found it extremely inconvenient to carry on their activities in the East, where their founders were known and opposition to them was personal as well as religious. In fact, opposition shortly grew into overt hostility, with Smith himself indicted as a horse thief, so that the Mormons had little choice but to flee. Joseph Smith, of course, with characteristic ingenuity, conjured up a vision urging their departure.[1] Their first stop after they left Fayette, New York, where they had organized their original church, was in Kirtland, Ohio; there they began their initial co-operative venture. There they met Sidney Rigdon, a Campbellite minister, who was speedily converted to their creed; his revivalistic enthusiasms and ecstacies hypnotized his congregation and it was with little difficulty that he got them to accept the Mormon doctrine and become members of the new church.

Rigdon, it is important to note, had been influenced in his early years by Owen's socialist philosophy, which harmonized perfectly with Joseph Smith's conception of the United Order of Enoch, with its dream of a communist commonwealth.

Kirtland did not provide the divine retreat that Smith and his cohorts had anticipated. Their venture proved relatively short-lived. They were unable to meet their debts, unable to meet any of the emergencies they faced. For a time they organized enterprises, established stores, constructed a church, but no New Jerusalem emerged, and in five years they left Kirtland and migrated farther west. While in Kirtland an attempt had been made to convict Smith and Rigdon on a banking charge, growing out of the collapse of the Mormon "Safety Society Bank";[2] both men were convicted, but they

[1] *A Short History of the Church of Jesus Christ of Latter Day Saints*, published by the Church of Jesus Christ of Latter Day Saints, p. 36.
[2] William Alexander Linn: *The Story of the Mormons*, 1902, p. 150.

appealed the case and left the state before the second trial was held.

The most interesting development in Kirtland, of which more will be said later, was the beginning of the Mormon economic and social system. The Mormons were not communists in the Labadist or Ephratist sense of the word. They began as economic individualists and developed a co-operative economics only after a severe struggle. In Kirtland the first stage in that adaptation occurred. There Smith had a revelation, instructing all Mormons to deliver their property to the church. "Thou shalt consecrate all thy properties," the Mormon Commandment read, "that which thou hast, unto me, with a covenant and deed which cannot be broken." Instead of demanding all property, however, Smith adopted the Biblical recommendation of a tithe, and thereafter every Mormon had to surrender one-tenth of his income and wealth to the Church of Zion.

A new settlement was begun at Colesville, in Thompson County, Ohio, where the Colesville Saints strove to duplicate the achievements of Kirtland. There twelve men, representing the twelve apostles, and at the same time the twelve tribes of Israel, laid the foundations of another Mormon community. All these undertakings were precarious and perilous, as was illustrated by the tarring and feathering of Smith and Rigdon in Hiram, in which the mob tried to kill the Mormon leaders, but succeeded only in making them greater martyrs. Smith was almost beaten to death, a bottle of nitric acid was broken against his teeth; Rigdon was dragged head-downward for miles and remained in a state of delirium for days afterward.

In the meanwhile, the Mormons despatched missionaries to the outlying country, and sent a special group to convert the Indians. Although the latter endeavor proved futile, the group learned a great deal about the western territory, which assisted them when they later ventured into the lesser known parts of the West. The Mormons were among the greatest missionaries of their time, and if they did not succeed in building up a following like the Methodists and Baptists, it was because of peculiarity of their creed, and not lack of effort. Their missionaries preceded their communities, breaking the ground and preparing the new converts for their arrival. They hazarded all directions, north, west, and south, and even penetrated Canada, where they achieved remarkable success within a very brief time. In some cases they converted whole groups and congregations with a single sermon; in others the task was more difficult; in still others, it proved a dismal failure.

The Jackson County Saints, in Missouri, were mercilessly attacked by the frontiersmen; their houses were burned, their barns destroyed, their stores robbed. A battle was waged on the Big Blue River, in which several men were murdered and many others wounded. Smith sent reserves from Kirtland to aid the Jacksonites, but too late to rescue their possessions, and the Mormons were forced to retreat across the river, where they tried to re-establish their settlement. Soon they pushed on farther into the interior of Missouri, then toward the western part of the territory. But persecution and attack followed them wherever they went. In the Battle of Crooked River men were killed on both sides, and Smith and four of his associates were arrested, tried, and sentenced to death. Only because General Doniphan refused to shoot them were the Mormons saved. They were kept in jail for a number of months, but eventually they escaped.

NAUVOO THE BEAUTIFUL

From Missouri the Mormons ventured into Illinois, where they built the settlement of Nauvoo, which means "the beautiful." Nauvoo flourished from the very beginning, and within a decade its population leaped from six thousand to twenty-five thousand, and it became the hub of the surrounding ter-

ritory. It became incorporated as a "city state," [1] established
an independent judiciary, organized a university, and created
the Nauvoo Legion, five thousand strong, to protect the inhabitants against any further attacks. Freedom of worship
was guaranteed in the town, as also was freedom of speech
and the press. "It is beautifully situated. . . . I never saw
more abundant proofs of intelligent industry and quiet domestic thrift than were presented by the appearance of these
houses and farms." [2]

THE MURDER OF THE PROPHET

The more successful Nauvoo became the more it inspired the
hostility of its neighbors. Unable to attack the town forth-
rightly because of its defenses and its independent militia, its
enemies strove to extradite its leaders, get them back into
Missouri, where they could be prosecuted, imprisoned, and
hanged. Several attempts were made to achieve that end,
but all failed. When the Saints nominated Joseph Smith as
a presidential and Sidney Rigdon as a vice-presidential candidate, the battle broke out in desperately violent form. Smith
advocated the purchase of all slaves by the United States
Government, which should then grant them immediate emancipation. This was enough in itself to start a small civil war,
and it did.

Smith advocated a national bank, in which the officers should
be elected each year by the people, with only two dollars a day
salary—a recommendation, harking back to Jacksonianism,
which was most challengingly progressive. In addition, he
urged, with a sagacity which was truly clairvoyant, if, alas,
not prophetic, that all lawyers should be disbarred and then

[1] *A Short History of the Church of Jesus Christ of Latter Day Saints,*
p. 73.
[2] *Private Papers and Diary of Thomas Leiper Kane.* Edited by Oscar
Osburn Winther, 1937, pp. 6, 7.

despatched "to preach the Gospel to the destitute, without purse or scrip." Disputes were settled by the bishop, who functioned as a material as well as spiritual arbiter. Lawyers were considered parasites, as likewise were all middlemen. Lawyers and bankers made their living, according to Smith, by robbing those who worked. In a land where "God was the landlord," [1] lawyers could scarcely find a crevice into which to crawl. Needless to say, no lawyers ever joined the Mormon Church or, when they did, they not only forsook their profession but also denounced it.

Such ideas were too progressive for their time, and all bankers and lawyers naturally attacked the Prophet, as did the rest of the populace. Smith was in advance of his time in social vision.

When Smith, with his forward-looking ideas and ideals, ran for the presidency, advocating, among other challenging theses, the emancipation of the Negro slaves, he was attacked by everyone except his own followers. The Christian churches scorned him as a maniac, the government condemned him as a trouble-maker, and the press denounced him an enemy of "freedom." [2] More than that, he was decried as "a proclaimed culprit," a "fugitive from justice," [3] and his people were attacked as guilty of the most "abominable [of] thieving operations." [4]

It all resulted finally in the massacre of Smith, his brother, and another comrade, in Carthage, where a mob invaded the jail and shot down the Mormon leaders defenseless in their cells. Smith's brother was the first to die, as a bullet struck him from the window. Joseph Smith himself dashed to the window to face the hate-throbbing mob, but was killed by two perfectly aimed bullets before he could open his mouth in

[1] Bishop Albert Carmichael: *The Elements of Stewardship and Our Social Program*, 1927, p. 25.
[2] "The Mormon Circular," *Quincy Herald*, Vol. I, No. 20, Feb. 3, 1842.
[3] *Ibid.*: Vol. I, No. 51, Sept. 8, 1842.
[4] *Sangamon Journal*, Vol. 14, No. 21, Feb. 13, 1845, Springfield, Ill.

protest. Dr. Richards succeeded in achieving his escape through a secret passage whereby he managed, after great hardship, to get back to his people and report the details of the massacre.

All during the pre-Utah days the Mormons had been accused of organizing anti-government forces, independent groups which repudiated all governmental authority.[1]

ENTER BRIGHAM YOUNG

After Smith's murder Brigham Young became the new Prophet and led his people from Nauvoo into the Far West and finally to Utah, where they found their promised land. Young had joined the Mormons as a convert back in the Ohio days when Kirtland was their haven, and had since become a conspicuous figure among the Saints. He was a thick-set man, with tiny, darting eyes, a narrow forehead, a sharp chin, and a voice that could both caress and challenge within the same second.[2] In the name of expediency, he could be all things to all men. His practical mind stood out in sharp contrast to that of Smith. He was more interested in work than faith, in achievement than vision. He was not a dreamer, had little concern for revelations, but much concern for material provender. He reverenced Smith for his revelations, but had little interest in those that were not practical. His ambition lay in making the Mormons into a successful group, organizing their lives in such a way that they would be invulnerable to attack, free to be themselves, unmolested and unassailed in their own domain. Smith insisted upon being first in Rome or nothing, and consequently incurred the animosity of myriads; Young was willing to be second in Rome, but first in the hearts of his followers. The result was that Young succeeded, where Smith

---

[1] *Documents Containing the Correspondence, Orders, etc., in Relation to the Disturbances with the Mormons,* pp. 9, 10. (Published by order of the General Assembly, Missouri, 1841.)

[2] W. E. Waters: *Life among the Mormons,* 1868, p. 180.

had failed, in building up a Mormon state and spiritual empire which has lasted till this day.

There can be little doubt but that part of the friction between the "Gentiles," as the Mormons described all non-Mormons, and the Mormons, had been due to Smith's grandiose, megalomaniacal dreams of conquering the country and the world. "The plan of said Smith, the Prophet, is to take this state; and he professes to his people to intend taking the United States and ultimately the whole world," declared Thomas B. Marsh (originally one of the Twelve Apostles of the Mormon Church, who later returned to the Church) and added that "Smith's prophecies are superior to the law of the land." However distorted or exaggerated Marsh's testimony may have been, the fact remains that the frontiersmen of the time believed in it and were convinced that Smith, like the Pope in Rome, was determined to capture the country and enslave it to his dictatorial whim.

Brigham Young avoided such misconstructions and misinterpretations of doctrine. He was a simpler man, free from such worldly ambitions as being president of the country or ruler of the world. He merely wanted the Mormons to find their New Canaan, settle there, build themselves a sound and secure home, and found it upon rock instead of sand, so that it should endure over the centuries.

Utah proved to be that home, the real promised land.

THE SALT LAKE VALLEY PROJECT

Once they had arrived in the Salt Lake territory and begun to establish their settlement, Brigham Young immediately mapped out its physical and economic contours. Always a pragmatic person, he planned the Utah community with modern technocratic precision, determined to utilize its infinitesimal as well as its infinite possibilities. In order to give the ground Biblical blessing, the river running through it was christened the Jordan, while other sites were similarly hallowed.

Few groups had undertaken such an extended trek westward at that time, and the Mormons themselves scarcely realized at first how far they had traveled in order to escape the assaults and attacks of the Gentiles. When they began to calculate distances, they knew they were over a thousand miles removed from the nearest eastern settlement. But they were unafraid. There were Indians about them, but they were certain they could live happily with them, and they knew also that they had in Great Britain over forty thousand converts, all of whom they expected to follow them into the desert land and make it a living Eden. There were other colonies, too, which would join them in time, and when they were all united, they would build up such a model community that all the world would bow before it.

Joseph Smith's plan for his City of Zion is worth quoting:

> "The plan provided that all the people should live in the city, that the city should be a mile square; that the blocks should contain ten acres, cut into half acre lots, allowing twenty houses to the block; that the streets should be eight rods wide and intersect each other at right angles . . . that the middle tier of blocks should be fifty per cent wider than the others (these were to be used for schools, churches and public buildings); that stables and barns should be outside the city; that farm lands should be laid off north and south of the city, that no lot should contain more than one house, that all houses should be set back twenty-five feet from the street, and some other specifications." [1]

MORMON ECONOMY

In Utah as well as the earlier settlements the Mormons worked out an economy which represented a combination of individualism and collectivism. Individuals were allowed to

[1] Lowry Nelson: *A Study in Social Origins,* 1930, p. 18.

own private property, but its control was always subject to the theocratic state. They not only had to donate a tithe of the income to the general economy, but they had to be prepared at any time to surrender it all, if need be, to the common weal. Every man "was entitled to whatever was necessary to maintain himself and his dependents in comfort and decency, but whatever he earned in addition to his needs he was to turn over to the community, to be used for the benefit of the group life." The Mormons were imbued with faith in the same co-operative ideal which prevailed in the other communist colonies. If their communism was somewhat modified, it was not because they did not believe in the supremacy of the group over the individual, but because they believed that the interests of the group and the individual could be thus best harmonized. They worked out for the advantage of the individual, but for the good of the whole. The land belonged to the people, as also, according to Brigham Young's dictum, did the mountains and all that resided in them, the rivers, the valleys, and the horizon which stretched beyond.[1]

[1] "This co-operation," writes Warner, "has given us farms, orchards, homes and population; it has given the people [Mormons] renown for patience, endurance, and success; it has testified to moral courage, to industrial unity, to religious influence. . . . Our first lumber mills, factories, as well as our settlements, were founded on the principles of co-operation." To this Mr. Warner adds: "The essential element of co-operation as it exists in Utah cannot be found elsewhere. Nevertheless, in the chapters of our history there are lessons for the sociologist and the political economist, the statesman, the philosopher, and the religionist, separately or combined. The unique experience of Mormon co-operation, its successes and failures, its present and future, could best be studied on the spot. It is only regretted that ignorance and prejudice are so combined that almost none believes that any good can come out of this despised Nazareth of our magnificent country. Our people are not anxious to place themselves under the tyranny of monopolists, particularly if this has to be done at the expense of self-help—the boast of freemen—or of that united help, which supersedes the motto of 'live and let live,' by the more Godlike one, 'live and help live,' which is as much the key to Mormon history in the past as it will be to the triumphant vindication of its principles in the future." Warner: *Co-operation among the Mormons*. Publications of American Economic Association, Vol. II, No. 1, 1888, pp. 114, 115, 116, 117.

Among the Mormons an individual did not venture off and seize a space of land and call it his own, regardless of the interests of others. On the contrary, land was sacred, and its division depended largely upon how it could best provide for the community as a whole. Co-operative enterprises were established in order to facilitate this way of life. Capitalist influences intruded, and there were times when many of the Mormons succumbed to them, but their prophets and their church did not. They remained inviolable. The Mormon Church, with its various and accumulating monies, soon played an important role in this process; it lent money for the erection of mills and factories, and in the case of the manufacture of sugar, its success was phenomenal.

In Nauvoo, the Mormons had built a prosperous city out of a swamp; in Utah, they built a magnificent city out of a desert. The following description of Salt Lake City, printed in the New York *Tribune,* as early as 1849, by a gold-digger, who had little if any affection for the Mormons, is most striking:

"The company of gold-diggers which I have the honor to command, arrived here on the third instant, and judge our feelings when after some twelve hundred miles of traveling through an uncultivated desert . . . we found ourselves suddenly and almost unexpectedly in a comparative paradise.

"Descending the table land which bordered the valley, extensive herds of cattle, horses, and sheep were grazing in every direction. . . . The whole space for miles, excepting the streets and houses, was in a high state of cultivation. Fields of yellow wheat stood waiting for the harvest, and Indian corn, potatoes, oats, flax and all kinds of garden vegetables were growing in profusion. . . . We passed on amid scenes like these, expecting every moment to come to some commercial centre, some business point in this great metropolis of the mountains, but we were disappointed. No hotel, sign post, cake and beer shop, barber pole, smoke-house, grocery, provision, dry-goods or hardware store distinguished one part of the town from another. Not even a bakery or mechanic's sign was anywhere discernible. Here, then, was something new; an entire people reduced to a level and all living by their labor—all cultivating the earth or following some branch of physical industry.

"This territory, state, or as some term it, the Mormon Empire, may justly be considered as one of the greatest prodigies of our time and in comparison with its age the most gigantic of all republics in existence.

"I this day attended worship with them in the open air. Some thousands of well dressed, intelligent-looking people assembled. . . . The beauty and neatness of the ladies reminded me of some of our best congregations in New York. They had a choir of both sexes who performed extremely well, accompanied by a band who played well on almost every musical instrument of modern invention. . . . Then followed various business advertisements read by a clerk. . . .

"The Mormons are not dead, nor is their spirit broken, and if I mistake not there is a noble, daring strain and democratic spirit swelling in their bosoms which will people these mountains with a race of independent men, and influence the destiny of our country and the world for a hundred generations. In their religion they seem charitable, devoted and sincere; in their politics bold, daring and determined; in their domestic circle quiet, affectionate and happy, while in industrial skill and intelligence they have few equals and no superiors on the earth." [1]

The Mormons have been so libeled by their enemies, so satirized, caricatured, and condemned, that few people know today that Joseph Smith was one of America's first utopian socialists, that his economic vision was far in advance of those of his contemporaries, and that his concept of society, afflicted though it was with the theocratic virus, was far more concerned with human values than that of his individualistic neighbors. If men are "not equal in earthly things," he

[1] Quoted from Henry Mayhew: *The Mormons*, 1851, pp. 262, 263.

declared, "how then can they be equal in obtaining heavenly
things?" Equality was his challenging credo. Whatever an
individual owed, Smith contended, was only because of the
existence of the group, of society, and he owed all that he had
to society, which in his eyes owned everything. Individual
man was merely a "steward," taking care of possessions and
properties which did not belong to him, but to all the people.[1]

MORMON COMMUNISM

Brigham Young, following Smith's decree, declared shortly
after the Saints arrived in Utah, that "no man here has any
land to sell. He does not own it. *We* own it. And every
head of a family shall have his land measured out to him—
all he needs and can take care of. The water goes with
the land. The timber in the mountains, also, belongs to us all,
not to one man only, and we shall say when and under what
circumstances it may be cut."[2] More than that, every Mormon was entitled to a livelihood, to an equal share in the
wealth of the community. He had to work for it if he could,
but work was always there for all; if he was ill, he received
the same as the others as long as he was incapacitated, even
if for life. This explains why the Mormons never had any
poor among them, never had any doles, never had to resort to
the state for aid in slum-clearance, or other rehabilitation
projects.

The Mormons believed, like the technocrats of today—and
like the Socialists, Communists, and Anarchists—that there

[1] Quoted from *The Book of Mormon*: Mosiah, Chap. 4, p. 144: "I
would that ye should impart of your substance to the poor, every man
according to that which he hath, such as feeding the hungry, clothing
the naked, visiting the sick and administering to their relief, both spiritually
and temporally, according to their wants.

"And see that all these things are done in wisdom and order; for it is
not requisite that a man should run faster than he has strength. And
again, it is expedient that he should be diligent, that thereby he might
win the prize; therefore, all things must be done in order."

[2] John Henry Evans: *Joseph Smith, an American Prophet*, p. 238.

was enough for all, enough land, enough resources, enough products. They declared time and again, through the lips of Joseph Smith, Brigham Young, and their succeeding leaders, that every man had a right to a livelihood, that the state owed it to him, was responsible for it, and that he had a right to sue the state for it.

Reduced to the lowest common denominator, what it meant was that the Mormons believed that every community possessed enough means to provide the common necessities of life for every individual. If it did not provide them with such, it was because the few robbed the many. The Mormon communities were organized as they were in order to avoid that miscarriage of justice. They were not pristine communists, in the apostolic style; they were more modern and more subtle. They sought to amalgamate the social necessities of the group with the personal appetencies of the individual. They wanted to achieve an amity between opposites, a synthesis of antitheses. In short, they wanted to preserve individual initiative within a collectivist economy.

They wanted every individual, or rather every family, which was their common unit, to own its own home, its own tools of production, its own clothes and all the other necessities which are associated with a modern livelihood. A man, they believed, should have as much as he could eat, and so also his wives and children—likewise with clothes, medical attention, and other social necessities. Beyond such necessities, the individual or the family was entitled to nothing. Such surplus belonged to the common stock, to be divided up among the less fortunate in the community. It was that surplus which kept the Mormons from developing the common evils of modern communities: impoverished groups, slums, crime, and destitution. The money provided by the rest of the community was always sufficient to prevent such catastrophes. In fact, often it was more than was needed, and when that was the case it was used for expansional purposes. Unemployment was unknown among them because the United Order could always find work for everyone.

These semi-communist experiments, for which the Saints have never received due recognition, began in the early days of their advance. It was back in Thompson County, removed slightly from Kirtland, where Joseph Smith first experimented with his concept of the United Order of Enoch, a society based upon theocratic communism, the original vision of which he derived from apostolic Christianity.[1] The Order was also set up in the Jackson County settlement, but it was never able to develop in either place, because the Mormons were driven out before they had a chance to work out the details of their experiment. In Glenwood, however, no such interruption occurred, and the experiment proved an amazing success. John Henry Evans' description of it affords an excellent picture of how the people lived:

> "The community numbered about five hundred persons. . . . A bishop presided over the 'ward'. . . . There was no political government. Each head of a family . . . owned his home, the town lot on which his house stood, and the furniture in his home. That was a part of his 'stewardship.' Also he had his own vocation—which was whatever he felt himself best fitted to do. . . . No lawyers were needed in that community, for the bishop settled all the disputes for nothing, and the midwife not only brought babies into the world, but saw to sick people. . . . Thus division of labor was carried to its most practical ideal.
> "Household necessities were supplied in a unique way. Every so often the farmer came to the door with flour and potatoes, the butcher with meat and lard, the poultry-grower with chickens and eggs, the dairyman with butter and cheese and milk, and so on. Each asked . . . "How much of this do you need?" Whenever the children required new shoes or the old ones mended, they were sent to the shoemaker. Or in case they needed a new frock or a pair of overalls, they went to the store.

[1] Evans: *op. cit.,* p. 242.

"No mention was made of money. Nobody there had money or needed it. All the men and boys got their pay in 'credits.' What they bought went down on the debit side of their account, and what they earned on the credit side. At the end of the year the books were balanced, and the men knew where they stood.

"Every able-bodied man worked. He had to or be expelled from the Order. If anyone played sick . . . he was waited upon by a committee. . . . Boys, too, had to work, if they were able.

"As soon as the boy got to the stage when his voice was fully changed, he was expected to do two things: to select a vocation and look around for a wife. . . .

"When the couple returned home, they found a house to live in . . . furnished with home-made tables, chairs, and other necessary things. After that the farmer, the butcher . . . and the rest had another customer.

"On Sundays everybody went to the church—Sunday School in the morning and a religious service in the evening. And once a week men, women, and children went to the village dance, where only 'square' dances were allowed." [1]

In Utah various communities were organized on the principles of the United Order. Brigham Young early organized a series of co-operative chain stores so that the people could buy things at the lowest possible prices, and every head of a family owned stock in them. In Brigham City, Lorenzo Snow instituted a co-operative plan in which the people owned almost all the larger industries, which made it possible for them to get their necessities at astonishingly cheap prices. In Orderville, a settlement in the southern part of Utah, there was no individually owned property at all except clothes. Everyone ate, as they did among the other communal groups, in a common hall, had the same food, leaders as well as followers.[2] As in

[1] *Ibid.,* p. 246.
[2] For illustrative evidence of the socio-paternalistic character of Mormon economy, see Dean D. McBrien: "Economic Content of Early Mormon Doctrine." *Political and Social Science Quarterly,* Vol. VI, No. 2, Sept., 1925, pp. 188-190.

Glenwood, money did not exist. Payment was always in the form of goods for labor and energy expended.

BELLAMY'S VISIT

So impressed was he by what he had heard of the co-operative, semi-communal way of life of the Mormons that Edward Bellamy visited them in Utah in 1883. He had conferences with various Mormon leaders and conversed with Lorenzo Snow in detail about the new economic system the Mormons had introduced. Bellamy was inspired by much that he saw, and when he wrote *Looking Backward,* he embodied many Mormon ideas in his utopian scheme. At the time Bellamy visited Utah, he had already written *The Duke of Stockbridge,* a novel which depicted the struggle between the agricultural and financial interests active in Shays' Rebellion. In *Looking Backward,* his most popular novel, he tried to embody the most progressive ideas of the time, and among those incorporated were those of the Mormons. In all the Bellamy societies which were organized after the publication of *Looking Backward,* Mormon economic doctrine was not only respected, but it was also studied as representative of the advanced social planning of the day.

POLYGAMY AMONG THE SAINTS

Although the Mormons were moralists, they were far more latitudinarian in their concept of good and evil than either the Pilgrims or Puritans. They lacked the morbid asceticism of the New England pioneers. They did not object to dancing; they had cotillions and balls, although they preferred square dances to all others; they liked the stage and in time developed one of the best theaters in the country. Appreciating the value of the stage, Brigham Young constructed his theater before his Temple, and had his sons and daughters become performers to encourage the rest of the population to follow in their footsteps.[1] The Salt Lake Theater, which involved an expenditure of over one hundred thousand dollars, was begun in 1861. While religious plays only were staged at first, it was not long before the barriers were removed, and the theater became a cultural center for the whole region. Maude Adams, one of America's greatest actresses, was born in Salt Lake City, and derived from this background.

In music, the Mormons were notably progressive. Although they resorted often to popular and regional music in order to win the interest of their less cultivated followers, their Temple, unlike that of the New England theocrats, was filled with the refrains of the great European composers: Wagner, Mozart, Bach.

But it was not because of their lenient attitude toward the theater, dancing, and music that the puritanic-minded frontiersmen became so enraged whenever they heard the word "Mormon." The Mormons were strangers to them because they lived differently, believed differently, swore by an alien God. *The Book of Mormon* was a foreign book, even though Joseph Smith declared he found it on American ground, in the State of New York. These frontiersmen had never read it, and anything they had never read was evil in their eyes. In addition, envy was an important factor. Mormon communities succeeded far better than Gentile settlements; ergo, some wicked force must be working on their side, conspiring in their favor.[2]

Worse still was the sex factor. There envy was reduced to its lowest common denominator. The Mormons in time became polygamists, with many women instead of one to adorn their households, which was what most of the frontiers-

[1] Katherine Fullerton Gerould: *The Aristocratic West,* 1925, p. 61.
[2] As Frederic L. Paxson wrote: "It [the Mormon government] was an efficient government; more so than the spontaneous governments of Oregon or Franklin had been. And Non-Mormons passing through its jurisdiction often had reason to be glad of its existence." (Frederic L. Paxson: *The History of the American Frontier,* 1924, p. 349.

men unconsciously desired, but consciously opposed. Their hostility was uncondonably vicious, as is always the case when unconscious motivations are unearthed and challenged. Most men, as Freud and a score of other psychologists and anthropologists have shown, are polygamous by nature, and have had to regulate their polygamy within the elastic realm of monogamic *mores*. Prostitution and spinsterhood have been the casualties. In other words, women have suffered much unhappiness to uphold a moral code obnoxious to man's nature.

The Mormons turned toward polygamy—they did not officially adopt it until August 29, 1852—only after Joseph Smith had a vision in which God told him that his Latter Day Saints should live as did the Jews of Biblical times: Abraham, Jacob, Moses, Solomon, all of whom had numerous wives. Smith was opposed to adopting it officially because of the added antagonism he was certain it would create on the part of the Gentiles, and it was not until a number of years after his assassination that the Mormon Church sanctioned it. No doubt part of Smith's interest in polygamy can be traced to his deep-rooted sex urge and to his disappointment in his wife's lack of fecundity. She had borne him one child who had died in infancy; for many years she did not bear him another, and those were years when Smith reflected upon the sadness of his lot, married to a woman who could not provide him with the children necessary for celestial glory. Smith was obsessed with the belief that man's future in heaven was dependent to a large extent upon the number of progeny he could bring before the throne of God. As a father he had proved an abysmal failure. To assure himself of the parenthood necessary to win favor in God's eyes, he had to have other wives, just as the ancient Jewish patriarchs did. He had been reflecting upon this necessity for a long time before God spoke to him and provided the *revelation* which has since become so famous. Part of the words which he claimed God said unto him are as follows:

"Verily, thus saith the Lord, my servant Joseph . . .
Abraham received concubines, and they bare him children, and it was accounted unto him for righteousness,
because they were given unto him and he abode in my
law; as Isaac also, and Jacob, did none other things than
that which they were commanded. David also received
many wives and concubines, as also Solomon and Moses,
my servant, as also many others of my servants, from the
beginning of creation until this time."

For a long time after Smith himself and several of his
Apostles began to practice polygamy—they always resented
the word "polygamy," and spoke of it as plural marriage,
Smith himself insisting that it be called "celestial marriage"—
they kept it a secret in order to prevent the Gentiles from attacking them for the practice. Most of Smith's celestial wives,
beginning with the exquisite Louise Bemen, and including the
talented Eliza Snow, and the irresistible adolescent Lucy
Walker, were morbidly and fanatically devoted to him.[1]
Within a few years he had twenty wives,[2] most of them living
with him in his own house, putatively as his relatives or adopted
sisters. He was still afraid to confide the truth to his initial
wife, Emma, who learned the truth only when several of her
husband's enemies disclosed it to her. She was an unintelligent

---

[1] Abundant evidence has been gathered to show that the majority of
Mormon women preferred polygamy to monogamy. Evans: (*op. cit.,*
pp. 266-275) cites a number of women who all declared they believed
plural marriage was superior to single. "The principle of plural marriage
is true," one of these women stated, "and, if properly lived, would redeem
woman from slavery and put her on a higher plane than she has ever
occupied before. There would be no prostitution in the world, and every
normal woman would have a husband and children." Another Mormon
wife avowed that "a Congress composed of polygamic men who are true
to their wives would confer a far higher honor upon a nation, and would
perform better service to this country than a Congress composed of
monogamic, unreliable husbands."

[2] For an excellent description of Smith's marital maneuvers, see Vardis
Fisher's *Children of God,* which, though a novel, is sound as history in
most respects. Fisher expatiates upon the characters of the respective
wives, and provides a picture of Smith at that time which is extraordinarily
illuminating and revealing.

woman who denounced his other wives as prostitutes and bawds, and threatened to expose him to the whole country if he did not rid himself of their presence. He compromised, and despatched all but two of them back to their homes. Emma reluctantly allowed these two to remain, to assuage her husband's amorous ardor.

The Saints did not immediately approve of Joseph's revelation or of his attempt to carry it into practice. There were rumbles of protest from many quarters, men and women denounced it in the streets of Nauvoo, meetings were held, defections occurred, and for a while chaos threatened. When the Apostles returned, however, and Smith explained to them the revelation, they began slowly to understand. Brigham Young at first decried the idea as bordering on the insane, but later he was one of the first to test out its extremes. Others denounced the Prophet, as Joseph Smith was most commonly known, as lecherous, vile, and vicious. Smith, however, succeeded in weathering all their gales and storms of denunciation, and within a relatively short time convinced the majority of the leaders of the Church that celestial marriage was a categorical imperative. After that all the leaders practiced it, but entirely in secret, because they had suffered enough persecution from the Gentiles and did not want to add more for this reason.

Monogamy, Smith declared, exalted one woman and left others—sweethearts, mistresses, prostitutes, spinsters, unexalted; polygamy exalted all women equally. Polygamy made it possible for all women to be married and bear children. It also enriched and irradiated the family institution and gave new possibilities to personality development among children, Orson Pratt, as well as Joseph Smith, maintained.

Smith made the mistake of asking various women to become his wives, several of whom later revealed the fact to others, and it was not long, as revulsion and revolt against the new credo spread, before the Gentiles learned of its practice, and thereafter the Mormons were more persecuted and harassed than ever. The Gentiles were now convinced that the Mormons were demons, fiends, befoulers of Christian principle and practice, and had to be destroyed. Guerrilla attacks multiplied, state governors denounced the Mormons as agents of disorder and treason, and no Saint's life was safe from mob or militia.

Joseph Smith had anticipated all this, but he had not been shrewd or careful enough to avoid it. His belief in polygamy was more than personal; or at least he rationalized it into other spheres wherein it had diverse justifications. Above all, he hated prostitution, which prevailed in every Gentile community, in hamlets, villages, and towns, as well as in large cities. It was the price the Gentiles had to pay for their factitious monogamy. He wanted a community without prostitution and he achieved it. Plural, or celestial, marriage made it possible for every woman to get married and bear children—which was not possible under the monogamous system of morality. This convinced him more than ever that God had inspired him to lead men away from the vice of monogamic marriage into the virtue of celestial marriage. Besides that, the hypocrisy of adultery was avoided. Instead of sinning with women, men could marry them, and officialize their affections. This eliminated the "back-street" sweetheart or mistress, who had to conceal herself from the wife's scrutiny. No woman would any longer have to be a spinster or a whore.

Joseph Smith did his best to fulfill his prophecy and before he was murdered he had twenty-five wives, although he was never sure of their count, most of them ranging in age from sixteen to fifty; his premature death, however, prevented him from achieving the maximal triumph of Brigham Young, his successor, who had twenty-seven wives, but, more important, fifty-six children, and almost countless grandchildren, who still govern society in Salt Lake City, where his statue stands as the great monument dominating the face of the land.[1]

Joseph Smith had confined celestial marriage at first to the leaders of the church, himself, Brigham Young, Rigdon, and the other Apostles; in time, however, they found that the rest of the members resented this sexual privilege and demanded that they be included, if it was to be accepted as a prevailing Mormon custom. The bureaucrats, who had tried to preserve the privilege for themselves, had no choice. They made polygamy official and legal, and from that time on, 1852 until 1890, it became the regular custom in all Mormon communities. It was the remoteness of the West that made it possible for them to practice polygamy with relative impunity.[2] But it should not be thought they had no difficulties in maintaining the custom. After Brigham Young's famous speech, informing the world that the Mormons believed in plural marriage because it was authorized by the Bible and sanctioned by a revelation from God to Joseph Smith, a whirlwind of denunciation swept across the land.[3] Preachers condemned the Mormons as adulterers and fiends, vile products of the Devil; Congressmen urged their extermination as so many sacrilegious rodents; newspaper editors crusaded in favor of sending an army to subdue and destroy them; humble people frightened their children, their wives, and their mothers by crying, "Look out, there's a Mormon." Not until 1882, when the Edmunds Bill was passed, forbidding polygamy in the

[1] From all evidence available, it would certainly seem that the marital relationships, polygamous though they were, succeeded even better than the monogamous ones among the Gentiles. (*Cf.,* Juanita Brooks: "A Close-up of Polygamy," *Harpers,* Feb., 1934, pp. 303-305.)

[2] Ephraim E. Ericksen: *The Psychological Aspects of Mormon Group Life,* p. 76.

[3] One group of Mormons left the Church and founded the Reorganized Church of the Latter Day Saints; this group contended that Smith considered polygamy "a cursed doctrine." (Elder Jason W. Briggs: *The Basis of Polygamy.* Plano, Illinois, 1875, pp. 2-6.) Other pamphlets published by the same group emphasize the same doctrine. (*Cf.,* Alexander H. Smith: *Polygamy,* 1899, pp. 1-5.)

nation, and threatening with imprisonment any who practiced it, were the Gentiles able to force the Mormons to give up officially their celestial marriage ideal. Of course, outsiders knew nothing, or at least very little, about the real life of the Mormons. That a vast group of people dared live differently, economically as well as domestically, from the way other people did, was a sufficient indictment, an indisputable proof of their alliance with the forces of evil. The more the Mormons were hated, the more they believed in their moral superiority and their destined triumph over the wicked Gentiles. Few Mormon women objected to polygamy. Life in a polygamous society was no happier, but at the same time scarcely more miserable, for wives than in a monogamous one.[1] Women, like men, adapt themselves to prevailing conditions.

BRIGHAM YOUNG: DICTATOR

The Mormons were secure in their desert fastness and felt equipped to defend themselves against their worst adversaries, even the soldiers of the national government. The national government had betrayed them so often in the past, state militias had imprisoned them and given Joseph Smith over to the Gentile dogs to be destroyed in the blood of the Lamb; they were willing to clash swords and bayonets, meet cannon with cannon, with anyone who attempted to rob them of their homes and plunder them of their possessions. Joseph Smith had been a patient Prophet, long-suffering, gentle to the point of softness, forgiving, kind; Brigham Young, however, was made of sturdier stuff. He was the opposite, shrewd, canny, unforgiving, hard. Joseph Smith finally had a Nauvoo Legion, but he never knew how to use it to best advantage.

[1] Louis W. Larsen: "Childhood in a Mormon House," *American Mercury,* August, 1933, pp. 480-483. As Mr. Larsen shows, "the typical polygamist was the man with two wives," which is really not widely different from the so-called monogamous practices which persist today.

All his military ventures, which were fortunately few, proved futile. Young, on the other hand, never failed in what he set out to do. When in the early days the Mormons were attacked, Young conveniently and ingeniously disappeared, or at least arranged it so that he was not in the dangerous places. When Joseph and Hyrum Smith were murdered, Young was miles away from the scene. His absence was not due to cowardice, but to sagacity. He did not relish the prospect of becoming a martyr. Joseph Smith had always said he would have to give up his blood so that the Mormons might live. Young preferred sacrificing the blood of the Gentiles to that of the Mormons. Although he admired Smith's courage in going to Carthage, where certain death awaited him, he was convinced that a wiser course would have been for him to continue his flight to the West, and rebuild his church there.

Brigham Young wasted little time in moving the Mormons to the safer territories of the West, where he rebuilt the church and established the center of the Mormon empire. To protect what his people had achieved he never hesitated to fight and kill. They had been murdered in sanguinary abundance in the past; hereafter, he decided, if they were attacked, they would defend their homes to the last man. Mormon soldiers were equipped with the best military arms of the day; they built up the best army in the West. Their secret service, their regiments of avenging angels, their infantry and cavalry, struck terror in the hearts of their enemies. No one but the armies of the national government dared tackle them.

THE MORMON WAR

Opposition to the Saints multiplied in such monstrous proportions throughout the country that President Buchanan, in 1857, despatched a formidable section of the national army to Utah to conquer Brigham Young and his followers and destroy his experiment. This marked the beginning of what became known as the Mormon War. Few officials in Washington ever dreamed that there would be any serious difficulty involved in the conflict. But that was because they knew little of the Mormons. For years the Mormons had been the most peaceable of peoples; under Joseph Smith's leadership they had believed in Christ's doctrine of turning the other cheek. For years Smith had defended the doctrine of peace at all costs, even that of death. Christ's career had been his inspiration. Persecution and attack, however, forcing them upon repeated occasions to forsake the homes and communities they had built, hardened them, and year by year they came to realize that force had to be met by force.

First there had been the Danites, frequently known as the Destroying Angels, led by Dr. Avard; they had dedicated themselves to the destruction of their enemies by fire and sword. Smith had expelled them from the Church, because he believed in peace instead of war. In Utah, when Young instead of Smith ruled, the old Danite tactics were no longer condemned. Bill Hickman and Porter Rockwell, the two best shots and bravest men among the Mormon fighters, found abundant opportunity for their skill. They became scouts, minute-men, and avenging angels.

The first thing the Mormons did when they heard of the approach of the American military was to ambush them, disarm them, and burn their trains of food and other supplies. The army generals, unaccustomed to such bold tactics on the part of an enemy, and equipped to fight in West Point instead of western style, could not believe their eyes. The Mormons had whipped them in this first stage of the battle without firing a shot. From that time on their respect for the Mormons as soldiers increased with terrifying rapidity. They had thought they were going to fight some religious fanatics who were brave but stupid, and who could never compete with trained military men.

It was not long before it became apparent that the Mormons

were not only skillful fighters, but that they had, in addition, a geographic advantage in their Salt Lake Basin with the mountains surrounding it, which made their position almost impregnable. Slowly it became clear that all the government's armies couldn't get through the Echo Canyon without being chopped to pieces by Mormon artillery and sharpshooters. The American officers reported that they would far rather battle with ten thousand furious Indians than with a thousand Avenging Angels. Indian aim was unsure, but Mormon aim was mortally accurate. As a peaceful, non-resistant people, the Mormons had been driven from place to place, but as a fighting organization they were well-nigh unconquerable.

Sam Houston's Philippic

"The more men you send to the Mormon War," Sam Houston, the Texan emancipator, declared in violent tones upon the floor of the Senate, "the more you increase the difficulty. They have to be fed. For sixteen hundred miles you have to transport provisions. The regiments sent there have found Fort Bridger and other places heaps of ashes. They will find Salt Lake City if they ever reach it a heap of ashes. Whoever goes there will meet the fate of Napoleon's army; for these people if they fight will fight desperately. They are defending their homes. They are fighting to prevent the execution of threats that touch their hearths and their families; and depend upon it that they will fight until every man perishes." [1] All over the country similar sentiments were uttered. And when Houston, old fighter that he was, added, "As for troops to conquer the Mormons, fifty thousand will be as insufficient as two or three thousand. I say your men will never return, but their bones will whiten the valley of Salt Lake," he increased the fears felt in many quarters. The

[1] Quotation taken from Vardis Fisher: *op. cit.*, p. 531.

defeat which the army had received when their trains were burned had already made the newspapers call the expedition "Buchanan's Scandal," or "Buchanan's Blunder."

YOUNG'S STRATEGY

Realizing its plight, the Federal Government sent in emissaries to mediate with the Mormons, but for a good while Young refused to consider their propositions. The Mormons had been betrayed by so many Federal and State officials before, he could see no reason why he should trust this new crop of them. Although he knew he could prevent the Federal army from invading his land, he also knew that in killing American soldiers he would only aggravate the hostility of the nation, and before long armies would descend upon him from the West as well as the East, and the Mormons would be completely surrounded. He decided, therefore, upon a shrewder tactic —one which would win him the sympathy instead of the antipathy of the nation. This tactic was to burn the city the moment the soldiers started their march, raze it to the ground, so that when they arrived in the valley, it would be as desolate as when the Mormons first saw it.

Young had worked out a strategy so clever that no sudden move, change of position, or shift in attack could prevent its success. For days, weeks, and months the Mormons were busy collecting their supplies and personal possessions, boxing their records, crating their wares, packing their arms, in preparation for their hegira southward. Hundreds of them set forth in advance to found their new Mecca. In one train alone there were almost a thousand wagons. An endless procession of men, women, and children hastened on from the valley into the interior, singing as they sped. Many of them were accustomed to such flights and had learned to endure them without protest or complaint.

Young was correct in his diagnosis of the response which would follow. The press of the nation for the first time took up the cudgels in defense of the Mormons, attacked the government for threatening to drive a peaceful people from the soil they had cultivated and developed from a desert into a garden of prosperity. Soon the European press came to the Mormons' defense, and it was no longer possible to prosecute the Mormon War as a great moral crusade. The Mormons, and not the Federal military, had won the sympathy of the nation and the world.

A Peace Commission was consequently despatched by President Buchanan to the Mormons in hopes of achieving a truce in which neither side would be disgraced. Young met the Commissioners, McCulloch and Powell, and had a long conference with them. Both of the Commissioners were depressed by what they saw: a deserted city with only enough men left in it to light the torches and the fires necessary to destroy it within a few hours. They had never met people like this before. The frontiersmen they knew were made of different stuff. They possessed no such idealism. Their concern was for money, goods, land, and each individually tried to seize and hold as much as he could. They had none of the social vision of the Mormons, who shared rather than seized things, and who were willing to destroy all they had rather than sacrifice their principles and faith.

The Commissioners insisted that Young allow General Johnston's soldiers to come into the valley and settle themselves there for a period as guardians of the territory. At first Brigham Young laughed at the suggestion, reminded the Commissioners of the sufferings his people had been forced to undergo from previous armies of occupation; later, however, after profound reflection, he decided to accept their suggestion. He didn't want his people to move again, and he didn't want to see more bloodshed, even though the Mormons proved the victors.

Such was the motivation which governed his decision to allow Johnston's soldiers to enter the valley. The Commissioners, in order to win this victory, had been forced to promise that the army would behave itself in the most disciplined manner, would not interefere with Mormon life or enterprise, and would act only in a supervisory capacity. Young had no illusions about what would really happen, but it was better he believed to risk their presence than murder them and arouse the animosity of the nation, or burn up the valley and reduce it to a vast blistering cinder.

The army had not settled itself in Salt Lake City more than a month when whorehouses made their appearance, bars flourished, gambling became a common practice, and life as a whole became as crude and gross as it was in other frontier communities.

The Mormons shook their heads and sighed, whispered among themselves about the evil ways of the Gentiles, but were powerless to alter the situation. Civilization, as Brigham Young observed, had arrived. The Christians had come, and with them all the corruptions of anti-Christ. "If you tell a Christian a Mormon has two wives, he is shocked," said Young in one of his eloquent discourses, "even though he takes a fresh woman every night! Christian nations license women to open their doors and windows and carry on this abominable practice. New York City alone has fifteen thousand prostitutes and we haven't a single one here, yet they yelp to God of our immoral conduct. The miserable, nasty hypocrites."

Even when Brigham Young became "smitten" with Harriet, later known, as she insisted, as "Amelia," he did not lose his cognizance of the situation, or divorced his emotion from his intellect. He did erect the famous "Amelia Palace," and he did spend more evenings with Amelia than with his other wives, but he never forgot his social role as leader of the community, not even to the day of his death.

REPUDIATION OF POLYGAMY

When the Civil War broke out, the pressure upon the Mormons relaxed, and after a correspondence between Lincoln and Young, the Mormons found themselves able to continue for a brief period with their work. In some communities the United Order of Enoch was expanded, in others different forms of co-operation developed. The whole Mormon colony made great progress during this interval.

After the Civil War, unfortunately, the attacks were renewed, and by 1890, when most of the founders of the Mormon sect were dead, Woodruff, the president who succeeded John Taylor, signed a document repudiating polygamy as a marital practice. This resulted in a schism among the Saints. The majority of the veterans, aged friends of Joseph Smith and Brigham Young, left Utah, disgusted, as they declared, with Woodruff's "sell-out" to the Gentiles. They went to found Mormon communities of their own in the untracked wildernesses, among strange valleys and hills, remote from Gentile authority. Some ventured into the exotic mountainlands of Mexico, where they were certain that the suppressive hand of the American Government could not interfere with their religion.

Those who remained adapted themselves as best they could to the new regime. They did not all give up polygamy, and to this day, in inconspicuous and unsanctioned form, polygamy continues to survive. The younger Mormons, however, have accepted the monogamous *mores,* to the sad disgust of their elders, and officially monogamy reigns. The government, because of pressure from various quarters, mainly ecclesiastical, had to combat polygamy on principle. In actuality, most government leaders didn't care if the Mormons practiced it privately so long as they repudiated it publicly.

With the passing of polygamy as a marital ideal, other ideals vanished also. The United Order of Enoch, Joseph

Smith's socialistic dream, has disappeared, and even the co-operative economics practiced under the Young dynasty no longer prevail. The present-day Mormons have become almost as capitalistic as other Americans, with this exception, that theocratic controls remain, and each Mormon still must contribute his tithe to the Church, and as a result of that contribution the Church managed during most of the recent depression to take care of its idle and impoverished, and did not have to call upon the national government for fiscal aid until long after all the other states. Even today, there is less poverty in Mormon communities than in any others in the land.

In that way, at least, Smith's dream bore fruit. The Mormons never lost their belief in social solidarity, and even when their economics developed a competitive instead of a co-operative turn, they clung to their ecclesiastical ideal. Today, for example, there are many socialists among the Mormons, who hope soon to reorganize the United Order of Enoch in order to translate their Prophet's aspiration into reality.

CHAPTER XI

Beyond the Horizon

"Wipe out earth's furrows of the thine and mine,
And leave one green for men to play at bowls,
With innings for them all."

MRS. BROWNING

"Things will never go well in England so long as goods
be not in common and so long as there be villeins and
gentlemen. By what right are they whom we call lords
greater folk than we? On what grounds have they de-
served it? Why do they hold us in serfage? If we all
came of the same father and mother, of Adam and Eve,
how can they say or prove that they are better than we,
if it be not that they make us earn for them by our toil
what they spend in their pride? They are clothed in velvet
and warm in their furs and their ermines, while we are
covered with rags. They have wine and straw and water
to drink. They have leisure and fine houses; we have pain
and labour; the rain and the wind in the fields. And yet
it is of us and of our toil that these men hold their state."

JOHN BALL

Modern historians have striven constantly to prove that
radicals are communists in theory but individualists in practice. Consequently, it is a curious irony to discover, as we
have done, radicals who are individualists in theory but communists in practice.

Such were the majority of religious communists who settled in this country. They believed that their individual
souls were separate embodiments of the Lord, that every hair
on their heads was a special extension of heavenly design,

168

that every gesture, motion, action, was a result of God's unwavering will.

They were willing to sacrifice everything for the common good, except their personal right to interpret God's word as they individually wished, to come to God in their own individual way. In other words, they were economic communists but psychological individualists. They were unconcerned with economic privileges, but very much concerned with psychological independence. They would not surrender the slightest iota of their religious freedom—because religion was far more important to them than economics.

This was true of all the religious communist colonies settled in this country. They were acquisitive in a spiritual but not in a material sense. Wealth meant nothing to them. They wanted to live like the Apostles, without any possessions at all, trusting always and only in the Lord. They knew that God would take care of their bodies, but they themselves had to take care of their souls. What they were acquisitive about was their individual salvation. Like Bunyan's Pilgrim, they were concerned with immortality, with the new life immediately ahead of them when Christ returned from heaven. "Life, eternal life," Bunyan's Christian cried as he flung wife and children aside in his mad race to the Celestial City. It was his own salvation which alone consumed him. The fear of death, the extinction of his ego, had come upon him, and he was afraid. That fear possessed him day and night, now that he had to meet the universe alone, and not, as Catholics did, with the supporting hand of the priest. Now he had to create within himself, out of the flame of his own emotion, a new way out for his soul. What the priest and the Church had once done for him, he now had to do for himself. The individual was saved by himself, and himself alone, and not by any outside authority.

Later, humble people shared the same emotions, sensed the same significances. They all sprang from that intimate

vision of Christ which was so common in that day. A cobbler,
George Fox, wrote:

"I kept much as a stranger, seeking heavenly wisdom
and getting knowledge from the Lord; and was brought
off from outward things, to rely on the Lord alone. As
I had forsaken the priests, so I left the separate preachers
also, and those called the most experienced people; for I
saw there was none among them all that could speak to
my condition. And when all hopes in them and in all men
were gone so that I had nothing outwardly to help me,
nor could tell what to do; then, oh, then I heard a voice
which said: 'There is one, even Jesus Christ, that can
speak to thy condition.' When I heard it my heart did
leap for joy. Then the Lord let me see why there was
none upon the earth that could speak to my condition.
I had not fellowship with any people, priests, nor pro-
fessors, nor any sort of separated people. . . . But when
Christ opened to me how he was tempted by the same
devil, and had overcome him, and had bruised his head;
and that through him and his power, life, grace, and
spirit, I should overcome also, I had confidence in him."

Bunyan's revelations were similar:

"Now did my chains fall off my legs indeed; I was
loosed from my afflictions and irons; my temptations also
fled away; so that from that time, those dreadful Scriptures of God left off to trouble me; now went I also home
rejoicing, for the grace and love of God. . . . Now could
I see myself in Heaven and Earth at once; in Heaven
by my Christ, by my Head, by my Righteousness and
Life, though on Earth by my Body or person. Christ
was a previous Christ to my soul that night; I could
scarce lie in my bed for joy and peace and triumph
through Christ."

It was out of such spiritual substance that these communist
groups and colonies were born. When the individual feels
himself part of a group, and identifies his interests and affections with its direction and destiny, he does not suffer from

that sense of spiritual and economic insecurity which assails
him in societies predominantly individualistic. The absence of
that insecurity makes it possible for him to live in the main
an extrovert instead of an introvert existence. The group
provides him with a form of strength and endows him with
an element of courage that he would otherwise not possess.
It supplies him with a source of power, through the agency
of its socialized religion, that makes it possible for him, as
we have seen, to face the hostilities and horrors of the universe with a measurable degree of fortitude. Instead of being
willing to forsake everyone and everything for the sake
of his individual ego, as was Bunyan's Christian, he is more
willing to sacrifice his ego for the sake of the group. Like
the Florentines, who, in their battle with the Pope, held, in
Machiavelli's words, "love of their native city higher than
the fear for the salvation of their souls," the individual in
earlier societies believed more in the survival of his group
than in his own physical preservation.

It meant little to these simple, zealous people to sacrifice
economic advantage for spiritual gain. They wanted to preserve their eternal souls, not their temporal pocketbooks. They
wanted little of life because they believed it had little to offer.
After all, most of them were convinced that Christ's return
was imminent, and that the more they lived like Christ on
earth, the better they would fare in heaven. They chose to
live like the Apostles because they hoped to be the new apostles
in the world beyond. They were willing to endure the tribula-
tions of this world in order to enjoy the rewards of the next.

They adopted a communist way of life because that was the
way of Christ's disciples, and the way they wanted to live.
They did not become communists merely because they believed
communist endeavor would sustain and profit them more
than capitalist enterprise. They gave little thought to such
distinctions. Oddly and interestingly enough, their economic
enterprises sometimes proved remarkably successful, and many

of their colonies, as we have already seen, prospered and flourished through the years and were the envy of their capitalist neighbors. Few of their colonies failed as economic ventures. When they dissolved, it was because some individual or individuals among them grew avaricious and disrupted the organization, or because the young people resented the discipline and restriction necessary to that way of life. They did not fail because they were communistic. The reverse was the case. They succeeded in building up more prosperous groups than those founded by the individualistic, "devil-take-the hindmost" settlers, and many of their communities were shining examples of efficiency, thrift, and sound economic planning.

Their excessive religiosity, however, limited their intellectual perspective and inhibited their cultural progress. Few of them were interested in education, except insofar as it served a practical purpose. Higher education, with its study of the classics, was not encouraged. Science, except to the degree that it was utilitarian, as in the case of the use of steam and the construction of the steam engine, did not interest them. They were too concentrated on religious concerns and preparations for eternity, to interest themselves in mundane education. In their schools religion was the main subject, although along with it went the three R's, necessary to the individual in managing the day-to-day business of the colony. Beyond that their intellectual interests faded.

Their communism was that of peasants, small tradesmen, and artisans, good, gentle, and humanitarian. It was definitely lacking in the incentives necessary to the social and economic progress of industrial civilization. Their creed insisted that men surrender individual wealth to the community, not only in order that all men should benefit from it, but because poverty was good for men's souls.

In short, their communism was based upon religious idealism instead of economic reform. They believed in the sub-

jugation of individualism rather than in release from economic
bondage. Modern communism, on the other hand, is material
rather than spiritual in its appeal. It does not exalt poverty
as an ideal but condemns it as an evil. It aims to eradicate
poverty, not encourage it.

Admirably intentioned as were these religious communal
groups, their economic outlook was unprogressive. They
looked for progress in the next world, not in this. It would
have been impossible to develop out of them the industrial and
scientific society of our day; invention, initiative, speculation,
all prerequisites of modern civilization, were neglected. The
America we know could never have evolved from such communities as the Labadists, Ephratists, Rappites, or Shakers,
representing as they did the segregated and isolated aspirations
of sects.

It would be a grave error to belittle the efforts of these
early communal groups. They represent the matrix of ideas
destined to color and compel much of the thought of the
future. It is impossible to understand the contradictions and
paradoxes underlying American social philosophy without
an awareness of the significant role played by these communal
groups and colonies in shaping the character and determining
the spirit of the country.

ECONOMIC UTOPIAS

CHAPTER XII

The Owen Adventure in Happiness

*"I am come to this country to introduce an entire new
state of society; to change it from the ignorant, selfish system to an enlightened social system, which shall gradually
unite all interests into one, and remove all cause for contest between individuals."*

ROBERT OWEN

*"He heard that a number of people were going
To live in the Wabash with great Mr. Owen;
He said to himself, 'I must now have a care,
Circumstances require that myself should be there. . . .'*

*"The devil then mounted again on the ice,
And dashed through the waves, and got home in a trice,
And told his fell imps whom he kept at the pole,
Circumstances required they should widen the hole!"*

PHILADELPHIA GAZETTE, January 1, 1826

More important, if less lasting, than the religious colonies,
were the economic utopias created by the curious and motley
collection of radical enthusiasts who came to this country in
the nineteenth century. They were uninterested in religion;
they were, in fact, more often anti-religious in philosophy than
pro-religious. Their founders were not concerned with the
millennium or with protracted futures of any variety; they
believed in the present, in exploiting its infinite possibilities in
order to create a society in which men could realize themselves
as men and not as angels.

As in the case of the religious groups, most of the founders
of the economic utopias came from Europe; they were convinced that the new world was the only place in which angels

177

dared to tread. The new world had the advantages of limitless land, freedom from a molesting government, and incalculable chances for success impossible elsewhere. Almost every
European who entertained dreams of a new society thought of
it exclusively in terms of America. The old world was sold
out; its territory was owned by feudal landlords, or landlords who had acquired it from feudal estates. The new world
was reasonably free from such ownership; in it, land could be
acquired almost without money. It held few landlords to
demand returns from its produce. It only required people to
work the land to make it their own. Such an opportunity had
not existed for centuries. Poor people had already taken
advantage of it. Now reformers, utopians, dreamers, came to
convert it into paradise.

Enter Robert Owen

One of the most notable of the Europeans who ventured
into this country to found a utopian colony was Robert Owen,
an English monetary monarch in the textile industry, who
was prepared to invest a large part of his profits in establish-
ing a co-operative colony built on the socialist ideal. Owen
was influenced by the romantic, economic doctrines of his day;
like Rousseau, Helvetius, Holbach, and Diderot, he believed
in the perfectibility of man, if only the difficulties and impediments of his environment could be overcome. Change
the environment, and you change man, and alter the race!
Few people have entertained such an optimistic view of the
potentialities of the species.

Let us consider Owen and the Romantic creed. Why did
he believe in the perfectibility of man once freed from the
bonds of civilization? Why did Owen concur with Rousseau
in the myth of the "beautiful savage"? The answer is simple.
Nature and civilization were conceived as opposites, because
Nature allowed for a freedom which civilization prohibited.
Nature gave man the liberty of spiritual as well as physical

locomotion; civilization deprived him of that liberty by erecting artificial fences to circumscribe his movements and forging
chains of convention to repress his emotions. But why was
freedom demanded at just this time? Why not before? After
all, such fences and chains had existed for hundreds of years,
and, in somewhat different form, for thousands.

The reason it seemed imperative in the eighteenth century
was that an old society, based on a feudal mode of production,
had become unable to sustain itself, while a new order, based
on a capitalistic mode of production, struggled to supersede it.
The middle class, developing the capitalistic spirit in the
maw of feudal society, needed freedom of economic enterprise
—laissez-faire economics—to extend and expand its class interests. With civilization still handicapped by the economic
regulations and restrictions of feudalism, the middle class was
naturally altogether in favor of returning to Nature.

Nature was thus more than a mere point of reference, to be
cajoled into idyllic form by Locke or beatified by Rousseau;
it was the battle-cry of the epoch. Class philosophy and intellectual outlook were appraised by their attitude on the question
of Nature. Those who agreed with the Hobbesian view of
Nature were the stand-patters, the philosophic defenders of
the landed class; those who adopted the concepts of Locke and
Rousseau were the revolutionaries, spiritual allies of the middle
class. The former sought to perpetuate the old world, with
its old rigidities and regulations, its old rulers, and its old
conventions. The latter sought to create a new world, with
new conceptions freed of the rigidities and regulations of the
old, and with new rulers who would break the ground for the
new way of life.

OWEN'S PAST

Owen started his reforms, as all men should, in his own
back yard, improved the conditions of his Lanark Mills, paid
his workers full wages during a four months' lay-off caused

by an American embargo, provided medical and educational opportunities previously unknown, shortened the working hours and lightened the tasks of his laborers, and tried to make life in his mills at least endurable if not joyous. Himself the son of a worker, Owen never forgot his background or tried to deny or conceal it. His father had been a saddler, and he was proud rather than ashamed of the fact. He proclaimed it in his speeches, mentioned it in his essays, discussed it in conversations. Part of his financial success was attributable to his marriage with the daughter of a millionaire, David Dale, but his ideas were certainly not derived from that source. His romantic and utopian conception of socialism was more original than that of most of his contemporaries. Osmotically, he had, as stated, imbibed many of the ideas of the French philosophers, but his original inspiration came, actually, from a book of John Bellers, *Proposals for raising A Colledge of Industry of all useful Trades and Husbandry,*[1] (1696), from which he drew a vivid idea of the possibilities of co-operative enterprise, if planned by a central authority. From that time on, he devoted himself to co-operative instead of competitive living, and his American experiment was an expression of that ideal.

"I am come to this country," he wrote, "to introduce an entire new State of society; to change it from the ignorant, selfish system to an enlightened social system, which shall gradually unite all interests into one, and remove all cause for contest between individuals."[2]   In the Constitution adopted by the Society, that ideal was confirmed:

"[The Constitution] is particularly formed to improve the character and conditions of its members, and to prepare them to become associates in Independent Communities, having common property.

[1] Ernest Sutherland Bates: *American Faith,* 1940, p. 370.
[2] *New Harmony, an Adventure in Happiness—Papers of Thomas and Sarah Pears.* Edited by Thomas Clinton Pears, Jr. Indiana Historical Society, 1933, p. 8.

"The sole objects of these Communities will be to procure for all their Members the greatest amount of happiness, to secure it to them, and to transmit it to their children to the latest posterity."

Owen purchased New Harmony from the Rappites, which fact enabled him to build upon the structures and properties included by George Rapp in his bill of sale.

DECLARATION OF MENTAL INDEPENDENCE

Within a brief period, Owen had attracted eight hundred people to his colony, and without fanfare or pyrotechnics the project was begun. Colonists presently arrived in such irrepressible abundance that laws had to be passed prohibiting the admission of further members, unless exceptionally qualified for the great task confronting them. Owen felt certain that New Harmony would mark a milestone in the history of mankind. His colony was not, to him, just an experiment; it represented a new epoch in human relations. Men would never look upon themselves in the same way again; the competitive conflicts which had rendered their natures uncongenial and bitter, would vanish; goodness, kindness, generosity, and spiritual cooperation would take their place. On July 4, 1826, Owen proclaimed his Declaration of Mental Independence, which, he believed, was destined to stand beside the earlier Declaration of Independence as an equally significant turning point in historical affairs. "I now declare to you and to the world," he wrote, "that man up to this hour has been in all parts of the earth a slave to a trinity of the most monstrous evils that could be combined to inflict mental and physical evil upon the whole race. I refer to private or individual property, absurd and irrational systems of religion, and marriage founded upon individual property, combined with some of these irrational systems of religion. . . . Our principles will spread from community to community, from state to state, from continent

to continent, until this system and these principles shall over-
shadow the whole earth, shedding fragrance and abundance,
intelligence and happiness upon all the sons of men."

Unfortunately, Owen's dream was discouragingly short-
lived. Within a year, he was compelled to admit that his hopes
had proved futile. He found that men and women accustomed
to the vitiating influences of a competitive environment, were
not easy to transform into co-operative, social beings. The
carry-over was too great to overcome in a short span of time.
Owen was still convinced that he was right in theory, but
wrong in calculation. The time element intervened. Men
needed more breathing-space for such a revolutionary re-
adaptation of personality.

Owen spent a great deal of money and an even greater
amount of energy in his attempt to realize his ideals. He
was something of an eccentric to begin with. As one of the
first English socialists, one could hardly expect him to be
altogether British in his philosophy. "He is a remarkable
man," wrote Adin Ballou, of Hopedale, describing Owen as
he knew him: "In years, nearly seventy-five; in knowledge
and experience, superabundant; in benevolence of heart, transcendental; in honesty, without disguise; in philanthopy, un-
limited; in religion, a skeptic; in theology, a Pantheist; in
metaphysics, a necessarian circumstantialist; in morals, a universal excusionist; in general conduct, a philosophic non-
resistant; in socialism, a communist; in hope, a terrestrial
elysianist; in practical business, a methodist; in deportment,
an unequivocal gentleman. He embraces the whole human
race in ardent affection. He holds no human being an outlaw,
an alien, a stranger, to be cast off, overlooked, or injured. He
knows no enemies to hate, persecute or punish. He loves all,
seeks the good of all, labors for all, hopes for all." [1]

Like many Englishmen of his time, he believed in Jeremy
Bentham's theory of "the greatest good for the greatest num-

[1] Adin Ballou: *The Hopedale Community*, pp. 146, 147.

ber," but he could never swallow the Utilitarian therapeutic. He believed, like most of the Encyclopedists, that it was folly to talk about the greatest good for the greatest number in a society which provided for just the opposite; unless you changed that society, the greatest goods would always be acquired by the smallest number. Consequently, the only alternative was to change the society.

To that end, Owen spoke in the American Congress, his Bergeracian nose protruding like a warning sentinel, his voice pitched like that of an untutored tenor, challenging the country and the world to re-awaken to the new possibilities inherent in the race. He did not suspect, then, that his experiment was to prove abortive. Owen talked far and wide across the land in a vain attempt to convert it to his convictions. He was not, unfortunately, a pleasing man to look at, with his Gargantuan proboscis, his pathetic smallness of stature, his exasperating uncertainty and jitteriness of gesture, all of which weighed against him in his proselytizing. Nevertheless, he did influence people of intelligence and vision, who were more interested in the impersonality of his ideas than in the inadequacies of his personality. Among such people was Frances Wright, one of the greatest of the woman reformers of her time, who declared, "He will do much good here, where almost nothing is known of the system of social co-operation."

Owen's greatest influence was among intellectuals. If he had confined his colony to intellectuals and imbued them sufficiently with his ideas and ideals, the colony might have proved a success. The trouble was that New Harmony, unlike Rapp's old Harmony group, accepted anybody and everybody who was willing to swear by the elastic tenets of the regime. Most of them were land-grabbers or money-grabbers at heart, and once they were left to their own devices, they violated every ideal of the community. The religious commonwealths had succeeded because most of their members had been tested and tried abroad, and no irresponsibles such as infested New

Harmony were ever allowed to join them. They were idealists, pure and simple; the New Harmonists were, largely, pure materialists.

It was not long before many of Owen's best friends, people who had ventured forth from remote parts of the country to join the new community, became disgusted with its fruitless prospects. Instead of a New Canaan, it developed into an economic Sahara. In a letter to her uncle, Benjamin Bakewell, Mrs. Pears, wife of Thomas Pears, one of the charter members of the community, wrote to this effect:

"Mr. Pears tells you that our government is an aristocracy. He ought to have called it a despotism. Our feelings are perpetually irritated by some or other of their acts and Resolutions; and if we should unfortunately be so bold as to express our sentiments upon them, we are told that we are liable to expulsion. It makes my blood boil within me to think that the citizens of a free and independent nation should be collected here to be made slaves of. I believe Mr. Pears' chief crime was the freedom with which he spoke his sentiments, and because he scorned to cringe to the Committee, or to turn informer, —of which gentry there is an abundance here. Ah, my dear Uncle, how do I regret that we ever left Pittsburgh. If ever I should be fortunate enough to get into civilized society once more, I think I should never wish to leave it again." [1]

Owen tried to remedy the dissensions in New Harmony by bringing over with him the famous "Boatload of Knowledge," composed of a number of distinguished intellectuals, among whom were the scientists, Thomas Say, Gerard Troost, the explorer, Lesueur, and William Maclure; the educators, D'Arusmont and the irrepressible Madame Fretageot. D'Arusmont set himself immediately to the task of organizing his School of Industry, which soon became a fascinating institution. During its brief existence, it succeeded in combining

[1] Pears: *op. cit.,* pp. 40, 41.

work with education; every pupil acquired not only knowledge, but also earned from his daily work more than enough to cover the cost of his education. Such an educational technique was far ahead of its time. D'Arusmont claimed that he made his educational plan earn actually more than it cost. If the rest of Owen's experiment had been as expertly conducted, the colony might have proved a lasting venture.

So impressed was Frances Wright with the wonderful work achieved by D'Arusmont that she decided to establish similar schools wherever she settled. What moved her most was that the students in this school proved so remarkable as to be able, without the facilities of more prosperous institutions, to compete successfully with the best students in Europe. Frances Wright, in those days, was interested in her Nashoba venture, wherein she hoped to educate emancipated Negroes into a new state of manhood by giving them the wherewithal to earn their living as independent beings. D'Arusmont's plan of combining learning with making a living promised a solution to her problem. He believed in transforming education into practical experience.

Both D'Arusmont and Madame Fretageot were disciples of Pestalozzi, that strange, sphinx-like figure, more gargoyle than man, who had revolutionized education, robbed it of its upper-class prerogatives, and endowed it with lower-class possibilities. Madame Fretageot, in her ability to convince parents that their children needed this new education, was a remarkable pedagogue, fresher by far than the wilderness tang of the American hinterland.

Americans knew little of education in those days, and nothing of Pestalozzi, but through this violently determined woman they learned more of what was good for them in that direction than from a score of theocrats. She was concerned with female education, whereas D'Arusmont was concerned mainly with males. Her job, obviously, was more difficult. To transform women into educated bread winners was, in the nineteenth century, an almost insuperable task. Women were not supposed to be educated in the masculine sense; they were to be taught to play the piano badly and speak French worse, but beyond that nothing but manners and mannerisms counted. Madame Fretageot's idea was different. She insisted that women should use their brains—a revolutionary conception in those days. When we remember that Mary Ann Evans was afraid to sign her novels with a feminine name, and that Mary Somerville, one of the nineteenth century's most remarkable talents in mathematics, hid her astronomical calculations beneath a basket of crochet-work, it is easy to realize the prevailing tragic state of feminine education. In New Harmony, Madame Fretageot had a fresh opportunity of testing out her Pestalozzian theories. She was able to teach her girls not only to learn to be mothers, to knit and sew and cook, but also to milk cows and plow the fields. Madame Fretageot combined her work with that of D'Arusmont, and tried to make her girls as efficient as men. They were to be men-women, able to endure men's hardships, suffer their travails, triumph over their adversities.

Frances Wright, later to be so helpful in the reform movement, could hardly believe her eyes. The achievements of Madame Fretageot were utterly miraculous. They opened up new worlds of possibilities.

Even after the colony had failed, and the dream died, Frances Wright decided to carry on its spirit in her own adventures and attempts at settlements.

Undedicated Men

Despite the "Boatload of Knowledge," which Robert Owen brought with him, the colony could not succeed. Something cancerous ate at its roots. Its people lacked the dedication necessary to succeed in such an enterprise. Their demands were material rather than spiritual, where the religious colonies had been the exact opposite. The spiritual utopians had been dedicated to apostles of a millennial dream. They strove to be selfless instead of selfish in their psychology. They believed that labor was not only necessary, but sacred, and were hence willing to toil endlessly to organize and establish their communities. If the economic communities like New Harmony had been similarly inspired, their record might have been one of triumph instead of defeat. New Harmony was organized on a communal pattern, anticipating Marx in its theory that everyone should get all that he needed, and no one more. It had, for a considerable time, a common cash box open to every colonist. Owen believed that no one who did not need help would put his hand in the box, but he soon found himself wrong. Members began taking money with such freedom that soon nothing was left. All this discouraged Owen, who had witnessed the growth of the colony from its early days, and lent it every resource essential to success. The colonists were both undisciplined and unethical. Too many preferred to steal from the general treasury, instead of contributing to it any of their earnings.

Curiously enough, the only people who succeeded in utopian ventures were those who combined a religious with an economic ideal. Owen attempted, like the religious utopians, to build an agrarian commonwealth. His people enjoyed complete freedom of religious worship. Men and women, wedded or unwedded, lived in the colony as equals. Children suffered from no restrictions or discriminations because of color or creed. Owen expected New Harmony to be merely the first of thousands of similar colonies. He wanted them to spread far and wide, throughout the earth.

While Owen was present, the colonists labored daily to make the colony prosperous. If they didn't get up as early as some of the religious utopians, they worked at least as hard, when Owen was around. They had their dances, their little theater, their band, and they knew how to enjoy rather than repress man's best instincts and affections.

They were an industrial as well as an agrarian group, and the mills and factories were also held in common. Owen's departure greatly hindered progress. At first the colony seemed destined to achieve a marked success; but after Owen left it deteriorated rapidly. The members lost their enthusiasm, and before long it was in the red, instead of the black. Owen returned too late. Nothing, then, could save it.

THE ROLE OF RELIGION

Religion may very well be, as Pomponazzi asserted, a means of keeping the poor virtuous and servile, or as Marx described it, "the opium of the people"; it may dull the mind of the race and impede intellectual and cultural progress, but there can be no doubt that it moves the hearts of men, and drives them to work with greater ardor and zealotry, to realize the things in which they believe. This ancient combination of body-energy and mental-drive, the latter born of the fanaticism of other-worldly devotion, produces a synthesis of personality fecund with power and passion. Religion always gives man an illusion of power, by making him believe that the world was created for his benefit and is working in his favor. It has always served, despite the unawareness of its votaries, as a power-phenomenon, a substitute for man's own inadequacy.

Long before the organization of the American utopias, men had been cognizant of the significance of the role of religion as a power-factor. The best testimony was that of Cassius to Brutus, before the Battle of Philippi, when he said: "How I wish that there were gods so that we might have confidence not only in our arms but in the justice of our cause." Religion has been a psychological extension of the instinct of self-preservation, subtilized and sublimated into dramatic form. Cicero recognized the importance of religion when he stated, in describing the triumphs of the Romans: "By reverence and religion we have subdued all nations and races." Even

Napoleon, that supreme Machiavellian, condemned religion as unnecessary for intellectuals, but insisted on its necessity for the masses. Voltaire's insistence upon keeping the peasants on his estate religious, and erecting a church for their worship, so that they would work harder and not tend to revolt, was but another expression of the same philosophy. The Duke of Weimar's decree, forbidding his subjects "to reason [meaning to question religion] under pain of correction," was another illustration. Necker's counsel, voiced on the eve of the French Revolution, was equally revealing: "The more the increased taxation keeps the people in dejection and want, *the more essential it is to give them religious education,* for it is in the restlessness due to misfortune that there is most need of stout fetters and daily consolation."

And so it was with the religious communists that settled here. They rejoiced in their allegiance to their cause, their alliance with the Almighty, their identification with the infinite. Like the Jews who believed they were the "chosen people," like the Dissenters certain that they were sprung from the loins of the Lord, like the Hitlerites convinced that God is with them, familiar characteristics of all people who view themselves as fortunate proliferations of divinity, these religious communists were convinced, one and all, that their role, in whatever community, was sacred and final.

This was not true of the economic colonies. There a different motivation was involved. The majority of the members of the various economic communities were, to put it mildly, unreligious; there were, to be sure, some religious people among them, who refused to abandon their faith, but they were viewed by the rest of the group as mental cripples.

It should be said, in qualification, that the religion which these economic utopians opposed was that of organized Christianity. Most of them were theists, like Thomas Paine, and if they did not go to the extremes of Paine and organize, as he did in Paris in the hectic year of 1797, a "Church of

Theophilanthropy," they did not deviate far from his religious concepts. Robert Owen's belief in a Supreme Power was by no means dissimilar to Paine's, and was typical of the religious outlook of both these idealists. Owen's belief was in "rational religion," which he hoped would redeem the race. His "rational religion" consisted, he said, "in promoting to the utmost of our power the happiness and well-being of every man, woman, and child, without regard to their sect, class, party, or color, and their worship, in those inexpressible feelings of wonder, admiration, and delight, which, when man is surrounded by superior circumstances only, will naturally arise from the contemplation of the infinity of space, of the eternity of duration, of the order of the universe, and of that Incomprehensible Power, by which the atom is moved, and the aggregate of nature is governed." [1]   Owen's words might have been written by Paine, they coincide so completely in spirit and outlook. But Owen had no desire to open a church, and did not like that gesture on Paine's part. Churches, he believed, were the destroyers of religion, not the creators of it. Religion, in his opinion, was a private and not a public affair. Religion to him was identification with a Supreme Power, who under proper conditions would evoke the best in human beings; the task of man was to create the proper conditions under which that best could be evoked.

OWENITE EDUCATION

Owen believed in beginning at the beginning, which is the only way to begin: namely, with the children in the community. During their first five years they were to be trained physically, to learn how to use their bodies most expertly and efficiently; during the next five, they were to be taught in terms of experience, education by observation, with varied employments to give their education a practical turn; after that they were

[1] Quotation taken from George Browning Lockwood: *The New Harmony Communities,* p. 82.

to be instructed in definite occupations, edified in the divers philosophies, trained in the three R's, and equipped with a general knowledge in accordance for the most part with the best scientific views of the day. Later, the students were to be given technical training, and by the time they had undergone all this instruction, it was hoped that they would prove valuable citizens of the community.

Influenced by the radical ideas of that day concerning the future dissolution of the family, Owen urged the organization of communes as the basic social unit; each commune, as he envisioned it, was to consist of at least two thousand people, and everyone in each community was to be provided with equal opportunity to develop his personal and economic resources without impediment. Owen wanted to get away from the ingrown relationships of the family, which made parents and children such a close unit that societal interests became secondary. He wanted them to think in social instead of personal or familial terms. All these communes were to be self-subsistent, and were to be governed by their own councils. Owen believed that, in this way, the prevailing capitalist system of society with its "fundamental errors on which society is based—errors producing all manner of inequality, vices, crimes, and misery, making man an inferior and irrational being, and the earth a pandemonium"—would disappear and be replaced by a socialist order, in which fulfillment instead of frustration would predominate. Owen was afflicted with an inspired and superb naïveté. He could not understand, for example, why the human race should any longer maintain "such a heterogeneous mass of folly and absurdity, and doom their offspring, through succeeding generations, to be inferior, irrational men and women, filled with every injurious notion, and governed by most ignorant and misery-producing institutions, while excellence, superior external circumstances and happiness lie directly before them and easy of attainment." He thought of man constantly in logical instead of psychological terms. He failed to see him as a product in considerable degree of mental inertia and cultural lag. And that explains in large part why New Harmony proved such a quick failure.

The Declaration of Principles, which was a preamble to the Constitution, embodied the noblest sentiments of the day, of all days, and is typical of Owen's idealistic approach to society and life. The following quotations from it are representative of its spirit:

"Our object is that of all sentient being, happiness.
"Our principles are:
"Equality of rights, uninfluenced by sex or condition, in all adults.
"Equality of duties, modified by physical and mental conformation.
"Co-operative union in the business and amusements of life.
"Community of property.
"Freedom of speech and action.
"Sincerity in all our proceedings.
"Kindness in all our actions.
"Courtesy in all our intercourse.
"Order in all our arrangements.
"Preservation of health.
"Acquisition of knowledge.
"The practice of economy, or of producing and using the best of everything in the most beneficial manner.
"Obedience to the laws of the country in which we live.
"We hold it to be self-evident:
"That man is uniformly actuated by a desire of happiness.
"That no member of the human family is born with rights either of possession or exemption superior to those of his fellows.
"That man's character, mental, moral and physical, is the result of his formation, his location, and of the circumstances within which he exists.
"And that man, at birth, is formed unconsciously to himself; is located without his consent, and circumstanced without his control.

"Therefore, man's character is not of his own formation, and reason teaches us that to a being of such nature, artificial rewards and punishments are equally inapplicable; kindness is the only consistent mode of treatment, and courtesy the only rational species of deportment.

"We have observed, in the affairs of the world, that man is powerful in action, efficient in production, and happy in social life, only as he acts co-operatively and unitedly.

"Co-operative union, therefore, we consider indispensable to the attainment of our object.

"The departure from the principle of man's equal rights, which is exhibited in the arrangement of individual property, we have seen succeeded by competition and opposition, by jealousy and dissension, by extravagance and poverty, by tyranny and slavery.

"Therefore we revert to the principle of community of property.

"Where the will and the power exist, the result produced is proportioned to the knowledge of the agent; and in practice we have found that an increase of intelligence is equally an increase of happiness.

"We seek intelligence, therefore, as we seek happiness itself.

"As the first and most important knowledge, we desire to know ourselves.

"All members of the community shall be considered as one family, and no one shall be held in higher or lower estimation on account of occupation. There shall be similar food, clothing and education, as near as can be furnished, for all, according to their ages; and as soon as practicable all shall live in similar houses and in all respects be accommodated alike. Every member shall render his or her best services for the good of the whole, according to the rules and regulations that may be hereafter adopted by the community. It shall always remain a primary object of the community to give the best physical, moral and intellectual education to all its members." [1]

[1] Quotations taken from Lockwood: *op. cit.*, pp. 122-125.

First Prohibitionists in the New World

All the various communities organized under the aegis of the Owenite system were dedicated to the same propositions. In addition to their co-operative economic programs, they were all prohibitionist—Owen, in that regard, was in advance of the prohibitionist movement which was later to surge across the United States—and threatened to expel any members who partook of alcoholic stimulants. Owen was convinced that alcohol was an evil, a disrupter of man's resolves, a destroyer of goodness, generosity, and vision. There was only one way in which man could be brought to a clear understanding of himself, Owen believed, and that was by emancipating himself from all baneful influences, of which, in his eyes, alcohol was one of the most destructive. Never having drunk himself, he believed that alcohol was a poison to the soul as well as the body, and if his fight against it was not as melodramatic as, later, that of Carrie Nation, it was no less determined.

Das Ewig Weibliche

Since Owen felt that the family was a moribund institution, he believed, naturally enough, that all the members of the family should be equal in the new organization of society which he conceived. Women should suffer from no inequalities in relation to men. He was not the first in the country to advocate that equality; earlier colonies had provided it also, notably the Shakers, but Owen wanted such communism to be material rather than spiritual at base. The Shakers shared everything equally, but it was in terms of a millennialist aspiration. Owen's dream was an earthly one. He was opposed to marriage because it was "founded upon individual property." Owen believed it was almost impossible for people in our capitalist society really to marry for love. Horace Greeley, prissy moralist that he was, attacked Indiana in general, and Owen in particular, with the accusation of setting up a "paradise of free lovers." Frances Wright later took up the cudgels and strove to carry out Owen's principles. Her reputation was, by that time, however, so unsavory among the so-called respectable people, that she simply provoked further attacks upon the group. Owen's son, Robert Dale Owen, carried on the fight, and succeeded in introducing into the Indiana legislature the most advanced divorce laws in the nation, that secured rights for women to which no other state would, at that time, even give consideration. It was there that Frances Wright carried on her most ardent fight for woman suffrage, and made the issue a national one.

Owen lost interest in his colony after he realized that it could never fulfill his dream. He sold his land to the groups remaining at fantastically minute figures; what land they could not purchase, he sold to speculators, who robbed him at every turn. The land remaining, estimated at thirty thousand dollars in value, he bequeathed to his four sons with the single stipulation that they provide him with an annuity of fifteen hundred dollars, which they gladly consented to do. Altogether, he lost close to two hundred thousand dollars in the venture. His son, Robert Dale Owen, who was in love with Frances Wright, tried hard to carry on his father's ideal, and his failure was due to no lack of zeal on his part.[1]

Here was a colony which had started off with utopian aspirations, all the people dressing alike, everyone sharing equally in everything, music, painting, literature, provided for the many instead of the few, yet it developed old vices rather than new virtues. "I had hoped," Owen said, in bidding farewell to his dream, "that fifty years of political liberty had prepared the American people to govern themselves advantageously. I supplied land, houses, and the use of capital . . . but now upon my return I find that the habits of the individual system were so powerful that these leases

[1] Elinor Pancoast and Anne E. Lincoln: *The Incorrigible Idealist*, p. 8.

have been, with a few exceptions, applied for individual purposes and individual gain. . . .   This proves that families,
trained in the individual system, have not acquired those moral
characteristics of forbearance and charity necessary for confidence and *harmony*."

It was a sad confession for Owen to make.   It broke his
heart.   But he was an honest man and refused to close his
eyes to what he saw.

And what he saw was the death of his dream.

CHAPTER XIII

Brook Farm

(1841–1847)

THE DREAM OF THE LITERATI

"An original Yankee attempt to embody Christianity as understood by Unitarians and Transcendentalists . . . feeling its way toward co-operation by the light of experience and common sense."
                                    JOHN HUMPHREY NOYES

"All comers and the most fastidious find Brook Farm the pleasantest of residences."
                                    RALPH WALDO EMERSON

Of all the utopian colonies founded in this country, there was only one which gained the immediate and ardent affection of the intellectuals, and that was Brook Farm. Brook Farm was more than a colony; it was an experiment in a new way of life for people who were disillusioned and disgusted with the old. The founders of Brook Farm were unlike the religious utopians; they had nothing in common with Labadie, Kelpius, Beissel, Ann Lee, Janson; they were made of different stuff and sought to convert the mundane world into a better place. Like all utopians, they were dreamers, but in their dream they envisioned man as closer to the angels than the demons. They believed in the perfectibility of the race, in the exaltation of the species; they had little concern for the other world, but great concern for this. The Brook Farmers adopted "the philosophy of Here and Now, on the spot with the goods at the moment, not yesterday, not tomorrow, but to-

197

day," wrote John Van Der Zee Sears, who knew the community well, and added that "this hour, this instant, is the appointed time to live for all you are worth. Put your heart in your work right Here. . . . This was their ideal." [1]

Brook Farm grew out of the dream of George Ripley, a Unitarian minister, whose whole life was dominated by his belief in the possibility of man's advance through the development of a Christian way of life. He believed that the Christian faith demanded sacrifice of self. Kelpius, Beissel, and Labadie were concerned with Christian economics only because it was a means of achieving eternal life. Ripley was concerned with the Christian way of life because it was a means of achieving a way of life as a road to a better mundane order. As a Unitarian he could not share in the enthusiasms and ecstasies of the millennialists; he wanted man to attain his millennium on earth. Heaven would (and could), he was certain, take care of itself. The earth, on the other hand, could be mastered only by an act of will. Man had to consecrate himself to its conquest. To do that, Ripley came to believe that a community wherein man could show other men how to live had to be organized, planned. "It seems to me," he said, "that anything would promote the spirit of Christ better nowadays than a church does—perhaps even meeting in an upper room or in a fisher's boat by the side of a lake." [2] Later, Ripley formulated his conception more concretely. "A community is to be formed," he declared, "to promote more effectually the great purpose of human culture, to apply the principles of justice and love to social organizations; to substitute brotherly co-operation for selfish competition; to prevent anxiety in men by a competent supplying in them of necessary wants; to guarantee each other the means of support."

[1] John Van Der Zee Sears: *My Friends at Brook Farm*, 1912, p. 141.
[2] Many of the quotations here of conversations and the like, are taken from Katherine Burton's *Paradise Planters*, which constitutes one of the best accounts of Brook Farm.

George Ripley founded Brook Farm because he was discouraged with the failure of his work as a minister and hoped to redeem that failure by organizing a colony wherein people might live in accordance with his preaching. Ripley was no more of a failure than any other minister of his time. In fact, he was one of the very best ministers produced on this continent. But he was a morbidly conscientious man and could not tolerate the discrepancy between men's Sunday and weekday lives. He wanted men to be the same all week round, all year round. He knew, however, that that would be impossible as long as men lived in a competitive economic world. On Sunday that world was closed up, and men could forget, or at least shelve temporarily their greeds and hates, their machinations and cruel strategies. Not until they could live on weekdays as they lived on Sundays would it be possible for man to achieve moral and social progress. What disillusioned Ripley was the realization that his preaching was not attaining that end. His congregation showed no moral or social improvement.

They listened to him Sunday after Sunday, admired him as a preacher, adored him as a personality, but did not change their lives or way of living. They remained, on the whole, the same satisfied, moderately rich, supremely contented people that they had always been, and despite Ripley's sermons they were never inclined to alter the character of their existence. That was what made Ripley so unhappy. He could not endure their smugness, their Philistinism. He believed that preaching had value only when it changed the lives of men. Elizabeth P. Peabody, one of the early members of the Farm, voiced Ripley's sentiments excellently when she wrote in *The Dial* (October, 1841): "One would think from the tone of conservatives that Jesus accepted the society around him as an adequate framework for individual development into beauty and life. . . . We maintain, on the other hand, that Christ desired to reorganize society, and went to a depth of principle and magnificence of plan for this end, which has never been appreciated except here and there by an individual, still less carried out."

Brook Farm represented Ripley's attempt to carry out that principle and plan.

When he left his congregation to undertake this new venture, he gave assurance in a farewell address which will never be forgotten, that he had not lost his faith, but had added to it. "I believe," he said, "in the omnipotence of kindness, of moral intrepidity and of divine charity." And then he remarked, "The followers of Jesus should be a band of brothers— a family who do not care about the chief seats in the synagogue or the greetings in the market place. Equality before God of all of us—that has been my preaching and it is real to me, not a speculative abstraction or a political party's watchword." Most challenging of all were his words that he felt that "the spirit of God is no longer in our churches. And so I shall have to seek it elsewhere. My sympathies are with the downtrodden and the poor—and our creed cares little about them. That is why I have been looking at the foundations upon which it is built. That is why I am leaving you today."

Channing, the great founder of Unitarianism, had planted the idea of a Christian community in Ripley's head, but it was Ripley and not Channing who had the courage to organize and develop it. It would be a place, as Ripley explained to Emerson and Margaret Fuller, where "we could gather and show the world how to live."

Curiously enough, it was not to be a communist colony. Ripley was opposed to communism on principle. "Capital will never be ruled from the governing of our community," he stated; "we mean to have a true freedom, a freedom that will make people kind and unselfish. . . . We want to break the family caste but leave the family inviolate. . . . We are to be a community of property, but we shall exclude competition and the ordinary rules of trade." In other words, Ripley believed it was possible to organize a co-operative community upon a private-property basis. It was that belief that attracted to him so many of the New England intellectuals: Emerson, Hawthorne, Margaret Fuller, Theodore Parker, Orestes Brownson, Bronson Alcott. He promised them that he would give birth to "a new life, a new spirit. . . . I can see the young men welcoming it as the angels were welcomed at Christ's birth, for it is singing the same words of peace and good-will. I feel their creed is mine. I believe in the divinity of labor. . . . I want to harvest my flesh and blood from the land. . . . I want a society of friends, working, thinking, and living together, with no strife, except that of each to contribute the most to the benefit of all."

Among those who at first were most enthusiastic about Ripley's scheme was Ralph Waldo Emerson, whose words in praise of it were never forgotten. Your community, Emerson said, will be "a substitute for our failing churches, our closed temples, where once a week we tell man of his Maker. Your community will be open all the time, as the foreign churches are, where the tired wayfarer can come in and be soothed by the thought of a better world when he is weary of this one."

THE EARLY SETTLEMENT

In 1841 Brook Farm was begun with the organization of a stock company and the purchase of land in the vicinity of Roxbury, Dedham, and Watertown, Massachusetts. Less than fifteen thousand dollars were involved in the initial investment. Among the earliest of those to accompany Ripley to his planned paradise was Nathaniel Hawthorne, who was then a utopian in spirit. He plunged into the venture as wholeheartedly as he could, believing that Ripley had struck upon something new and significant in social relations. He played "chambermaid to a group of cows," "milked the transcendental heifer," as he dubbed one cow that he believed had an inordinate liking for him, became adept with the pitchfork and the sickle, and declared that "such a delectable way of life as that in Brook Farm was never seen on earth since the days of the early Christians." He worked so hard and so zealously he was called "the prince" by his co-workers. He introduced many of the poetic euphemisms which became popular in the colony. Most rememberable of these was his description of the manure pile, which he called "the gold mine." He even succumbed to the feminist jargon of the group, averred that he hated to be ruled by his own sex, and added that he would "love to be ruled by a woman." Marianne Dwight, one of the leading feminine members of the community, heartily approved. She insisted that "nothing less than the elevation of woman to independence and an acknowledged equality with man," which Brook Farm encouraged, could make civilization truly civilized.

Even when Hawthorne decided to leave the Farm, because he found he couldn't write effectively there, it was with heartbroken reluctance. "Some day," he prophesied, "I will write a book about Brook Farm [and he did], and have supermodern inventions coming from it—a machine that makes heat from moonbeams, one that makes music from building blocks, one that makes women's dresses out of sunset clouds." *The Blithedale Romance* scarcely did all that, but it did immortalize Brook Farm in fiction. No doubt Hawthorne's picture would have been more laudatory had he not changed so markedly with the years. Instead of believing in the creative potentialities of a co-operative commonwealth, he came to believe in the superiority of monarchy. "Our government grows more intolerant every day," he wrote in 1854. "I wish it might be changed to a monarchy." Later he confessed that he felt "more at home and familiar there [in England] than even in Boston, or in old Salem itself." [1]

[1] For further details concerning Hawthorne in this connection, see Newton Arvin's *Hawthorne*, p. 226, and the author's *Liberation of American Literature*, pp. 274-275.

Despite Hawthorne's withdrawal from the venture and Emerson's refusal to join it even after he had given it his endorsement, the Farm survived. It was a striking sight to see George Ripley, slim and graceful of figure, his tousled hair stringing out of his quaint, weather-worn straw hat, walking about in cowhide boots, leading his flock to labor. It lent inspiration to everyone. Each member of the Farm worked sixty hours a week from May to October, forty-eight from November to April. For a few years the colony managed to keep out of the red. During its first year it had over four thousand visitors, among whom were such distinguished personages as Henry James, Horace Greeley, Emerson, Thoreau, Frances Ostinelli, Margaret Fuller. Its actual members were of various extractions and denominations. There were, as C. J. Thomas wrote, "some who are of the Roman Catholic Church; some from the Jewish; some Trinitarians; some Unitarians; some from the Swedenborgian Church, some who are Liberals, some who are called 'Come-Outers.'" Thoreau was the only one disappointed with the place. In his characteristically sour way he snorted, "I'd rather keep bachelor's hall in hell than go to board in heaven if that place is heaven." One can picture him, his nose turned contemptuously upward, condemning these simple people who lived by a vision alien to his. Thoreau preferred the pigs in New York to the people.[1] But new members joined the group from time to time, one of the most interesting being young Charles Dana, who soon became a leading spirit in the colony.

These transcendental farmers, whose eyes were upon the stars even when their hands were begrimed with mud, were an adventurous lot, unflaggingly confident of the significance of their enterprise. John Van Der Zee Sears, who had been sent to the Brook Farm School by his father, a follower of Ripley, has left us a most interesting picture of the routine of the colony, especially that of the school:

[1] Henry Seidel Canby: *Thoreau*, 1939, p. 183.

"We bathed, dressed and breakfasted at 8 A.M.   At
9 A.M. Dr. Ripley was in his office and I in the schoolroom.
In the evening two hours more were given to the cows.
I liked the work, liked the cows, and especially liked to
be with Dr. Ripley.   His flattering report that Cedar
could milk like a streak secured for me the maximum
wage, ten cents an hour, so that, at twelve years of age
or thereabouts I was earning enough to pay the cost of
board and lodging.

"The milkers were necessarily late at breakfast and
supper and these meals we took with the waiters, the
pleasantest company in the dining room.   Dr. and Mrs.
Ripley were charming table companions and the bright
girls were merry as happy children.   Perhaps Cedar did
not fill Hawthorne's place quite so well at table as in
the stable, but there were no intimations given to that
effect.   Making the most of the present moment was in
order.   Looking backward was not." [1]

In their simple, economical dress, the men of Brook Farm
with their colorful blouses and caps, the women with their conveniently curled hair, their knickers, their light, free walk,
presented an odd, fantastic sight to their neighbors and visitors.
Bostonians were horrified when they saw these strange-looking
creatures, apparitions of Satan, as many thought them,
dressing and living in violation of established New England
mores.   Preachers thundered denunciations of the Brook
Farmers from scores of pulpits; politicians attacked the colony
as a center of free love,[2] newspapers satirized it, magazines
caricatured it, but no one in Brook Farm was either concerned
or worried.   It was only their own opinion that counted.
The world might criticize; they were content to create.

Ripley's school was one of the most advanced of the
day, anticipating in many respects ideas and techniques which
constitute part of the cornerstone of modern, progressive

---

[1] John Van Der Zee Sears: *op. cit.,* p. 114.
[2] The truth of the matter is, as Noyes stresses, (*op. cit.,* p. 143) there
was never "any attempt on the part of Brook Farm to meddle with the
marital relation."

education; it went so far beyond the education of that day
that contemporary educators attacked its teachers as miseduca-
tors, destroyers of the young. They introduced the kinder-
garten in America long before the name itself was known
here; [1] they anticipated John Dewey and the early Bolsheviks
with their theory of learning from experience; they taught
their children from life and not from books, from observation
and not from authority. They studied the land, examined it
as infantile geologists, scrutinized its flora and fauna, traced
their origin, determined their destiny. They studied birds
and other animals in the same intimate, personal way. School,
consequently, became a place of joy and gaiety, of exhilarating
exploration, and inspiring discovery. George Ripley himself
taught philosophy and mathematics and directed the school as
a whole; it offered a six-year course which prepared one for
college, three of those years being spent in agricultural pursuits. Combining the practical with the theoretical was its
great aim.[2]

No wonder that these were happy people, that the children
grew up with joy in their hearts, that everyone sang as he
worked, that the evenings were rich with music, plays, dramatic
readings, and other entertainments, which lent a radiance to
their intellectual and esthetic lives. As Elizabeth Peabody
pointed out, "This community aims . . . to live in all the
faculties of the soul." [3] Brook Farm was no somber colony
with the ascetic and cenobitic taboos of the *Woman in the
Wilderness* group, the Ephratians, the Shakers. It was alive
with dancing, games, performances, and a countless variety of
entertainments, one more exciting than another, in which
everyone participated with increasing glee. Curiously enough,
"there were no sedentary games in our repertoire," wrote
John Van Der Zee Sears, not because there was any "prejudice

[1] Burton: *op. cit.*, p. 149.
[2] *Early Letters of George William Curtis to John S. Dwight*, 1898, p. 3.
Edited by George Willis Cooke.
[3] *The Dial*, Vol. II, No. 3, January, 1842, p. 364.

against cards or chess, or any other game so far as I know, but no one cared for any form of amusement that separated two or four from all the others."[1] They were not waiting for a new world in which to realize their ecstasy; this world which they had created on Brook Farm *was* their new world, and it sufficed them. "The weeds were scratched out of the ground to the music of Tennyson or Browning," wrote George Curtis, "and the nooning was an hour as gay and bright as any brilliant midnight at Ambrose's."[2] They loved nature and animals as well as men. "Nature and the animal creation," wrote Marianne Dwight, one of the earliest and most interesting members of the community, with a distinguished talent for painting, "here seemed to be in advance of humanity. Nothing speaks to me more eloquently of the repose and the love spirit that shall prevail in Association, than the social state of animals with us. I have spoken to you perhaps of our domestic animals, our cats and dogs—who go from house to house and are equally at home in either—a thing I never observed in civilization. A gun is never fired here—not a child on the place appears to have the least disposition to molest a bird's nest—and the birds are in consequence surprisingly tame—they do not fear our steps, they come to us to be fed. Last night a whippoorwill took shelter in our back room. Mr. Klienstrup and Mr. Allen take much satisfaction in their pet squirrels and quails, which come out of the woods to make them daily visits."[3]

Although Brook Farm was primarily a product of Unitarianism, the philosophy it adopted became familiarly known as Transcendentalism. The transcendentalist philosophy derived directly from Emerson, who was its leading American apostle, but indirectly from Kant, Carlyle, and Coleridge. Their ideas

---

[1] John Van Der Zee Sears: *op. cit.,* p. 102.
[2] Early Letters of George William Curtis to John S. Dwight, p. 9., *op. cit.,* p. 9.
[3] Marianne Dwight: *Letters From Brook Farm,* pp. 98-99.

on the theme went through many changes in the hands of their followers before they reached Emerson, who in turn gave them still another twist to imprint his own personality on them. Emerson himself stated that his Transcendentalism owed more to Kant than to anyone else, although he traced it back to Hellenic as well as Germanic sources. Plato and Plotinus were part of its inspiration. Transcendentalism represented a reaction against the materialistic and realistic philosophies of the eighteenth century; instead of stressing the predominant influence of outside forces, telluric environment, inherited tendencies, cultural controls and compulsives, or the physical supremacy of sensations, reactions, habits, reflexes, it concentrated its emphasis upon soul—hence Emerson's concept of the Oversoul—the superiority of mind over matter, the overmastering power of will. It was opposed to Locke's theory that nothing existed in the brain, except the contribution of the senses; it affirmed the presence of ideas, realities, forces, outside of and superior to the sensory factor. Man's power resided within him; he could make of himself what he wished. Instead of being a slave to external forces and factors, or to his sensations and habits, he was master over them, and needed only to exercise that mastery to be a free man.

Ripley believed in the same philosophy and though his interpretation of it varied often from that of Emerson, he seldom differed with the latter on fundamentals. The Brook Farmers not only had their "transcendental heifer," but also their transcendental philosophy to live by. They had no special denominational God on whom to anchor their faith; they had no belief, as did the Marxians of later years, in an economic curative which would elevate man by improving and transforming the environment. Such advance, they believed, was not up to God or the environment, but up to individual man himself. Brook Farm simply made better individuals, endowing them with transcendental vision and power. By encouraging a co-operative instead of competitive milieu, it released hidden potencies within the individual and converted him into a new man.

ORESTES BROWNSON

One of the unique figures interested in Brook Farm, in fact, so interested that he not only came there from time to time and talked and lectured, but sent his son there to be educated, was Orestes Brownson. Brownson was not a Transcendentalist in the Emersonian sense of the word, yet he was one in his own conception of what it meant; whatever he believed in, and that ranged ultimately from labor politics to the Roman Catholic Church, he viewed as a transcendental necessity. He could not believe in anything which did not possess transcendental meaning. As one of the first persons to apprehend the significance of class relationships and of the whole class struggle, anticipating Marx by over a decade, his significance in American history is definitely established. His vision was wider and deeper than that of the rest of his contemporaries. Even his worst enemies admitted his vigor.

Brownson was torrential, thundering down mystic mountains and inundating far-flung plains with his eloquence. Nothing that he said or wrote was insignificant. That he was often wrong-minded, eccentric, irresponsible, was undoubtedly true. But about his worst deviations and aberrations of vision, there clung something of the impassioned wisdom of a prophet. Without having written a line of poetry, Brownson was a poet in his own right. A strange, queer, contorted poet he was, more interested in substance than form, and continuously fascinated by the illusion of the infinite and the eternal.

Everything in life interested him, and always it was the enduring which he sought. He was one of the first of the New England intellectuals to identify himself openly with the Workingmen's Party and to declare himself in favor of the working class. At a time when William Ellery Channing defended the middle class against the working class, Brownson defied him and denounced his position as reactionary. Channing had utilized the ancient argument that the working class was better off than the richer classes because it did not have to worry about the uncertainty of its wealth. "To me," Channing wrote, "the matter of complaint is not that the labor class want physical comforts . . . but that they live only for their physical nature." Despite Channing's exalted position as the greatest of the Unitarians, Brownson fired repeated salvos of attack against him in an attempt to annihilate his Philistine security. In his famous essay, "The Laboring Classes," Brownson had broken ground for the radical movement and prepared it for the long fight ahead.

It is no wonder then that Brownson exhibited more than a casual interest in Brook Farm. The very fact that George Ripley had announced that Brook Farm was to be a humanitarian and co-operative, but not a communist, colony immediately attracted Brownson's interest. Curiously enough, Brownson had never been a communist; despite his sympathy with labor, he had been consistently anti-communist. Like Madison, he saw society divided into classes, based on property relations, and, like Guizot, he realized that these conflicting relations determined the direction and destiny of history. Brook Farm represented in his eyes something challengingly new; it seemed a colony in which property relations might disappear, and people be able to live as human creators, not creatures of property. He never accepted Brook Farm in its entirety; even when he visited it he blustered against it, but never without an understanding of its ultimate aim. In his article in the *Democratic Review* of November 18, 1842, he praised it for its rustic virtues and its sweet simplicity.[1] He admired it because it was so unthreatening to established institutions. It did not attack private property, the organized state, the church, the family. It was an ideal experiment based

[1] Arthur M. Schlesinger, Jr.: *Orestes A. Brownson*, 1939, p. 151.

upon a most ideal compromise.[1] Because it was such an ideal compromise, it attracted not only the irascible and splenetic Brownson, but also a multitude of other geniuses and eccentrics, among whom were the romantic and arresting Margaret Fuller, the transcendentalist-minded baker, Isaac Hecker, the philosophic peddler, Bronson Alcott, the courageous and defiant editor, Horace Greeley, the utopia-haunted citizen, Albert Brisbane, and the visionary ecclesiastic, Adin Ballou.

For many years these people found Brook Farm a happy haven. Although some of them did not live there, they visited it, spent periods there, shared in its ideals. It was the kind of dream that children conjure up, in which there is plenty of time for play and in which worry has no place. Isaac Hecker, who later was to join the Catholic Church and become the founder of the Paulist Fathers, wrote to his family:

"The scenery around is beautiful; a more pleasant situation could not be selected. The people are all very kind and Mr. Ryckman would do anything for me with the greatest pleasure, so there is nothing of that kind of help that I may need but what will be bountifully supplied."[2]

Until Hecker left to joint Alcott's Fruitlands colony, he was considered a most important member of the Brook Farm Community.

But, alas, the finances of the place concerned them but little. George Ripley was responsible for that detail, which, however, they never realized was a fundamental. And it was the difficulty of finances which forced George Ripley, before long, to change Brook Farm from a venture in personal improvement into one in social reform.

[1] The fact that Brownson later became a Roman Catholic and renounced most of his earlier progressive ideas, has nothing to do with the validity of his previous convictions. They remain as sound today as they were in his day.

[2] Rev. Vincent F. Holden: *The Early Years of Isaac Thomas Hecker,* 1939, p. 101.

The Fourier Invasion

It took a long time for George Ripley and the rest of the Brook Farmers to succumb to the social compulsion. They fought it off as long as they could. They were American people with a Christian background, and European utopianism held little appeal for them. They had all heard of Fourier, but few of them had ever taken him seriously. What changed their minds was the coming of Brisbane, accompanied by Greeley, plus the fact that they could not manage their colony successfully in its existing form. They needed financial aid and financial reform in order to continue.

And that was what Brisbane promised them. Alas, he never fulfilled his promise, though he talked much about it.

Emerson himself considered Fourier's conception of society a military ideal. Others considered it a menace to society. People were divided about its meaning and significance. But Brisbane and Greeley would not be denied. "Your scheme has elements of Fourierism in it, but undeveloped," Greeley insisted; "now that many are taking it up so ineptly, why don't you turn your Farm into a phalanx and show them a real one?"

His words stuck. They revolutionized Ripley's mind. Dana was unmoved by them, but Ripley was never the same thereafter. Fourier gradually became his new inspiration. Another influence was Channing, who was propagandizing for Fourierism in his magazine *The Present,* and anything that Channing said or wrote was bound to move Ripley. Both Channing and Ripley were impressed by the fact that Fourier had been a profoundly religious man. Unlike Marx, who declared religion to be "the opium of the people," Fourier believed that it was impossible to achieve a co-operative world except through religion. "The love of God," he wrote, "will in our new order become the most ardent love among men."

By the organization of phalansteries, each of which in turn

had its respective productive groups, freed from the exploitations of all middlemen, Fourier envisioned the structure of a new society which would ultimately attain the ideal unity of men with God. Brook Farm, following Fourier's idea, organized a group entitled the Sacred Legion, to be composed of the most heroic and self-sacrificing members, who would undertake of their own free will to do the more arduous and unattractive tasks.

When Brook Farm tried to put Fourier's ideas into practice, in a modified way, it lost a goodly number of its members, and its school, famous throughout New England, suffered still more in that respect. After the community had been centralized, and individuals assigned to their special Series, some to the Festal Series, others to the Cattle Series, others to the Amusement Series, and so on, everyone realized what a profound change had come over the character of the community. It was no longer the individualist co-operative venture of George Ripley, but the non-individualist co-operative venture of Fourier. George Ripley had traveled a long way before he came to this turn in his philosophy. No longer did he believe, as the colony had originally, that "community of property is the grave of individual liberty." [1] Fourier, it is true, never believed in wholesale communization of property, but his scheme was far removed from the regime of private property which Ripley had originally advocated and practiced on the Farm. Individual initiative and independence were largely blotted out in the Fourier scheme. Instead of everyone making a place for himself, everyone had a place made for him. The element of chance was practically eliminated from the structure of a Fourier community. "The elements of the heavenly bodies are not left to chance," declared Channing, "so why should the destiny of any human being be left to chance now or hereafter?" Noyes insisted that it was this new alliance "by which Brook Farm was signally related

[1] John Thomas Codman: *Brook Farm*, 1894, p. 38.

to the great socialistic revival of 1843 and the whole of American Socialism" which made it unforgettable.

The Convention of the Associations of Hopedale, Northampton, and Brook Farm, at which Channing spoke, was dedicated to "a united contemplation of the wonderful progress . . . of the great truths of Social Science discovered by Charles Fourier." [1] The Brook Farmers never denied the validity of their previous principles; they always contended that Fourierism was only an addition to them.   Ripley made a determined attempt to get the Hopedale group to join the Brook Farm community.   The exchange of correspondence between Ripley and Adin Ballou, the head of the Hopedale organization, illuminates the differences between the two groups.   In that connection Adin Ballou's letter to Ripley is worth quoting.

"DEAR BROTHER RIPLEY:

"We are unanimous in the solemn conviction that we could not enlist for the formation of a community not based on the distinguishing principles of the standard of practical Christianity, so called, especially *non-resistance,* etc.   We trust you will do us the justice to think that we are conscientious and not *bigoted.*

"We love you all and shall be happy to see you go on and prosper, though we fear the final issue. . . .

"Affectionately yours,

"ADIN BALLOU" [2]

With the advent of Fourierism, Brook Farm was subjected to a series of attacks, one more vicious and violent than another, in newspapers, magazines, and on public platforms. Among the leaders in the attack were the New York *Express* and the New York *Observer;* other papers that followed suit were the *Courier* and the Buffalo *Advertiser.*   So long as it remained just an idyllic community, interested in a quiet, co-

[1] Zoltan Haraszti: *The Idyll of Brook Farm,* 1937, p. 27.
[2] Codman: *op. cit.,* p. 143.

operative way of life, it had been tolerated by the New Englanders, who considered it an adventure of eccentrics. But
when it came under the influence of a foreigner, a French-
man whose name they could never satisfactorily pronounce,
that was too much. There were some politicians who wanted
to see the colony exterminated. There were others who
swore that it had become a hell-hole of infidelity and a cess-
pool of free love. The canards invented became worse and
worse as opposition to the experiment grew. The Brook Farmers, however, refused to be alarmed or frightened and went
their way defiantly and with determination.

In *The Harbinger,* the paper published both in Boston and
on the Farm, they advocated a new order of society, and
viewed their Brook Farm Phalanx, the name adopted by the
colony in March, 1845, as a great pioneer experiment in social
progress. It called not only upon Americans, but the whole
world for support. "We want people to join us," Ripley
insisted, "of whatever nation to whom the doctrines of universal unity have revealed the Destiny of Man." It also urged
that "our brothers of the different associations in the United
States will not regard *The Harbinger* as the exclusive organ
of the Brook Farm Phalanx. . . . It is intended that it should
represent as far as possible the interests of the general movement which is now spreading with such encouraging progress
throughout the land. . . ." [1] *The Harbinger* was a highly
serious magazine; it lacked humor, gaiety, wit. It possessed,
however, an infectious enthusiasm for Fourier's ideas, and it
swiftly gained a most intelligent if somewhat limited audience.
Emerson wrote for it, as did also Dana, Dwight, Lowell, and
Whittier. Many of its contributors refused to sign their
names to articles, preferring anonymity as representative of
a higher form of social consciousness. Though Fourier was
far from a Marxian communist, he did not believe in the encouragement of individualistic impulses and passions; he

[1] *The Harbinger,* Vol. I, No. 3, June 28, 1845.

wanted the individual to find his place in the whole, find joy
in it, but make no attempt to leap beyond it and carve his ego in
a special niche above it.

Margaret Fuller, always the flaming advocate of freedom,
quickly recognized the change that had taken place on the
Farm. "The community," she said, "begins to seem a
mechanical attempt to reform society, instead of a poetic attempt to regenerate it." Emerson also realized the change
and remarked to Ripley that "if Fourier's system were really
carried out we should all be reduced to a set of machines and
individuality would become a lost word in the English language." But Ripley, encouraged by the fact that there were
estimated to be as many as two hundred thousand Fourierists
in America,[1] was unmoved by Emerson's words. To begin
with, he denied their implication,[2] and in the second place, he
was convinced, like a multitude of others, that it would not
be long before all the country became Fourieristic. By this
time he had forgotten, or at least almost forgotten, the Brook
Farmers had stated in their original creed that "we take human nature as it is—as God made it. We do not propose to
remake it; that is the folly of reformers and theorists and
more especially moralists in and out of the church. The
desire, the personal desire to acquire property is a fundamental trait of character more or less strong in every individual. If society cannot be adjusted to that trait, it will
fail."[3]

Ripley had now become a reformer, a theorist. He no
longer believed in the intrinsic significance of environmental

[1] Lindsay Swift: *Brook Farm, Its Members, Scholars and Visitors*, 1904,
p. 275.

[2] "We are prepared to take the ground," declared *The Harbinger*, "that
there is not and never can be individuality so long as there is not association. Without true union, no part can be true. The members are made
for the body; if the whole body be incoherent, every member of it will
be developed falsely." *The Harbinger*, Vol. I, No. 17, 1845, p. 265.

[3] Codman: *op. cit.*, p. 62. Quoted from Mr. Ryckman, one of the Brook
Farmers.

forces. He now realized that the individual had to be fitted into a social pattern to give him significance. To stand alone, as Emerson urged, was something alien to his personality.

Emerson embodied, in its highest and most extreme form, the essence of individualism. He was not against co-operation on principle, but he was violently opposed to any venture, co-operative or otherwise, which threatened to curb the individualistic spirit. Like the well-known Brook Farmer, he agreed that "the great problem is to guarantee individualism against the masses, on the one hand, and the masses against the individual on the other." No man believed more profoundly in the potency of individual man. However outmoded his philosophy may have become today, it was the great challenge of that period, and George Ripley had to meet and combat it with all the wit and intelligence at his command. "All the men in the world," said Emerson, "cannot make a statue walk and speak, cannot make a drop of blood, or a blade of grass, any more than one man can." His faith was in "the infinitude of the private man." More than that, he even declared that a "man is stronger than a city." In religion he believed that "nothing is at last sacred but the integrity of your own mind. Absolve you to yourself, and you shall have the suffrage of the world. No law can be sacred to me but that of my own nature."

What all this meant was that Emerson, who had been so interested in the Farm in its beginnings, and who had continued to show concern for it for years afterward, even though he never joined it, was growing farther and farther away from it. Ripley was sorry, because he had such deep affection as well as admiration for the Concord sage. He had originally counted on both Emerson's and Margaret Fuller's joining the Farm and had been most deeply disappointed when he had finally realized that they would not. With regret he had been forced to admit the truth of Hawthorne's observation that Emerson "stretches his hand out of cloudland for something real, nor knows when he has it. And the fact he thinks he holds in his hand, melts away in his grasp." Emerson's description of Hawthorne, that he was an "everlasting rejecter of all that is, and seeker for he knows not what," was hardly more flattering.

Emerson's reaction to the Farm was more than individual; it was barometric. Gradually, many of the best friends the colony had won began to lose interest in the enterprise. Already the Farm had become crowded with an increase of a variety of artisans and mechanics who showed little interest in the original ideas of Ripley, Dana, Dwight, and their disciples; the former were attracted to the place when it became Fourieristic, because it offered a more convenient and comfortable way of life than they could find elsewhere. But they had no interest in poetry readings, meetings of mystic dreamers beneath the New England stars, intellectual peregrinations among the ancient philosophers, discussions of religious visionaries, and inspired talk of transcendental and eternal things. This was all alien to them, and they ridiculed rather than reverenced it.

This conflict augered the imminent dissolution of the colony. It was a psychological rather than an economic breach. And, it was not, alas, a breach that could be hurdled. It increased rather than decreased with the years. The original group soon began to feel that they were foreigners in the very community they had organized. They moved dubiously across the soil they had first plowed, stared with incredulous eyes at the houses they had constructed with their own hands, debated with themselves whether they had been fools or wise men, and were unable to decide. So few literary outsiders came to visit them now, they were grateful for the sight of an intellectual face, and when Robert Owen, founder of New Harmony, dashed in, in his charming but conquering way, they were so delighted they could scarcely conceal it.

Owen was disappointed at the lack of communist zeal at Brook Farm. He conversed with all the leaders, but had his longest conversations with George Ripley, who found great delight in his observations. Owen at first shocked a number of the Farmers by declaring that Fourier had acquired most of his doctrines from him. "He got his truth from me," Owen said dogmatically, "and the rest of his scheme is imagination and a banker's imagination at that." Owen was convinced that the Brook Farmers would never succeed because they were afraid to pursue their beliefs to their ultimate conclusion—which was communism. Communism, Owen insisted, was necessary for perfection. With "the right circumstances given," Owen added, "we shall grow perfect." But the Brook Farmers would not be convinced. They had already condemned John Collins' communist group at Skaneateles, New York, because it was based upon socialization of property. No Fourierist could approve of such a community—and Owen's community fell into the same category.

Although they disagreed, Owen could not but like the Brook Farmers and the latter in turn could not but like him. They both had one thing in common: a desire to reform the race, to elevate it to a higher plane of existence, free it from its petty, crass interests and impulses, and infuse it with loftier ideals.

Although George Ripley still continued to be the main inspiration of the colony, Albert Brisbane began to compete with him in influence. Brisbane, tall, thick-bearded, high-browed, piercing-eyed, became known as the Great Apostle, and was able in that role to exercise considerable power in shaping the destiny of the group. Behind Brisbane, to be sure, was always the shadow of Fourier, whose bust and picture were now conspicuous decorations in the place. By this time Fourier's name had acquired a sacred significance. He was adored and worshiped, and his books were read and discussed as reverently as the Bible. In fact, his work had become a new Bible. He was even alluded to upon one occasion at Brook Farm as "Fourier, the second coming of Christ."

But Fourier was now dead, and Brisbane violently alive.
He was active in translating and publishing the works of
Fourier, and did more than anyone else to popularize them in
America. Horace Greeley gave him a column in his *Tribune,*
in which to promulgate his theories. He lectured widely and
effectively, and was instrumental in organizing over two score
communities. He was so haunted by Fourier's doctrines that
he lived as much among the stars as on earth. It was not
uncommon for him to refer to the sidereal spheres with an
intimacy which was almost incestuous. Saturn, Venus, Jupiter
were his spiritual allies; they were closer to him than India,
Greenland, or Madagascar. With a wave of his long-fingered
hand he could conjure them to his side, and melt them down
or freeze them up to achieve celestial rapport. Many people
who listened to him were certain that he was a heavenly
emissary, in touch with supernal things, a weird magician of
the skies. A thousand years were no more to him than the
passing of a second, ten thousand no more than the deep
breath of a giant. "I love those great worlds up there," he
ejaculated, as if he had some particular claim upon them, as
if they owed him tribute. The Brook Farmers were overawed
by his eloquence; the fervor and ferocity of a prophet lived
in him. He spoke like one inspired. He had such fervid faith
in supernal and eternal things that he even "talked of our
meeting thirty-five thousand years hence under Saturn's ring;
and we agreed to do so! Thirty-five thousand years from that
very evening." [1]

Brisbane also introduced the group to many new European
ideas and authors. As Marianne Dwight says, "He gives us a
most beautiful and vivid picture of Paris, with its broad
streets, its palaces, fountains, statues, etc. He actually carried
us there with him and showed us all this magnificence and let
us see for ourselves what, even in civilization, the combined
efforts of men can do. He said he never witnessed so much

[1] Marianne Dwight: *op. cit.,* p. 93.

life and activity—never felt so truly the greatness of man."
He introduced them to the work of Eugene Sue, who was
then very little known in the country, and encouraged them
to read his novels, which, as he informed them, had been
read by a million people. He pointed out to them that Sue
was one of the first socialist novelists, and that he was breaking
ground for a new literary tradition. Living when he did, and
being at the time a disciple of Fourier rather than Marx, he
knew nothing of the proletarian literary tradition, of which
Sue later was to be accredited a founder.

Day by day, however, the hostility to Brook Farm increased.
Fourier became regarded as a devil, a destroyer of social
standards, especially of marriage. Brisbane did his best to defend his master in this respect, but without great success.
Although Fourier's theories about marriage were far from
conventional, they were sufficiently nebulous to defy definition. Moreover, the Brook Farmers were never interested
in Fourier's ideas about sex, morality, and marriage. They
clung to their simple, middle class code of morality, and were
far purer than the Puritans in practicing it. Of all the
newspapers, only Greeley's *Tribune,* which advocated Fourierism, sprang to the colony's defense.

Everything might have gone well with the Farm despite
its innovations and the new members crowding into it, had it
not been for a physical tragedy: the burning of the Phalanstery,
upon which so many of the artisans and mechanics had been
at work for months and months. This building was to house
most of the community and to function as a vital center of
activity. The Brook Farmers had watched the structure go
up day after day, seen it acquire skeletal form, then body
and substance, and their hearts had been gladdened by every
sound and hum of construction. The whole future of the
Farm was wrapped up in this structure. It was the realization
of past, present, and future.

Minot Pratt, the head farmer, had left the place, as also

had Peter Baldwin, one of the oldest members, but even their departures, discouraging though they had been, would not have impaired the progress of the Farm had the Phalanstery not burned. When Cheever cried out, "The Phalanstery's on fire," he announced the doom of the community. The crowd which gathered to stare at the flaming structure, see its floors give way and crash one upon another, watch its beams sag and sink, its chimneys crumble and topple, knew in its heart that it was witnessing more than the burning of a Phalanstery—it was seeing its dream reduced to ashes. The two hours which it took for the building to burn to the ground were a living agony for the community. Every second was worse than the one before. Lack of adequate fire equipment made it impossible to stay the flames. Some of the women cried and screamed, others assumed an artificial, morbid calm; the men kept silent. There was the desperation of defeat in their eyes. Some, however, were fascinated by the poetic wonder of the sight. Marianne Dwight, in a letter to her friend, Anna Parsons, gives a vivid description of the catastrophe:

"Then came the sudden, earnest cry, 'Fire! the Phalanstery!' that startled us all, and for a moment made every face pale with consternation. I was in my room, just about writing to Dora. I ran to the front of the house. Flames were issuing from one of the remote windows, and spreading rapidly. It was at once evident that nothing was to be done. It seemed but five minutes when the flames had spread from end to end. Men ran in every direction, making almost fruitless attempts to save windows and timber. The greatest exertions were made to save the Eyrie, which at one time was too hot to bear the hand, and even smoked. Our neighbor, Mr. Orange, went first upon the roof and worked like a hero, and not in vain. But the scene! Here words are nothing—Why were you not here? Would I could convey to you an idea of it. It was glorious beyond description. How grand when the immense heavy column of smoke first rose up to heaven! There was no wind, and it ascended almost perpendicularly—sometimes inclining toward the Eyrie—then it was spangled with fiery sparks, and tinged with glowing colors, ever rolling and wreathing, solemnly and gracefully up—up. An immense, clear blue flame mingled for a while with the others and rose high in the air—like liquid turquoise and topaz. It came from the melting glass. Rockets, too, rose in the sky, and fell in glittering gems of every rainbow hue—much like our 4th of July fireworks. I looked upon it from our house till the whole front was on fire—that was beautiful indeed—the whole colonnade was wreathed spirally with fire, and every window glowing. I was calm, felt that it was the work of heaven and was good; and not for one instant did I feel otherwise. Then I threw on my cloak and rushed out to mingle with the people. All were still, calm, resolute, undaunted. The expression on every face seemed to me sublime. There was a solemn, reverential feeling, such as must come when we are forced to feel that human aid is of no avail, and that a higher power than man's is at work. I heard solemn words of trust, cheerful words of encouragement, of resignation, of gratitude and thankfulness, but not one of terror or despair. All were absorbed in the glory and sublimity of the scene. There was one minute, whilst the whole frame yet stood, that surpassed all else. It was afire throughout. It seemed like a magnificent temple of molten gold, or a crystallized fire. Then the beams began to fall, and one after another the chimneys. The end, where the fire took, being plastered, held out the longest, but in less than an hour and a half the whole was leveled to the ground. The Phalanstery was finished! Not the building alone, but the scenery around was grand. The smoke as it settled off the horizon, gave the effect of sublime mountain scenery; and during the burning, the trees, the woods shone magically to their minutest twigs, in lead, silver, and gold. As it was to be, I would not have missed it for the world. . . . And I do assure you, the moral sublimity with which the people took it was not the least part of it. . . . Engines could not help us much. There was such a rush of the world's people to the Hive! We gave them what we could—made hot coffee, brought out bread and cheese and feasted about 200 of the fatigued, hungry multitude. . . ."[1]

The Farm was never the same again. Something went out of it, as if consumed by the flames. Dana was in favor of closing the Farm immediately, the debt-accumulation now was so gigantic. Ripley, however, and most of the others wanted to stay on, and they did, but not for long. The membership of the group dwindled rapidly; six months after the fire there were only fifty people left of a previous hundred who had been there before the fire. Ripley found himself so harassed with debts that he had to sell the larger part of his excellent library to Theodore Parker in order to raise funds to meet some of the more immediate bills of the Farm. Neither he nor his wife could endure the sight of his empty bookshelves, so they concealed them with draperies and tried to forget their existence. It was not long before Ripley realized that he had to sell the Farm, a thing which he did, with heartbreaking expedition. But the money derived from the sale covered only a small part of the total debts of the colony. Ripley, with characteristic conscientiousness, assumed responsibility for all the remaining debts. After he had to give up *The Harbinger*, he spent most of his time writing articles for Greeley's *Tribune*, and for various magazines and journals. His most lucrative job was with the *New American Encyclopedia*, where he made as much as seventy-five dollars a week.[2] In time he paid back every cent that was owed.

Ripley's struggle in those days was more than an economic one. His mind was clouded with doubts and fears, which were doubled by the unexpected conversion of his wife to Catholicism. Sophia Ripley found in the Virgin Mary the Mother that she had always sought, and, following in the foot-

[1] Dwight: *op. cit.*, pp. 146-147.
[2] Codman: *op. cit.*, p. 238.

steps of Isaac Hecker and Orestes Brownson, she joined the Catholic Church. She tried to persuade her husband to join the church also, but George Ripley could not tolerate its dogmas. Hecker visited him, as also did Brownson; he listened patiently to them, admitted the wisdom in much that they said, but that was all. Although no doubt he regretted the fact that his wife had become a Catholic, he never reproached her for it, and throughout the rest of his life he continued to respect her decision.

To the end of his days, he maintained his religious independence. He was a courageous, but no longer a cheerful, soul. The failure of Brook Farm had signified in his eyes the failure of his life—the failure of a new way of life, which he had believed he could establish.

CHAPTER XIV

Hopedale

AN ADVENTURE IN RELIGIOUS CO-OPERATION

"Hopedale held on its way through the Fourier revival, solitary and independent, and consequently never attained so much public distinction as Brook Farm and other Associations that affiliated themselves with Fourierism, but considered by itself as a Yankee attempt to solve the socialistic problem, it deserves more attention than any of them . . . it commenced earlier, lasted longer, and was really more scientific and sensible than any of the other experiments of the Fourier epoch."

JOHN HUMPHREY NOYES

Few people today remember the name of Adin Ballou. Yet there was a time, less than a century ago, when his name was on the tongue of myriads, and his ideas were the challenge of a generation. They had a morning brightness and clarity about them that compelled admiration. Although not so important a thinker as Emerson, nor so interesting a personality as Alcott, he was in his day revered as much as they, and among many exalted above them. His was no minor name; it was a major force, and much of New England was shaken by its impact. Adin Ballou was guided and inspired by the Universalist ideas of his time; he was a spiritual son of the religious revolutionaries of New England, and his devotion to their ideals was as unwavering as his belief in a beneficent and beatific God. He would allow nothing to stand in the way of his ideal, and in that regard he was more

225

forthright and determined than most of the compromisers who preceded and followed him. He wanted a world, or at least a colony, upon which God could smile with pleasure and be convinced that His creation of Man was good. Man owed so much to God and, in return, gave back so little. By creating a little slice of heaven on earth he could give back a bit, however small, in repayment for his privilege. Such a slice of eternity would be eternal in itself.

Ballou's description of the origin of the colony is too revealing not to quote:

> "The Hopedale Community was a systematic attempt to establish an order of Human Society based upon the sublime ideas of the Fatherhood of God and the Brotherhood of man, as taught and illustrated in the Gospel of Jesus Christ. The primordial germ, of which it was the natural outgrowth and consummation, first manifested itself in my own mind about the time of the opening of the year 1839. . . . At that date I was Pastor of the First Church and Parish of the town of Mendon, Mass., a position I had occupied during the eight previous years. I had long before outgrown my early belief that the religion of the New Testament was chiefly concerned with the condition of Mankind in a future state of being. . . . I had come to see that the Teachings of the Master were essential to human well-being in this world as well as in the world to come; that it was one of Christ's labors to inaugurate the kingdom of heaven on the earth; and that it was the imperative duty of his disciples to pray and to work earnestly for that sublime end." [1]

Ballou had seceded from the Universalist Church because he did not believe in Christianity as merely an other-worldly prospect; he longed "most ardently to see New Testament Christianity actualized." But he did not confine his criticisms to religion. He was a social as well as religious reformer. To begin with, he was a pacifist, and that meant that he not only opposed war, but every form of activity which abetted it.

[1] Adin Ballou: *History of the Hopedale Community*, 1897, pp. 1-10.

He was condemned by multitudes for his pacifist position. But even when attacked he preferred, like John Halifax, to turn the other cheek rather than strike back at his opponent. And he practiced what he preached.

"The great overshadowing War System everywhere deemed essential of public order and the security of the common welfare, with its multiplex enginery of destruction," he wrote, "its appalling burden of degradation, poverty, and wretchedness, crushing the life out of vast multitudes of people; its manifold barbarities and cruelties, subversive of the essential principles and vital spirit of the Gospel of Christ, we unqualifiedly condemned and repudiated." But Ballou did not stop with his desire to eliminate war. That was only one of the reforms he advocated. He was one of the early advocates of the temperance movement which later developed into the prohibition movement, and if he never developed into a masculine fire and brimstone artist such as Carrie Nation, it was only because he did not believe in such violent technique. He was a Christian; he preferred to die on the cross of his beliefs rather than crucify his opponents. In that sense, he was one of the most angelic men of the century. There was a touch of Alcott about him, a flash of Emerson, a trace of Parker, a suggestion of Ripley, a flare of Channing—he wasn't as fine as any of them but as a composite he possessed something in himself that all the others lacked.

Like the rest, he was an early advocate of anti-slavery in sentiment and lent his aid to the Abolitionist movement, although he never became the flaming force that Garrison was, or Lovejoy, or Parker. Adin Ballou did not flame. He was too calm, too measured, too rational in his emotions.

Naturally, he founded his colony upon such convictions. Without being an anarchist, he was opposed to the powers bestowed upon governments in the outside world and, in Hopedale, government was divested of such sovereignty. The "subtle methods of control and usurpations of authority," of which government, or which cleverer political scientists would have called the state, was guilty, the "disregard of the requirements of the moral law and of the rights of the weak and defenceless" were not allowed to creep into the Hopedale community. All this, Ballou wrote, "was transcended and set aside by us in our declared loyalty to that kingdom which 'is not of this world,' whose officers are peace and its exactors righteousness, and wherein those that are chief and would be accounted greatest are servants of all." [1]

Pierrepont Noyes had complained that with all the co-operation which prevailed at Oneida, there had never been an attempt to curb the competitive spirit in games. No one in Oneida ever seemed to realize the significance of that fact, not even old man Noyes himself. Ballou did. One of his first regulations was to eliminate all competition from games as well as from the rest of life. He wanted to inspire co-operation in everything that his community essayed. Competition in itself, in any field, resulted, Ballou declared, "in class distinctions, in gross inequalities of condition, in revolting extremes of wealth and poverty, of prodigal luxury and famishing want, of gorgeous display and loathsome destitution, engendering discontent, ill-will, resentment, animosity, hatred, and sometimes the spirit of revenge and open violence." All this, Ballou contended, was "utterly opposed to our doctrine of human brotherhood, which [is] 'each for all and all for each.' " This was the only way in which they could "build a new civilization radically higher than the old."

No one with any sense of human decency could quarrel with Ballou's conception of a harmonious community. "Neither individual nor social good must be sacrificed," he stated; "both must stand on a common foundation." [2] Ballou had a logical mind and subjected man to a psychological as well as physical dissection. Man's wants, he concluded after

---

[1] *Ibid.*, p. 11.
[2] Adin Ballou: *Practical Christian Socialism*, 1854, p. 166.

extensive analysis, were seven: Individuality, Connubiality,
Consanguinity, Congeniality, Federality, Humanity, Uni-
versality. To get these wants, these rights, these privileges,
man must be a free man. And Ballou's dream was to make
man a free man.

In this regard Hopedale was more like Brook Farm than
it was like most of the other co-operative colonies. Brook Farm
did not aim to be communistic; neither did Hopedale. Brook
Farm derived from Unitarianism, Hopedale from Universalism, both products of the same religious schism, even though
Unitarianism was far more advanced in intellectual outlook
than Universalism. Both tried to fuse the best elements of
an individualistic and a communistic economy. In both
groups there was a continuous tug of war between the two
tendencies. The introduction of Fourierism converted Brook
Farm into what was, practically speaking, a communist colony;
Hopedale, though it became increasingly socialistic, never, in
any full sense, adopted that pattern.

Ballou disliked Fourier's teachings in that they placed
philosophy above religion; in Ballou's eyes religion was the
supreme philosophy. "My system," cried Ballou, or well-
nigh shouted, "ascribes supremacy to the Christian religion."
And after that there was no argument—at least, not with
Ballou. His system, he added, "aims at . . . perfect har-
monization . . . that lawful and innocent enjoyment is the
only true happiness; that temperance is indispensable to
health . . . that the cross precedes the crown, and that a
rational abstinence from sexual pleasure is the surest guaranty
of solid aggregate philosophy." [1]

Ballou was contemptuous of Owen because the latter did not
revere religion as the mainspring of human impulse and motivation. Ballou was neither an atheist nor an agnostic. He was
a religious equalitarian. He wanted men and women to live
humanly, within a socialist economic pattern. He was con-

[1] *Ibid.*, p. 485.

vinced that his society was superior to Owen's New Harmony because he placed religion highest in the intellectual scale of things. Owen was anti-religious, or at least non-religious. He was scornful of Christian metaphysics. Pantheism was intelligent, but Christian monotheism, which in Owen's eyes was really polytheism with its God, Son, and Holy Ghost, he would not consort with. Ballou, on the other hand, was a Christian and he would have no traffic with pantheists or any other "ists" of whatever variety. "Religion has ever been and ever must be the Lord of Philosophy," Ballou averred, "therefore my social system must be radically superior to Owenism." [1]

Ballou's career was far from a serene one. Many people, even many of his followers, opposed his propositions, and he had to carry on fight after fight in order to win his spiritual victory. His determination to take no part in politics, because it was a man-made and not a God-made matter, aroused hostility from the start; then his refusal to allow any members of his community to hold public office only aggravated the situation. In his semi-monthly publication, *The Practical Christian,* he declared his views and stated his beliefs in most unequivocal form.

Finally, a Constitution was drawn up to avoid further disputes. Because it is such an interesting document and reveals so much of Hopedale life, I shall quote various sections from it:

"Know all men:
"That in order more effectually to illustrate the virtues and promote the ends of pure religion, morality, and philanthropy; to withstand the vices and reform the disorders of the present social state; to secure to our posterity the blessings of a more salutary, physical, intellectual, and moral education; to establish a more attractive, economical, and productive system of industry; and to facilitate the honest acquisition of individual property for

[1] *Ibid.,* p. 521.

laudable purposes,—we whose names are hereunto an-
nexed do unite in a voluntary Association to be called

"THE FRATERNAL COMMUNION

". . . Each Community shall endeavor to provide suitable employment for every individual . . . which various
employment shall be adapted, as nearly as the case will
admit, to the genius and taste of the several operatives.

". . . All children and youth . . . shall be educated in
the most approved manner. . . .

". . . An ample fare shall be agreed on, provided, and
served by each Community . . . either in commons . . .
or private families, as may have been stipulated. . . .

". . . Each Community shall endeavor to grow, manufacture, or purchase at wholesale, all articles of necessary
consumption; . . . and every item sold out of the Community stores . . . shall be afforded at cost. . . .

". . . Every Community . . . shall stand forever
pledged to the relief and comfortable maintenance of all
its members who may become destitute of pecuniary resources; and also of their widows and orphans.

". . . Every member shall have one . . . vote on all
questions; and the concurrence of two-thirds of all the
members present shall always be necessary to a decision."

The actual organization of the colony was similar in most
respects to that of the other co-operative communities. Ballou
was not a Rapp or a Janson, nor did he seek to be. Nevertheless his authority, if less mystical, was scarcely less decisive.
He trained his followers to obey him, and this they did im-
plicitly; his word was sacred. In order to establish silence
on a scientific as well as ethical basis, he organized "the silent
band," which was a group that made silence into an industry.
At a word from Ballou, everyone would stop speaking and
silence would sweep over the place like some ominous bird
with noiseless wings. Not even a breath could be heard. It
was almost like a yogi seance.

Productive functions, planting crops, caring for them,
harvesting them, culinary activities, domestic tasks, educa-

tional projects, all were collectivized. Ballou himself admitted
that their facilities were woefully inadequate.   In fact, in
the beginning, he was opposed to collectivization or communization of any kind.   On June 8, 1843, he maintained at the
famous convention of co-operative and progressive colonies,
held in Boston, that "individual property grew directly out
of individual existence, was inseparably connected with it,
and would never be wholly abolished so long as man had a
stomach which must appropriate food exclusively to itself."
Then he added in the light of his conclusion, "the right of
individual property being a natural, inherent, and necessary
one . . . the question should not be shall we abolish it, but
rather, what are its proper limitations and uses?"   During
that conference, John A. Collins, a leading member of the
Anti-Slavery Society of Massachusetts, disagreed violently
with Ballou, and maintained that man's condition of infelicity
was entirely due to environment, and that it would only be
through change in environment that man could be changed—
to which Ballou retorted that Collins should go out and
test his theories, the result of which was the foundation of
the Skaneateles Community in central New York.   Unfortunately, it lasted but a few years, and its failure convinced Ballou, who was an intellectual prig in such matters,
of the original truth of his counsel.   No community could
succeed, according to Ballou, unless the souls of the individual men creating it were purged from the very beginning
of all thoughts of sin and all conceptions of evil.

Hopedale itself did not last very long, and Ballou took
its demise with philosophic fortitude.   It is a difficult task to
harmonize communism (or collectivism) with individualism,
and, I suspect, always will be.   "If we communized very
strongly some claimed too much at the expense of the whole,"
Ballou wrote, "and if we encouraged individualism beyond a
certain point, there was presently an annoying and reprehen-
sible manifestation of selfish egoism."   Ballou tried the cen-

tristic approach. "Finding ourselves in this latter condition," Ballou said, "we tried to get back to the center of the narrow strait in which we were obliged to sail."

A final compromise was effected in the organization of Bands and Sections, which purposed to give a social, if not a communistic, character to the group. These Bands and Sections, with their divers functions, their activities, their plans, their schedules, were conspicuously close to the collectivism of many of the other utopian colonies. Ballou, however, did everything in his power to minimize their collectivistic, and maximize their individualistic tendencies. He wanted to combine the socialism of Christ with the individualism of Paul.

In the beginning the community was successful. It started with a capital of four thousand dollars and at the end of the first year its capital had increased to sixteen thousand. From a single building with a few dilapidated barns, the community developed into a thriving enterprise. Within the year it became a village, had a dozen houses, excellently equipped barns, mill-dams, shops, and all the appurtenances which go with a progressive community. It was not long before there were forty-four persons, ten men, twelve women, and twenty-two children, besides numerous cows, oxen, steers, horses, and swine. But this success was short-lived. Restlessness and revolt developed, even marital infidelity occurred. The latter sin had worried Ballou so much he passed a resolution in which he condemned "free love as an immoral, wicked, and vicious practice." [1] Undoubtedly he was thinking of other colonies and their dread ideas on the subject, when he declared himself in such a forthright if not violent manner.

The final blow came when the Draper brothers, who had done so much to back the venture, decided that they had to discontinue their support. The pair owned three-fourths of the joint stock of the community, and realizing that they would have to increase their investment if Hopedale was to continue,

[1] *Ibid.*, p. 249.

they decided to call a halt, withdraw as much of their money as they could still collect, and let the colony smoulder in its own ashes.

It must be said to the great credit of Adin Ballou that, severe and tragic though this blow proved to be, he never condemned the Drapers. "Some have been disposed to censure severely . . . the Brothers Draper," he wrote, "[but] I have never sympathized with such imputations." But Ballou was, with all his other deficiencies, such a noble soul, that he went further, and said that even if "the Brothers Draper . . . had been willing to devote their rapidly accumulating property to the further development of the Hopedale Community, it would have sooner or later failed"—and then he added, in character with his whole philosophy, that the failure was due to "lack of moral qualification." More than that, he said, "No community can be a success except its membership consist of persons the like of which the world even now possesses very few."

It was that stress upon individual character, integrity, nobility, that made Adin Ballou into such a forceful figure in his time. He and Ripley had no quarrel on that score. It is not surprising, then, that he declared that "the failure of the Hopedale Community was a moral and spiritual, not a financial one."

Hopedale never succumbed to the Fourier "craze" which had swept across so much of the land; it clung to its Yankee insularity and provincialism to the end. As John Humphrey Noyes said, it was never tainted by foreign ideas or influences.[1] His words, as the founder of one of the longest-lived communist colonies in this country, are most interesting:

"If the people of this country were not so busy with importations from England and France that they cannot look at home productions in this line, his [Ballou's] scheme would command as much attention as Fourier's

[1] Noyes: *op. cit.*, p. 119.

and a great deal more than Owen's. The fact of practical failure is nothing against him in the comparison, as it is common to all of them."

From the lips of Noyes such words were high praise, indeed. After all, Noyes had organized one of the most successful colonies seen on this side of the world—or any other side, either, for that matter. Noyes could appreciate Ballou better, perhaps, than anyone else at the time. He even went so far as to admit that "if it were our doom to attempt community-building by paper program, we should use Adin Ballou's scheme in preference to anything we have been able to find in the lucubrations of Fourier and Owen."

Ballou was like most of the other founders of the utopian colonies in that he worked as well as guided and inspired. He did the hardest work as well as the lightest, and, like Ripley, worked longer than his followers at his respective tasks. Noyes wrote that ofttimes "he [Ballou] would be so tired at his work in the ditch or on the mill dam that he would go to a neighboring haystack and lie down on the sunny side of it, wishing he might go to sleep and never wake again! Then he would recuperate and go back to his work." [1]

Adin Ballou failed with his colony, but not with himself. To the end he remained faithful to his ideals, faithful to his dream of what man could be, and what an individual man could achieve in life if he had the spiritual resolution and courage.

[1] *Ibid.*, p. 130.

CHAPTER XV

Fruitlands

"There [in America], if anywhere, is that second Eden
to be planted, in which the divine seed is to bruise the head
of Evil and restore man to his rightful communion with
God in the Paradise of Good."

BRONSON ALCOTT

"The most refined and the most advanced soul we have
had in New England, [Alcott] makes all other souls appear
slow and cheap and mechanical."

RALPH WALDO EMERSON

Of all the co-operative colonies attempted in America, a
unique and most quaint one was that of Bronson Alcott.
He called his colony "Fruitlands," because fruit was to be
the main food of the community. It possessed a farmhouse, a
barn, and ten apple trees. Alcott and his followers were not
only vegetarians and fruit lovers, but they insisted upon living on only certain types of vegetables and fruits. The philosophy of the colony was far removed from that of Brook
Farm or the earlier utopians; it was, in Alcott's words, simply
that of "the narrow way of self-denial." "Diogenes and his
tub would have been Alcott's ideal, if he had carried it out,"
wrote Hecker. "Ripley would have taken with him the good
things of this life. Alcott would have rejected them all." [1]
In that connection it is interesting to note that Hecker contended that "Emerson, Alcott, and Thoreau were three consecrated cranks."

[1] Clara Endicott Sears: *Bronson Alcott's Fruitlands*, 1915, p. 83.

236

Alcott, who started his life as a peddler, wandering through strange parts of the country, selling queer, outlandish wares, was an ascetic by nature. He early discovered a joy in renunciation. He was far more like Christ than Thoreau, or any other New Englander; Christ's philosophy of poverty not only appealed to him, it fitted in with his whole psychology. He wanted to be like the original apostles.

Bronson Alcott was born of Yankee stock, but was not a Yankee in soul. He was, in his own words, "the Paradise-Planter," and as such he spent most of his life.

Fruitlands was an experiment in Alcottism. Alcott believed that the land should be "consecrated to the sober culture of devoted men. We plan to grow only enough of chaste supplies for bodily needs." He would have nothing to do with foods which necessitated the death of animals or robbed them of their supplies. He was vehement in his attack upon one of the new members of the colony who confessed that she ate cheese clandestinely and had succumbed upon one occasion to devouring the tail of a fish. No wonder that Ripley said in a gently satiric voice: "They are eating bowls of sunrise for breakfast, and it may satisfy the older ones, but surely will not be too good for the children." Alcott heard of Ripley's remark, but disdained to reply to it. His love of nature was so great that argument about it seemed futile. He would not force nature; he would wait for it to reveal its fertility. He even refused to permit the use of manure, because, as he declared, "it is base and corruptible and an unjust method of forcing nature." He even opposed the invention, manufacture, and development of steamboats, railroads, and telegraphs.

Fruitlands was the most American of all the colonies. Nothing foreign invaded it. It had no Fourier, no Brisbane, no Marx, no leader at all, except its sunburnt founder, Bronson Alcott. But Alcott was enough. He was inspiration, leader, Christ, a sublime composite. He was the colony. Without him there would have been nothing. Without ever assuming the role of dictator, he was the spiritual dictator of all that lay before him. Without raising his hand or voice, he dominated everything he saw. He didn't like Brook Farm because it did not possess a final aim or teleological design. It was governed by no theory of food, no theory of sex, no theory of knowledge. Alcott had theories about them all, about everything, which he wanted to see put into practice. Moreover, Alcott wanted to improve men rather than conditions; the Brook Farmers believed that improved conditions would make improved men. Alcott had faith in internal, not external improvement. He wanted to improve men by getting at their bodies and souls, not by changing the conditions of their life.

Undoubtedly Alcott suffered from a touch of megalomania; most writers, thinkers, and reformers do, though most of them conceal it. Alcott concealed nothing. He believed in his own importance and did not hesitate to proclaim it. "You write on the genius of Plato, of Pythagoras, of Jesus," Alcott said to Emerson, "why do you not write of me?" Isaac Hecker, the soul-probing baker, who had first lived on Brook Farm before he became a member of Fruitlands, said, "I don't believe he [Alcott] ever prayed. Whom could he pray to? Was not Bronson Alcott the greatest of all? He was his own God." [1] In his *Journals,* Alcott wrote, "My week's intercourse with Emerson has done me good. . . . I apprehend my genius the more clearly. . . . I am an actor and a sayer, rather than a writer. . . . I am of the race of the prophets. . . . I have more than the scholar in me. I am rather a study for scholars. . . . I cannot but think that my action will make an era in the history of man." [2] Despite

---

[1] Rev. Vincent F. Holden: *op. cit.,* p. 153.

[2] *The Journals of Bronson Alcott,* 1938, pp. 128, 129. Edited by Odell Shepard.

such notions, Alcott was the humblest of men, and certainly one of the most steadfast in the defense of his convictions. If he suffered from the impracticality of an American Micawber, it was only because money meant so little to him that the idea of paying debts seemed silly, if not sacrilegious. He would have nothing of the "filthy lucre," except to meet his immediate needs. "Mr. Alcott," wrote his wife, "cannot bring himself to work for gain."

In his Temple School, which had earned international fame, he would not dismiss a Negro, even though he knew the fate of the school would be jeopardized. He believed in the equality of all peoples, and the Negro in his eyes had as much rights as a white, brown, or red man. He had to close his school in consequence, but he did not mind. He would far rather close his school than continue it without the Negro child. That would have been compromising his conscience, which was something he could never do. It was alien to his nature. "I closed my school today," he wrote in his *Journals*, "it is quite obvious that labours like mine cannot take root in this community, and more especially in this city, until parents and adults are better instructed in the principles and methods of human culture." [1]

Few have recognized the significant role Alcott played in American education. In more senses than one, he was one of the first true educators this country has had. He was the founder of progressive education. Influenced by Pestalozzi, he insisted upon fitting education to the child's mind instead of forcing the child's mind to fit itself to educational dogma. He began what John Dewey later continued and developed into a new educational concept.

Alcott's attitude toward education was not a suddenly acquired thing. Typical of his reaction is the following conversation with his uncle when he was only thirteen:

[1] *Ibid.*, p. 131.

" 'What's the use, Uncle, of learning by rote when you don't understand it? I can learn words by myself. What I want the teacher to show me is how to understand things!'

" 'But the teacher will explain anything you ask about,' declared his uncle. . . .

" 'What I want the teacher to do is to train the thing that I understand with, so he won't have to explain what's in the lesson books.'

" 'You'd better get in the wood for the evening and not criticize your betters,' said Bronson's uncle.

" 'I've done my chores,' replied the boy. 'What I want to ask you, sir, is your permission to stop going to school and spend my time reading here in your library.'

"Why, you ungrateful young fool! Most certainly not! What childish evasion is this? Are you not the boy who is supposed to be eager for an education? Let's hear no more of this nonsense, Bronson.'

"Bronson's lips quivered and he made a move that was to be characteristic of all the rest of his beautiful, thwarted life.

" 'But, Uncle, I can educate myself, if you will give me leave to read all your books. And—and—if you don't give me leave, I—I shall go back home. For I don't want to be away from mother and deprive father of my help on the farm just to have my memory trained.'

"His uncle's voice was stern. It was a day when children were not allowed to express their preference.

" 'You will return home, then, tomorrow. When you are ready to take the discipline to which other children submit themselves, you may return.' " [1]

Needless to say, Alcott did not wait. He left immediately, and with characteristic impulsiveness fought his way home through a fierce, flying snow.

Although Harriet Martineau had ridiculed Alcott's King's Chapel School, and others attacked him mercilessly, he refused to lose faith in his future as an educator. Though his enemies

---

[1] Quoted from Honoré Willsie Morrow: *The Fatner of Little Women*, pp. 27, 28.

were numerous, he had also many friends. Samuel May, a
Connecticut clergyman, was only one of many admirers. May's
appreciation of Alcott is revealing:

"I wrote Mr. Alcott, begging him to send me a de-
tailed statement of his principles and methods in training
children. In due time came to me a full account of the
school at Cheshire, which revealed such a depth of insight into the nature of man, such a true sympathy with
children, such profound appreciation of the work of education, and was withal, so philosophically arranged and
exquisitely written that I at once felt assured the man
must be a genius and I must know him more intimately.
So I wrote inviting him most urgently to visit me.

"He came and passed a week with me before the end
of the summer. I have never, but in one instance, been so
immediately taken possession of by any man I ever met in
life. He seemed to me like a born sage and saint. He
was a radical in all matters of reform: went to the root
of all theories, especially the subjects of education, mental and moral culture." [1]

Most interesting of all was Alcott's theory of organizing
infant schools in divers communities. Though he never
achieved great success in this venture, it was not for want of
heroic labor. Illustrative of his approach to the whole problem of child education are his own words:

"The influence of kindness with which the young under
my care are treated, begins to show itself in their manners.
These affections are in a good state—I know not how long
an envious, gainsaying world will permit me to pursue
the familiar, affectionate manner in which I have recently
treated the scholars. Already it has become a subject of
discussion among their parents:—they know not what to
think of treating children in so kind a manner." [2]

Alcott was a man of firm and fanatic convictions. He loved
vegetables and fruits so much that he came to hate animals,

[1] *Ibid.*, p. 46.
[2] *Ibid.*, p. 57.

especially dogs, hogs, and cats. When pork was served to him he would turn up his nose, shove it away, and refuse to taste it.[1] Apples, apricots, pears, peaches were enough for him. All meat was tabu. "Life was given to animals not to be destroyed by men, but to make them happy," wrote little Anna Alcott, and then added, "Oh, how many happy lives have been destroyed and how many loving families have been separated to please an unclean appetite of men. Why were the fruits, berries and vegetables given us if it was intended that we eat flesh?" [2] More than that, Alcott himself, despite his personal aversion for animals, was violently hostile to their subjection and exploitation by men. He could see no reason why men should enslave horses to do their work for them; like the Hindus, he believed horses as well as men had souls. All such animal foods as cheese, milk, butter, eggs, and the like were forbidden to the Fruitlanders, because they belonged to the animals, and if humans ate them the animals would suffer. The milk belonged to the calf, and a chicken had a right to its existence as well as an infant, said Alcott, describing the attitude of the colony; and even the canker-worms that infested the apple trees were not to be molested. For a time they even refused to have a lamp at Fruitlands because animal fat constituted part of the oil. As Louisa Alcott's Diary shows, various sayings in regard to food were popular among the group:

"Vegetable diet
and sweet repose.
Animal food and
nightmare."

"Without flesh diet
There could be no
blood-shedding war."

"Apollo eats no
flesh and has no
beard; his voice
is melody itself." [3]

[1] Odell Shepard: *Pedlar's Progress*, 1937, p. 40.
[2] Clara Endicott Sears: *op. cit.*, p. 89.
[3] *Ibid.*

The Fruitlanders condemned the Brook Farmers because the latter kept cows and oxen, sold milk, and bought butter.[1] By retreating to a world of abstractions, by basing one's principles upon absolute realities, one is more easily able to escape the practical implications of one's logic. The transcendentalist movement in America profited by that device.[2] Arising out of the changing environment of the time, responding as it did to the individualistic impulse which, accelerated by the spirit of the frontier, swept over America like a predatory invader, it obscured its immediate identity by ascribing its origins to the ancient past. Plato, Plotinus, Proclus, Kant, all played their part in giving metaphysical and mystical form to its credo. With Alcott, it was the mystical element provided by Plotinus and Proclus which afforded him the chief inspiration of his ethics.[3] With Emerson, it was Cudworth, Berkeley, and Kant as well as Plato, who supplied in the main his transcendentalist ammunition. While the "Transcendental Club" was organized, as Bronson Alcott declared, "because its members imagined the senses did not contain the mind," [4] in refutation of the Lockian conception of the sensory origin of knowledge, the ideas which grew out of its discussions, and out of *The Dial*, which it inspired, had less to do with absolute principles than with concrete and mutable realities. Emerson's unforgettable aphorism: "Hitch your wagon to a star," came far closer to the kernel of his philosophy—and that of most of the Transcendentalists—than any of his muddled observations on "the Oversoul." Even Alcott, who

[1] Shepard: *op. cit.*, p. 370.
[2] For contrasting opinions, see Frothingham's *Transcendentalism in New England* (1876) and George W. Cooke's *Poets of Transcendentalism: An Anthology with an Introductory Essay* (1903)—and also his *Historical and Biographical Introduction to Accompany The Dial* (1902).
[3] Austin Warren: "The Orphic Sage: Bronson Alcott," *American Literature*, Vol. III. No. 1, March, 1931, pp. 1-13.
[4] A. Bronson Alcott: "Conversation" on the Transcendental Club and *The Dial*. (Reprinted in *American Literature*, Vol. III, No. 1, March, 1931, p. 14.)

244 WHERE ANGELS DARED TO TREAD

was an emanationist of Plotinian extraction, and a far less
practical man than Thoreau, Ripley, Parker, or Emerson, was
swayed by the chaotic clash of events which stirred America
at that time. The influence of frontier individualism penetrated into the most exalted heaven of his Plotinian fastness,
and filled it with the smell and impact of earth. His words,
"Where is the individual who boldly dares assert opinions
differing with pre-established notions—dares to think for himself? . . . Dare to be singular; let others deride," might have
been written by Emerson as easily as by himself. His defense of self-reliance, his contempt for institutions, his belief
in progress, his optimism, were manifested in his reaction to
the America of his day: "Yes, even here we find progress. . . .
'Tis no time to doubt. Indeed, is it not time for the liveliest
hope?" All this reflected the earthly reality of his doctrines, once
they were translated into action. In one way, however, Alcott
did differ from Emerson and most of the Transcendentalists;
that was in his advocacy of the socialization instead of the
individualization of personality. In his Fruitlands experiment,
he endeavored to put into effect his social ideas, fantastic and
futile though they were. Influenced by the utopian socialist
ideas of the period, which Emerson, we should not forget, had
repudiated, Alcott managed to escape enough of the seductions
of the individualistic philosophy, at least in its wilder extremes,
to see through its shams and to be cognizant of its consequences.
In one of his "conversations" before the Transcendental
Club, he delivered himself of several observations on this
score which show how well he understood certain of the dan-
gers which inhered in the individualist philosophy:

> "That tendency of our teaching, a good deal has been
> rather to favor individualism—to confirm the student or
> inquirer in what was peculiar to himself, more than to
> lead himself forth into what belongs to all mankind. . . .
> We are so very individual that we meet with dif-
> ficulty. . . . Well, very good, if we can at last get free of

our individuality, and become persons indeed—partake that which unites and relates us to one another. I suppose that all doctrines, heretofore, have been aiming at that; but, unfortunately, they dropped out the mother word. Socialism was an attempt to bring men together into institutions, but it was found by those who undertook it that men were too individual, and the success has not warranted the outlay. Each person has taken away in his own culture the fruit of his own experiment, but is left alone, where he was before he entered, in a great measure."

In other places, to be certain, he revealed the same individualistic tendency which he deplored in the foregoing "conversation." Like most of the Transcendentalists, Alcott's philosophy was caught up in a mesh of confusion and contradictions. He was overwhelmed by the world which confronted him, a world in which everything was in a sea of flux, in which tiny wires suddenly were made into the conductors of great energy, in which inert metals were made into moving machines, and in which all values were juggled about in a state of chaos, the new becoming old before it had a chance to crystallize and mellow. Trying to find oneself in that world, as the Transcendentalists primarily tried to do, was like trying to poise a stone in mid-air. It is no wonder, then, that Alcott and his Transcendentalist friends turned to the past for anchorage; it is no wonder they seized upon Plato, Plotinus, and Kant for intellectual stability, for it was only by such a retreat that they could establish the illusion of permanence. The confusion in their logic arose out of an unhappy attempt to reconcile their philosophy with the world in which they lived. Had they remained in their neo-Platonic towers of contemplation, they might have escaped that confusion, and retained a semblance of consistency in their argument. Descending to earth as they did, however, was too much for them; and, as a result, their logic lost all coherence, betrayed them into frequent contradictions.

Such logic degenerated into naïveté, as his daughter Anna showed when she wrote that "Father said that if a person wanted a thing very much and thought of it a great deal, they would probably have it."

Fruitlands was an experiment in the Alcottian way of life. It was based upon hatred of convention, cant, hypocrisy, and above all, the state. "I would it were possible," wrote Alcott, "to know nothing of this economy called 'the state.'" He hated restriction of all kinds, and the restrictions imposed by the state were what irked him most of all.

Fruitlands lasted only seven months, but its memory has outlasted its century, and will most likely last centuries longer. Although Alcott's English friends and disciples subsidized his venture, it never took on an English character. It was American to the core. The Alcott House, which his friends had opened in England in his honor, bore little resemblance to this new venture which was to provide a spiritual oasis for all those lonely wayfarers of the soul who could find no peace in a world in which *"things* were in the saddle." Like the Brook Farmers, they dreamed of utopia, but the Fruitlanders conceived of it less as a fulfillment than as a denial. Isaac Hecker, who lived in both communities, put it well when he thus described Alcott's community, "Instead of 'acting out thyself,' it is 'deny thyself.' Instead of liberty it is mutual dependence. Instead of the doctrine 'let alone,' it is 'help each other.' Instead of tolerance it is love. It is positive, not negative." [1]

Their way of life was simple. They did not have to milk cows as did the Brook Farmers; they did not have to consort with pigs, rabbits, horses, sheep; they had only berries, beans, peas, potatoes, and fruits to cultivate. Their hours of labor, therefore, were short. They worked, the men in their linen tunics and trousers, the women in linen dresses and wide-

[1] Vincent F. Holden: *op. cit.,* p. 164. (From the Hecker Papers.)

brimmed straw hats, in a leisurely yet absorbed fashion. Alcott, despite his predilection for conversation, was one of the
hardest of workers. He lived in the fields often from dawn to
dusk. He loved the smell of the soil, of the things that pushed
their way up from it, and rhapsodized every time he saw another fruit or vegetable slide into life. Lane, the English
convert who had put up all the money for the project, was
awe-stricken at Alcott's enterprise. He had never seen a
man with such indefatigable energy and resolve. Alcott was
a living Prometheus.

The other utopian colonies had devised planned schemes
of living, scheduled their lives with infinitesimal care and
caution; the Fruitlanders never attempted such a form of life.
They lived, despite their odd notions, more simply and more
naturally. They did not have to apportion tasks, precision production. They believed in nature and believed nature would
take care of them. One of the reasons why their existence
was so brief was that they put too much trust in nature and
too little in their own wits.

It was truly tragic to see such a striking venture go so
rapidly to seed. There were crackpots in the colony: men like
Sam Larned, who lived on wafers for a year, on apples for
another; Abe Everett, a lunatic of the higher dimensions, who
envisioned utopia as a cross between a meal-ticket and a
strait-jacket and wanted none of the latter; Isaac Hecker, the
baker, who preferred baking souls to baking bread, and consequently ended up in the Catholic Church, where he discovered a permanent job in purgatory, as an eternal baker.
The other members, however, were reasonably normal. Of
course, Mrs. Alcott confessed she thought there were times
when her husband was going out of his head, and she won-
dered what she could do to save his sanity. On the whole,
however, Alcott held on to his sanity fairly well in a world
which was far from sane in so many aspects. Lane was more
cranky and crotchety, more morbid in his philosophy than

many of his contemporaries, but he could scarcely be called insane. All the Fruitlanders were sane, relatively speaking; it was their strange idealism which led outsiders to view them as lunatics. Their insistence upon spade-culture instead of ox-culture naturally made their neighbors think they were a tribe of cranks and lunatics. The way they planted their trees would scarcely inspire farmers with faith in their efficiency; several were planted so close to the house they almost undermined it with their roots.

To watch them live, to be sure, would not convince the average New Englander of their normalcy. Their asceticism was well-nigh pathologic. They even traveled without money, took passage on boats or seats on trains and confessed they had no money—they considered money the source of all sin— and offered their services as lecturers in payment for the fare. Usually they were successful. Upon one occasion the people took up a collection for them, but they refused it, remarking, "You see how well we get on without money." [1] Their morning showers, followed by music and singing, and then by a breakfast of bread and water, combined with various fruits, would hardly have awakened the envy of a New England gourmet. The midday meal was scarcely more alluring— the only addition to the bread and water was a vegetable, or sometimes two vegetables, with the fruits excluded. No one could partake of such poisons as tobacco, whisky, coffee, tea, or milk. [2] After the meals long conversations often occurred, some of which were most revealing of the attitudes that prevailed in the colony. In one conversation, recorded by Hecker, Alcott named Innocence as the highest virtue, Larned named Thoughtfulness, and Lane, Fidelity. In another conversation that Hecker reports, which was concerned with the Highest Aim, "Mr. Alcott said Integrity; I [Hecker], Harmonic Being; Lane, Progressive Being; Larned, Annihilation of Self; Bower,

[1] Clara Endicott Sears: *op. cit.,* p. 165.
[2] Holden: *op. cit.,* p. 161.

Repulsion of the Evil in us. Then there [was] a confession of the obstacles which prevent us from attaining the highest aim." [1]

They awoke, ate, talked, worked, ate again, talked more, worked again, ate once more, and discoursed till midnight, devouring the intellectual manna of the gods. In Alcott's eyes this was the closest approach one could make to God, or whatever gods there were. This was life as other people could live it. It was ecstasy in daily experience. It was living among gods instead of men.

Imagine, then, the sad, sick disillusion which faced these men when they realized their economic scheme would not work. They had looked upon Fruitlands as something divine, something conceived beyond the skies, in the timeless and spaceless beyonds, something with eternity wrapped in its seed. Unlike the Owenites, who swore by an economic creed, these Fruitlanders swore by something as ageless as the elements, as perdurable as the sea. They knew they were walking down God's path. Although they did not expect the King of Glory to walk in, or the Lord of Hosts, they would not have been surprised at his entrance. He was part of their inheritance. Whatever else they were or weren't, they were Christians, Christians to the core—and beyond. Mohammedanism, Buddhism, or any of the Oriental creeds never meant anything to them. They wanted, like the religious groups of the previous century, to carry on the tradition of Jesus, to make the world into a holy thing. Nothing could be more ideal as an apostolic aspiration.

This fanatical determination to make their colony a New Eden, as they liked to call it, was what finally led them to consider the adoption of celibacy as an ideal. Everything they did was blessed with prayer—when the first load of hay was transported to the barn, one of the group bowed his head and said, "I take off my hat, not that I reverence the barn

[1] Hecker Papers. Quoted from Holden, p. 164.

more than other places, but because this is the first fruit of our labor." [1] And celibacy was blessed even more. The Fruit-landers spent many days, weeks, and months discussing, de-liberating, and praying over it before they adopted it. Lane was the one most responsible for it. He had stayed for a time with the Shakers, where he found celibacy exalted into a hallowed principle. Lane had always felt sex to be unclean, and Ann Lee, with her Shaker enthusiasts, had convinced him that purity could be acquired only by its elimination.

For a considerable time, Alcott was almost persuaded to Lane's point of view. Religious fanaticism finds its root in the principle of self-denial, and there are few denials greater than sex. Renunciation of sex has always won the admira-tion of the populace, because it is one of the things most diffi-cult to sacrifice. Throughout the ages and in every part of the world the practice of celibacy on the part of ecclesiastics has impressed and overawed the commoners, who naturally esteemed those who could deny themselves such a precious privilege. It has also had a haunting appeal to religious fanatics, a final challenge to their high resolve. And Alcott, though a thinker as well as a dreamer, was a religious fanatic. More than that, he was dominated by a curious and romantic conviction that women were spiritually superior to men, that sex was unimportant to them, that they lived upon a plane of existence close to the gods. Ann Lee, consequently, appealed to him and made him wonder whether she might not be the great religious leader of the century.[2] Lane argued that the reason why Fruitlands was proving unsuccessful was due to its uncelibate way of life. The Shakers had been successful for over half a century, and Lane accounted for that by their celibacy. Alcott had to admit that Fruitlands was a failure, but he couldn't quite convince himself that it was due to its uncelibate existence. Day after day Lane kept pounding

[1] Sears: *op. cit.,* p. 76.
[2] Shepard: *op. cit.,* p. 375.

away at the idea, and he might have made a convert of Alcott, had it not been for Mrs. Alcott's intervention. Mrs. Alcott was not an amorous woman, but she didn't like Lane, and she wasn't greatly impressed with the wisdom of celibacy. Lane, for a reason which might have been unconsciously homosexual, was determined to separate Alcott from his family, and celibacy was an ideal technique. Mrs. Alcott decided to put the issue to a test. If her husband preferred living the way the Shaker men did, apart from their wives and families, she would allow him the freedom to do so, although she didn't like the Shakers. "Visited the Shakers," she wrote, "I gain but little from their domestic or internal arrangements. There is servitude somewhere I have no doubt." [1] If he preferred living with her and his children, he would reveal it in action. She and her children moved away from Fruitlands to a house owned by her brother in the town of Still River, where she knew they could live in tranquillity.

Mrs. Alcott won. "She vows," Lane wrote, "that her own family are all that she lives for." Lane and his son left Fruitlands and went to join the Shakers; Alcott left Fruitlands and went to join his wife. Lane blamed the failure of the colony upon Alcott's "constancy to his wife and inconstancy to the Spirit, which has blurred over his life forever." [2]

The failure of Fruitlands not only broke Alcott's heart, but it also almost splintered his mind and destroyed his life. The Fruitlanders had not been adventurers but true ascetics. After the group Isaac Hecker persisted for a long time, living as abstemiously as possible on simple things, such as fruits, nuts, and water, and abstaining from meat. Alcott did the same thing. But this time he did not want to be abstemious; he wanted to die. He was so broken that "days and nights went by," as his daughter Louisa, later to become internationally famous as the author of *Little Women*, wrote.

[1] *Journals of Bronson Alcott*, p. 154.
[2] Shepard: *op. cit.*, p. 379.

"and neither food nor water passed his lips." The family practically gave him up for this world. They sat around, mournfully, hopelessly, prepared for the worst. But Bronson Alcott did not die. The presence of his family was a comfort and an inspiration. It was his wife who finally persuaded him to live.[1] Life for Alcott, now that his dream was dead, was worthless. Fruitlands had been to him what heaven is to a Christian. It had been realization and fulfillment, a vision become visual. He tried, it would seem, to die by starvation. Others have tried it; some have succeeded. Alcott's family saved him from it. The failure of Fruitlands symbolized the failure of all he believed in. But gradually, as he listened to the voices of his wife and children, he understood there were other things still to be conquered, he took hold of himself, decided to struggle on, and for forty more years remained an indelible influence in New England.

Although Alcott recovered from his mental sickness at the failure of the Fruitlands, he could never get the memory of the colony out of his system. He constantly kept reverting to it, and frequently visited other colonies in hopes of finding in at least one of them that *sine qua non* lacking from Fruitlands. But never did he find the gleam. Several of them had great virtues, but even greater vices. Often he could agree with them in theory, but not in practice. Mrs. Alcott's reactions were similar. She was disappointed in the Northampton venture, where she found life "quite elementary and aimless," in Hopedale, where she "could find nothing higher than living quiet, inoffensive lives," and in Brook Farm, where she could "see but little gained in the association in labour."[2]

Unlike Hecker and Brownson, both of whom found the solution in the Roman Catholic Church, Alcott wandered on down the years alone, hand in hand with no one but himself. His family, of course, was an aid and comfort, but not a

[1] Clara Endicott Sears, *op. cit.*, p. 127.
[2] *Journals of Bronson Alcott*, p. 157.

spiritual sesame. He could derive no solution for his intellectual problems from it.

To the end of his life he was still searching for another utopia. He could not adopt the easy solutions of Isaac Hecker, Orestes Brownson, and Sophia Ripley; there was no single church that could satisfy him, no single doctrine that could encompass his needs, no single religion that could fulfill his dream of the past, present, and future.

CHAPTER XVI

Oneida: The Love Colony

*"I am writing that all men should know that I have sub-
scribed my name to an instrument, similar to the Declaration of '76, renouncing allegiance to the Government of the
United States, and asserting the title of Jesus Christ to the
throne of the world."* JOHN HUMPHREY NOYES

Oneida was the only utopian colony in America which combined communism in economics with communism in sex. It
was the kind of colony that William Godwin and Mary Wollstonecraft would have acclaimed, indeed, would have been
willing to join and encourage. Since its founder, John
Humphrey Noyes, knew little if anything about either, it is
extremely unlikely that he was influenced by their works.
Besides, his approach, like that of so many of the other
American utopians, was religious, whereas that of Godwin and
Wollstonecraft was anti-religious. Noyes' original belief in
communal economics sprang from his belief in the superiority
of the apostolic way of life; Godwin's and Wollstonecraft's
derived from Rousseau and the French romanticists, who believed that the institution of private property was the source
of all the major evils in modern society.

Although John Humphrey Noyes was different in many
respects from the other religious utopians, and finally succeeded in organizing a community the like of which had never
been seen in the world before, he did not deviate markedly
from the paradisaical pattern. Like Labadie, Beissel, and
Janson, he took Christ as his model, and made a touchstone of

254

his ethics. He could not tolerate what the Christian Church had done to Christ's gospel. As a young man, he had protested against the authoritarianism of the organized church and urged emancipation from all dogma and ritual. The churchmen ignored him and viewed his ideas as expressions of youthful intemperance. Little did they anticipate how far-reaching his influence was to become and what a role he was to play as a social reformer and sexual revolutionary.

The same furious fervor blazed in him as in John Ball, Thomas Munzer, and other iconoclastic zealots who sought to make the world into the kind of place Christ would have loved. Noyes did not spend his time expostulating about eternity, but rather with the everyday issues which affected the lives of everyone. No important conflict of the time escaped him. Slavery, however, was the one which concerned him most. He could not abide the fact that millions of men were owned by thousands of other men; such a condition seemed to him a violation of decency, freedom, humanity. In his own way he was as much of a firebrand in his fight against slavery as Garrison, Whittier,[1] or Lovejoy. He believed that the struggle against slavery was a struggle for a new society, a free society, in which all men should be new men, born to a new heritage. But it was not only the Negro he defended; he supported all downtrodden people and that included in the United States the Indians as well as the Negroes. He resented and fought the white man's treatment of the Indians in this country; like the early Quakers, he felt that the Indian was far more Christian in spirit than the Europeans who came to steal his land—he knew that Christianity was a matter of spirit and not of affiliation, denomination, or consecration.

In that connection it is most interesting to note that none of the utopian colonies ever had any trouble with the Indians.

[1] For a most interesting and perhaps the best description of Whittier's Abolitionist activities, the reader should turn to Albert Mordell's fascinating life of Whittier: *The Quaker Militant.*

They dealt with them in the same way that the Quakers did, that Roger Williams did, and the Indians, always desirous of being friendly with the white men who wanted to be friendly with them, respected their attitude. One of the principal reasons why the Puritans hated the Quakers was that the latter treated the Indians like human beings, not savages; equals, not inferiors. This was too much—and men like Cotton Mather said so in language untrammeled and unmitigated in its condemnation. Mather considered white men superior beings, so ordained by God, and the Indians foreordained as savages. Mather was so hostile to the Quakers he denounced them as "another sort of enemies, which may with very good reason be cast into the same History with them [the Indians]." He even sneered at the fact that the Quakers considered the "Killing of the Indians or Murdering of them" an evil. The Indians, as he saw them, were not human, at least not Christian, and he urged that they be treated as savages, and murdered whenever necessary.

Noyes never succumbed to such vicious doctrine. His attitude toward his fellow man, unlike Mather's, was governed by no national or provincial bias. He wanted to help the whole human race, not just a specific race.

He was so violent in his opposition to slavery, he denounced the government of the United States and wrote to Garrison, the great anti-slavery leader:

"I am writing that all men should know that I have subscribed my name to an instrument similar to the Declaration of '76, renouncing allegiance to the Government of the United States, and asserting the title of Jesus Christ to the throne of the world."

Then he added:

"I will give you my reasons for this 'wild deed.' When I wish to form a conception of the government of the United States (using a personified representation), I picture to myself a bloated, swaggering libertine, tram-

pling on the Bible—its own Constitution—its treaties with
the Indians—the petitions of its citizens; with one hand
whipping a Negro tied to a liberty-pole, and with the
other dashing an emaciated Indian to the ground. On
one side stand the despots of Europe, laughing and mock-
ing at the boasted liberty of their neighbor; on the other
stands the Devil, saying 'Esto perpetua.' . . . In view of
such a representation, the question urges itself upon me—
'What have I, as a Christian, to do with such a villain?'
I live on the territory which he claims—under the protection, to some extent, of the laws which he promulgates.
Must I, therefore, profess to be his friend? God forbid!
I will rather flee my country. But every other country
is under the same reprobate authority. I must, then,
either go out of the world, or find some way to live where
I am, without being a hypocrite, or a partaker in the sins
of the nation. I grant that 'the powers that be are ordained of God,' and this is not less true of individual
than national slaveholders. I am hereby justified in
remaining a slave—but not in remaining a slaveholder. Every person who is, in the usual sense of the
expression, a citizen of the United States, i.e., a voter,
politician, etc., is at once a slave and a slaveholder—in
other words, a subject and a ruler in a slaveholding government. God will justify me in the one character, but
not in the other. I must therefore separate them and
renounce the last. Holding simply the station of a subject,
as a Christian I may respect the powers that be for the
Lord's sake, but I cannot make myself a partaker of their
ungodly deeds by mingling in their counsels or assisting
their operations. . . . I have renounced active co-operation
with the oppressor on whose territories I live; now I
would find a way to put an end to his oppression. But he
is manifestly a reprobate; reproof and instruction only
aggravate his sins. I cannot attempt to reform him, because I am forbidden to 'cast pearls before swine.' I
must therefore either consent to remain a slave, till God
removes the tyrant, or I must commence war upon him,
by a declaration of independence and other weapons suitable to the character of a son of God. . . ." [1]

[1] Quoted from Robert Allerton Parker: *A Yankee Saint*, p. 49.

Wild as this doctrine may have seemed, it was no wilder, no more inflammatory, no more dynamitic, than that of dozens of other Abolitionists, many of whom wanted to tear down the pillars of the church, uproot society, and destroy every semblance of the established order which supported the slave-regime. Even Lenin's diatribes, dedicated to an attack upon capitalism, were no more challenging than those of the men and women who believed that if slavery was not eradicated from America the country would become a land of indecency and inhumanity.

Noyes was not only one of them, he was one of the most important of them—and one of the most daring and courageous of them.

II

It was Christ's doctrine of love which inspired Noyes and his followers to adopt a communist way of life. As early as 1843, Noyes wrote that "a spirit of love naturally led us into a sort of community of goods." But his community had not begun with this principle, as had the millennialist communities. They had just worked into it naturally, inevitably, one might almost say, as they found it the easiest, simplest, most decent way to live. They were Perfectionists, as they described themselves, and economic communism was as close to perfection as they could find in that sphere of activity.

Putney, Vermont, was the place of their origin. They were only a handful when they first gathered there. In their hearts, and especially in that of John Humphrey Noyes, lived the same dream which had inspired the earlier utopians. "My father was a zealot; perhaps today he would be called a fanatic," wrote Pierrepont Noyes, the son of John Humphrey Noyes, but, he added, "reading his early letters one can follow the logic which led him irresistibly to the conclusion that the demon selfishness could not be slain in a world which worshiped riches. He preached the communism of the Primitive

Church and his followers accepted his logic." ¹ But John Humphrey Noyes, as we shall see, was more significant than the other utopian leaders; he had far more imagination, initiative, and courage. Beissel, Kelpius, Janson swore by the Christian fundamentals, those embodied in primitive Christianity, but there they stopped; Noyes was willing to challenge the fundamentals themselves and when he believed those fundamentals needed alteration, as later he did in the periphery of sex, he undertook it without hesitation or trepidation.

Putney was scarcely a place. With flattery it might be called a village. It was Noyes and his followers who gave life to it. They organized the "Putney Corporation of Perfectionists," an organization which was established to achieve *perfectionism,* as Noyes conceived it. The group began in 1838, but it was not until 1844 that a "Contract of Partnership" was drawn up, which stated that all the property owned by the group was to be shared in common. The total investment was $25,940, and the members of the Corporation thus established were exactly four: the two Noyeses, John and George, John Skinner, and John Miller. Undoubtedly the predominance of Johns among them gave them pause, but they believed it a holy omen. Christ's favorite disciple had been named John.

Without the dominant force of John Humphrey Noyes's personality the colony could never have grown. One of the first things he did was to arrange, with almost dictatorial authority, for his sister Harriet to marry John Skinner, and his sister Charlotte to marry John Miller. This added immediately to the membership of the colony, and potentially to an even greater membership when their respective children should be born. With all his spiritual vision Noyes was a practical man. He wanted his project to succeed, if only to prove that God's trust in him was justified. Soon others joined the group, children came, and the community became a colony.

¹ Pierrepont Noyes: *My Father's House,* p. 125.

Unfortunately, Noyes is known mainly because of his sex ideas, his belief in sexual communism, his theory of "Male Continence." Important as sex was, Noyes was awake to the fact that it was a part and not the whole of life. He was interested also in all life's other aspects. Nothing eluded his concern. He became involved with dietetic problems, the preparation of food, the digestive functions, the relationship between body and mind, the functioning of the total organism, and everything which demanded inquiry of a scientific character. Had he been born fifty years later, he would have become a scientist instead of a utopian. He insisted upon the superiority of cold meals over hot ones, mainly because they saved so much labor and freed women from the bondage of the kitchen. More than that, he issued an ordinance against the three-meal diet and urged his followers to adopt it as a new form of wisdom.

> "Believing that the practice of serving up in a formal manner three meals of heated food daily is a requirement of custom and not of nature . . . unnecessary and injurious to health and comfort . . . subjecting females almost universally to the worst of slavery . . . we hereby notify our friends that we shall omit, in our ordinary domestic arrangements, two of the usual meals, viz., dinner and supper, and instead of them shall keep in this pantry a supply and variety of eatables, which we invite them to partake of at such times and in such manner as appetite or fancy may suggest." [1]

This attitude toward food was characteristic of that which prevailed toward all things: economics, politics, sex. Curiously enough, the labor-saving element was always primary. Noyes wanted no waste of energy in any direction. The whole communal structure of the group was based upon his theory of efficiency of production, distribution, and organization. There must be no loose cogs in the wheel of the community. All must work for one and one for all.

[1] Quotation taken from Parker: *op. cit.*, p. 97.

Unlike Alcott, his attitude was more pragmatic than idealistic. Alcott believed in deprivation of personality, renunciation of self, sacrifice of desire, whereas Noyes believed in the
expression of personality, realization of self, enjoyment of
desire. Alcott, as we have seen, was a progressive educator,
a philosopher, and an advanced dreamer, whose dreams embodied enough of reality to make them the challenge of the
day. Nevertheless, to the end, Alcott remained a Puritan at
heart. He could not get the New England virus out of his
blood, he could not shake himself loose, to change the figure,
from the grip of the Puritan tradition. Noyes, on the other
hand, hated the Puritan tradition, loathed all that it stood for,
and fought it and all other traditions which had a theocratic
basis. He did not believe in the supremacy of the clergy,
which the Puritans tried to institute, because he was convinced
that the clergy was and would always be an enemy of freedom.
His faith was in the people and not in the preachers. He was
as suspicious of the clergy as any atheist could be; he distrusted its words, gestures, prophecies. He wanted men to
worship as they pleased and, if in his colony he was practically
a dictator, it was because his followers set him up as such.
Later, when a crisis arose, he was the first to withdraw from
the group and to allow it freedom of decision. Clergymen, he
insisted, "organize themselves, like fire companies, ready at
a moment's warning, with engine and bucket, firehook and
ladder, to rush forth and extinguish the flames of fanaticism
that will occasionally break out in every community."

Noyes wrote this in his publication, *The Witness*, and he
wrote many other things in a similar vein, bristling with challenge, and barbed with bitterness. He was not a naïve man.
He believed in a definite way of life, and he was willing to
labor and fight for it.

The economic organization of Oneida did not differ widely
from that of the other utopian communities. Noyes, to be
sure, with a sense of superb diplomacy, declared himself a

conservative, and put himself on record when he declared that "the reformers must sit down and count the cost of the war they were engaged in, and not only become, but prove themselves more truly conservative than their adversaries, or they will labor in vain."

Noyes, in this one respect, was a quibbler. He was not a conservative, and never had been. He was a radical and could be nothing else. It was Andrew Lang who wrote that the first man who asked, "Why, Why?" was the world's first radical—and John Humphrey Noyes was such a man. He was a true radical, even though many of his convictions would never have satisfied the self-appointed radicals of his day. Noyes, however, wanted to cling, as did the other utopians, to the radicalism of primitive Christianity and he thought he could be more successful if he called his approach conservative rather than radical. It was a form of intellectual camouflage which he thought would gain his end. But it didn't. No one who knew Noyes or was acquainted with his doctrine ever thought of him as a conservative. They knew him as he was, a religious sans-culotte, a moral incendiary, a political anarchist.

It is more likely, however, that he believed a true radical like himself might legitimately be styled a conservative. At all events, he considered most self-styled radicals hopeless visionaries and sentimentalists. Noyes himelf never lost touch with the earth in his plots and plans for a new race; cloudland concepts did not tempt him. He wanted to keep his feet upon solid soil and his hands on human beings and not on marionettes, silhouettes, or dreamettes. He believed that most of the utopian collectivists in the country were impractical enthusiasts, lacking in insight and ingenuity. He was determined above all to be a realist, an economic, moral, and social engineer.

Both Putney and Oneida, consequently, were organized upon a most scientific and efficient basis. One of Noyes's "pet" ideas in that connection was his belief in the principle of

"Mutual Criticism," which he was convinced would give community life new soundness and significance.   No better illustration of what "Mutual Criticism" meant can be found than in this description of it by one of Noyes's followers:

"The little school at Putney went through a long discipleship before the system of Mutual Criticism was instituted. The process was perfectly natural. Love for the truth and love for one another had been nurtured . . . till it could bear any strain. The year 1846 was known among us as the year of Revival. . . . In one of our meetings Mr. Noyes talked about the possible rending of the veil between us and the invisible world . . . but were we prepared to make music, with this glorious company? . . . We were . . . barbarians to the refined society of heaven. . . . But he said there was one chord of sympathy between us and them . . . and that was the spirit of improvement. . . . As one measure he proposed Mutual Criticism, which is now such a pillar in our system. The plan was received with enthusiasm and one of our most earnest members offered himself immediately as the subject of the first experiment. The others engaged to study his character, get their impressions clear and bring to the next meeting the verdict of their sincerest scrutiny. . . . When the affair transpired we were not prepared for its solemnity. If some of us were sportively disposed in the beginning, we were serious enough before the surgery was over. There was a spirit in our midst which was like the Word of God, quick and powerful, a discerner of the thoughts and intents of the heart. All that winter we felt that we were in the Day of Judgment. Criticism had free course and it was like fire in the stubble of our faults. . . . It was painful in its first application, but agreeable in its results. One brother who has a vivid memory of his sensations says that while he was undergoing the process he felt like death, as though he were dissected with a knife; but when it was over he felt as if he had been washed." [1]

[1] *Mutual Criticism.* (Office of the American Socialist, Oneida, N. Y., 1876.)

"Mutual Criticism" was to lend strength to sociality, weld individuals closer together as a solid whole. So intimate a part of community procedure did "Mutual Criticism" become, individual members would undertake it every morning and every night, insisting that their relatives or friends criticise them, reveal their weaknesses from day to day, in order that they might profit from their advice; before they undertook new tasks, ventured upon strange journeys, they subjected themselves to the process of "Mutual Criticism"; before they did anything, "Mutual Criticism" was imperative.[1] "Mutual Criticism" included the infinitesimal as well as the infinite, the microcosm as well as the macrocosm. Men were criticised for smoking tobacco as well as for their ideas and concepts of God. In that connection, it is interesting to observe that tobacco-smoking was popular among the group, until it was discovered through "Mutual Criticism" that women disliked it, whereupon the habit was abandoned. In one sense, their "Mutual Criticism" was like the "Bolshevik self-criticism" practiced by the Communists in Soviet Russia; the main difference was the Noyesites utilized it as a means of self-advance, whereas the Bolsheviks exploited it as a means of political extermination.

Such criticism was often carried to fantastic if not pathologic extremes, as in the case of Charles C—, who was forbidden to marry the woman he loved, because the community believed she should have another father for her children. The following description of what happened is most revealing:

"Charles C— was a young man of great ability and singularly noble character. He was deeply in love with Miss B—, who like himself had been brought to the community in early childhood; being a young man of ardent temperament, his affectionate nature led him into such relations with the object of his love that frequent criticism was necessary to strengthen him against temptations that

[1] Allan Estlake: *The Oneida Community*, 1900, p. 60.

might militate against his loyalty to Christ. This love was reciprocal and was so intense that it could not easily be made subordinate to the highest allegiance of all.

"The community, always solicitous to discourage selfishness in conjugal intercourse as in all departments of life, when Charles C— and Miss B— had both been welcomed as candidates for parenthood, deemed it prudent that she should become a mother by some husband of her choice and that Charles C— should choose some other sweetheart to woo for the purpose of paternity.

"Not only temperament but tendencies that were in any way objectionable were recognized as being undesirable qualities to intensify by the uniting of two parents having the trait in common. . . . This may have been a trial for Charles C— but he never harboured a jealous thought of the man who was united to the same woman.

"Miss B— had been an object of admiration not only to Charles C— but to many of us. She was a young lady of great beauty. . . . Motherhood ripened her into a most charming woman and my friendship gradually grew into courtship. Although Charles C— was aware of my affection for Miss B— he was so far from evincing the least resentment that our relations continued to be those of the most heartfelt friendship.

"One evening when I was in Miss B—'s room, her child was so fretful that our efforts failed to sooth it. The door opened and Charles C— taking the child from its crib so quietly that we were scarcely aware of his presence, carried it into his own room. . . . His solicitude lest our courtship be interrupted, his manly, yet delicate way of acting on so generous an impulse made an impression on my heart that can never be effaced." [1]

Noyes believed that progress was made faster by changing the hearts of men than by altering the conditions of society, and in achieving that end, he viewed "Mutual Criticism" as an invaluable aid. "As the mass of mankind cannot easily be moved to change, the only alternative is to secede and form small insulated associations," he wrote in *The Perfectionist*,

[1] *Ibid.*, pp. 74-77.

and then added, "The error which we conceive lies at the foundation of all these schemes [those of other utopian colonies] is a false view of the causes and nature of the evils which afflict society as it exists. The disease to be cured is supposed to be *objective*, when in fact it is *subjective*. Relief is sought in a change of *circumstances*, while it can be found only in a change of *heart*." [1] Once that change of heart is accomplished, man becomes one with the angels. Their communism was not man-made, but God-inspired. Into the initial records of the Oneida Community, words to that effect were written:

> "The Oneida Association regards itself as a branch of the kingdom of heaven, the exponent of the principles and servants of the spiritual will of the kingdom. It has no written constitution or by-laws—no formal mode of electing officers. . . . In place of all formulas it relies on inspiration and working *through* those who approve themselves as agents of God." [2]

In the same report it was declared that "love is the appropriate reward of labor; that in a just spiritual medium every individual by the fixed laws of attraction will draw around him an amount of love exactly proportionate to his intrinsic value and efficiency, and thus all accounts will be punctually and justly balanced without the complicated and cumbersome machinery of bookkeeping." [3]

This was what Noyes had dreamed, and what he realized in both Putney and Oneida. Unlike Owen's community, where members had betrayed the trust of the founder and had actually stolen his money, Noyes's colony was impeccably honest and virtuous. The devotion of his followers to the communist ideal was unimpeachable. Their attitude was earnest, steadfast, enthusiastic.

[1] *The Perfectionist*, Vol. II. No. 11, July 15, 1843.
[2] *First Annual Report of the Oneida Association to Jan. 1, 1849*, p. 12.
[3] *Ibid.*, p. 15.

III

Putney was the mother of Oneida, just as experiment is the mother of invention. In Putney, Noyes developed his communist conceptions of economics and sex. In economics his contribution was not especially singular or significant. To a large degree it followed the same economic pattern as the other utopian colonies. In sex, however, his contribution was so original and challenging it startled the ears of the world. He became an international pioneer. The country was aroused, and the whole world became excited by it. What he proposed was not a variation in the form of marriage, but the inauguration of an entire new system of it. What he proposed was not reformistic but revolutionary. Reformers were interested then in freeing marriage from many of its feudal encumbrances, making divorce a privilege for all, endowing women with the same rights in the marital contract as men; but beyond that few of them were willing to go. Of course, two generations before, as previously noted, William Godwin and Mary Wollstonecraft had urged the total reorganization of the marital system, advocated free instead of contractual love, encouraged women to have illegitimate children in defiance of convention, stressed the importance of lovers living apart instead of in the same domicile; but they had never got very far with their proposals. They were willing enough to practice them themselves, but became considerably alarmed when their daughter sought to imitate them. George Sand, too, and the so-called George Sandist movement were no less revolutionary in their challenge. But such ideas appealed to individuals rather than to groups and their influence was dispersive rather than concentrated. Noyes, on the other hand, was interested in group change, group marriage, and he strove to convert his ideas into a group ideal.

He was not interested in a variation in the form of marriage, but in the creation of a new marriage form. And he succeeded.

It all began with what became known as his Battle Axe letter, in which he expressed views among the most iconoclastic of his day. It appeared in a paper, edited by Theophilus Gates, called *The Battle Axe and Weapons of War*. The letter was written originally by Noyes to his disciple, David Harrison, a youth who believed that John Noyes would sit at the throne of God, adjacent to Christ himself. Few letters have initiated a more widespread international discussion. It is too important not to be quoted in part:

"When the will of God is done on earth, as it is in heaven, there will be no marriage. The marriage supper of the Lamb is a feast at which every dish is free to every guest. Exclusiveness, jealousy, quarreling, have no place there, for the same reason as that which forbids the guests at a thanksgiving dinner to claim each his separate dish, and quarrel with the rest for his rights. In a holy community there is no more reason why sexual intercourse should be restrained by law, than why eating and drinking should be—and there is as little occasion for shame in the one case as in the other. God has placed a wall of partition between the male and female during the apostasy, for good reasons, which will be broken down in the resurrection, for equally good reasons. But woe to him who abolishes the law of the apostasy before he stands in the holiness of the resurrection. The guests of the marriage supper may have each his favorite dish, each a dish of his own procuring, and that without the jealousy of exclusiveness. I call a certain woman my wife—she is yours, she is Christ's, and in him she is the bride of all saints. She is dear in the hand of a stranger, and according to my promise to her I rejoice. My claim upon her cuts directly across the marriage covenant of this world, and God knows the end. Write if you wish to hear from me."

Gates's paper was a curious concoction of radicalism, cultism, and religionism, the like of which had never been seen before on this, or perhaps on any, continent. Like so many others, Gates believed in the millennium, but it was the sexual side of it which was his main concern. His paper was dedicated to an examination of the fate of the sexes in paradise. "Men and women," he contended, "had better change their partners twenty times over, under the best regulations they can make with each other, so as at length to have one with whom they can live in harmony and be in the order of God, than to live in any kind of strife and disagreement and live in the order of the devil." [1] He and his wife consequently abandoned their artificial marital relation and decided to live within the law of God and not that of man—which in later days became familiarly known as a state of free love.

Noyes was both dismayed and furious when he learned that his acolyte, David Harrison, had been indirectly responsible for the letter falling into Gates's hands. Harrison had been so startled by the letter that he showed it to Simon Lovett, who in turn showed it to other people, and it was not long before it found its way into print. There was nothing in the letter which Noyes was later to disavow; in fact, he went beyond it in many of his later views. What was wrong was its premature publication—and also the place in which it was published. Harrison had not intended that the letter should be printed, and he was as unhappy as Noyes when he read it in Gates's paper. But then he added, with a twinge of sorrow in his voice, "The Lord gave me not liberty to suppress it." But this was not to be the last time that Noyes was to suffer from the stupidity of his friends.

It was this letter, which Noyes composed in the sequestered environs of Putney, that first shot him into the public eye, made him a cynosure of discussion across two continents, and brought upon him salvos of attack and praise which rang round the world. He no longer had any choice but to defend and justify his doctrine. In his paper, *The Witness*, he admitted the authenticity of the letter, and later admitted that

[1] Quoted from Parker: *op. cit.*, p. 54.

it was God's will that he should be summoned to defend "the doctrine of communism in love." Nevertheless, to shunt off some of the adverse criticism which had been vented upon him, he decided to get married; despite the impetuosity of his temperament, he did not lose sight of the practicality of circumstance. After all, marriage was economic as well as erotic. He decided that Harriet Holton, who had been donating with reasonable generosity to his paper, should become his wife.

Not for a second did Noyes question Harriet's willingness. After all, he was God's ambassador, and he was honoring Harriet by offering her the privilege of becoming his wife. Harriet accepted his proposal almost immediately, and a unique marriage resulted. Noyes's proposal was characteristic. He was as concerned as ever with marriages in heaven as well as on earth. "We can enter into engagements with each other," he declared, "which shall limit the range of our affections. . . . I desire and expect my yoke-fellow will love all who love God, whether man or woman, with a warmth and strength of affection which is unknown to earthly lovers, and as freely as if she stood in no particular connection with me."

Seldom has any such proposal or marital theory ever emerged since ancient times. It marked a revolution in *mores*.

Another episode in the evolution of this new *mores* was to be found in the first sexual contract ever drawn up in the history of man. The witty, dynamic, irrepressible Mary Craigin, wife of the ever faithful, ever dull George Craigin, had fallen in love with Abram Smith, who claimed clairvoyant and divine powers in his own right, and the feud which resulted could have been settled by no other person than John Noyes himself. Because of his desire to plumb the complexities of the situation, the motives involved, the heavenly factors at work, and achieve a solution satisfactory to all those connected with it, Noyes decided to draw up a contractual agreement which would resolve all contradictions.

The agreement read as follows:

"The transaction between Mr. Smith and Mrs. Cragin
was characterized by two vices—licentiousness and deception. Both were undoubtedly guilty of both. But I judge
from all the evidence I can get, that Mrs. Cragin took the
lead and was the principal agent in the licentiousness, and
that Mr. Smith took the lead and was the principal agent
in the deception. She kindled the fire and he excused and
justified and concealed it. This is exactly in accordance
with the respective tendencies of the two sexes. Woman
is strong in the department of susceptibility; man, in that
of intellect. Do parties heartily accede to this judgment?
J. H. Noyes.
  "I do subscribe most fully to the above decision and do
wish to take on myself the most of the evil. A. C. Smith.
  "I think that Mr Noyes is correct in his judgment; and
that I took the place of Eve in tempting and seducing
man, who is made in the image of God. I sincerely ask
Mr. Smith's forgiveness for having dragged him down
into sensuality. M. E. Craigin." [1]

From this time on, Noyes was to become increasingly involved in the sexual sphere. He not only had to solve the
sexual conflicts of his disciples, but also his own. To begin
with, he became concerned with the problem of children. As
he saw his wife become pregnant with appalling frequency, he
began to question the laws of nature. Why should women be
subjected to such continuous confinement and misery? Was
it man's duty to accept nature's law of infinite proliferation,
or was it to contravene it as far as possible? Noyes gave long
and deep thought to the question before deciding upon an
answer. That answer proved simple. Since man had spent
most of his time controlling and combating nature in the
material realm, there was no reason why he should not practice a similar procedure in the sexual realm. Thereupon Noyes
set about the task of circumventing nature to prevent undesired
pregnancy. In those pre-Margaret Sanger days (after all,
the American Puritans had no knowledge of the divers and

[1] Quoted from Parker: *op. cit.*, p. 87.

curious contraceptives employed by the dextrous Chinese or the sophisticated French), the idea of preventing conception seemed impossible. Noyes's discovery of such a technique made him into a miracle man.

The method which Noyes advocated became internationally known as that of "male continence." At this point it is better to let Noyes himself speak, because no one can describe his technique so well:

> "We begin by analyzing the act of sexual intercourse. It has a beginning, a middle and an end. Its beginning and most elementary form is the simple *presence* of the male organ in the female. Then usually follows a series of reciprocal motions. Finally this exercise brings on a nervous action or ejaculatory crisis which expels the seed. Now we insist that this whole process—up to the very moment of emission is *voluntary*, entirely under the control of the moral faculty and *can be stopped at any point.*

> "Suppose, then, that a man in lawful intercourse with woman, choosing for good reason not to beget a child or to disable himself, should stop at the primary stage and content himself with simple presence continued as long as agreeable? Would there be any harm? It cannot be injurious to refrain from voluntary excitement. Would there be no *good*? I appeal to the memory of every man who has had good sexual experience to say whether on the whole the sweetest and noblest period of intercourse with woman is not that *first* moment of simple presence and spiritual effusion before the muscular exercise begins.

> "But we may go farther. Suppose the man chooses for good reasons . . . to enjoy not only the simple *presence*, but also the reciprocal motion and yet to stop short of the final crisis? Again I ask would there be any harm? Or would it do no good? I suppose the physiologists might say and I would acknowledge that the excitement by motion might be carried so far that the voluntary suppression of the commencing crisis would be injurious. But what if the man, knowing his own power and limits, should not even approach the crisis and yet be able to enjoy the presence and the motion ad libitum? If you say

that this is impossible, I answer that I *know* it is possible
—nay, that it is easy. . . . In the normal condition men
are entirely competent to choose in sexual intercourse
whether they will stop at any point in the voluntary stages
of it and so make it simply an act of communion or go
through to the involuntary stage and make it an act of
propagation.

"The situation may be compared to a stream in the three
conditions of a fall, a course of rapids above the fall and
still water above the rapids. The skillful boatman may
choose whether he will remain in the still water or venture
more or less down the rapids or run his boat over the
fall. . . .

"The wholesale and ever ready objection to this method
is that it is unnatural and unauthorized by the example of
other animals. I may answer in a wholesale way that
cooking, wearing clothes, living in houses and almost
everything else done by civilized man is unnatural in the
same sense. . . . Until men and women find a way to
elevate their sexual performances above those of the
brutes by introducing into them moral culture, they are
living an *unnatural* degradation.

"But I will come closer to this objection. The real
meaning of it is that Male Continence in sexual intercourse is a difficult and injurious interruption of a natural
act. But every instance of self denial is an interruption
of some natural act. . . . The lover who stops at a kiss
denies himself a natural progression.

"The amative and propagative functions of the sexual
organs are distinct from each other and may be separated. . . .

"It is held in the world that the sexual organs have two
distinct functions, viz., the urinary and the propagative.
We affirm that they have three, the urinary, the propagative and the amative, i.e., they are conductors first of
the urine, secondly, of the semen, and thirdly, of the social
magnetism. . . . We insist that the amative function—
that which consists in a simple union of persons, making
'of twain one flesh,' and giving a medium of magnetic
and spiritual interchange—is a distinct and independent
function . . . superior to the productive." [1]

[1] *Bible Communism. Male Continence*, 1853, pp. 7-12.

But Noyes did not stop there. He believed so implicity in his discovery that he insisted that it converted sex from a function into an art. Not only an art, but a "fine art." "Amative intercourse," he swore, "will have a place among the 'fine arts.' Indeed, it will rank above music, painting and sculpture, etc., for it combines the charms and benefits of them all. The practice which we propose will give new speed to the advance of civilization and refinement. The self-control, retention of life and ascent out of sensualism . . . will raise the race to new vigor and beauty, moral and physical. And the refining factors of sexual love . . . will be increased a thousandfold when sexual intercourse becomes an honored method of . . . communion and each is married to all." [1] Even before this, Noyes had lost his standing with the orthodox religious groups; he had been dismissed from the Divinity School, and his license to preach had been withdrawn by the New Haven West Association. None of these attacks, however, had intimidated him. "I have taken away their [the clergy's] license to sin and they keep on sinning," he wrote, "so though they have taken away my license to preach, I shall go on preaching." [2] But this ecclesiastical onslaught was as nothing compared with what happened after Noyes released to the world—no less—his theory of male continence.

That doomed him in the eyes of the orthodox, the conventional, the conservative, for all time. Nothing but success could live that down—and though Noyes achieved success with his theory for a while, its ultimate failure resulted in the momentary burial of his dream. Later Madame Karezza was to revive it, unaware of Noyes's trail-blazing efforts in that direction, and for a period Noyes's theory of male continence became known as the Karezza method. [3] In more recent days, Noyes has received the credit that was due him

[1] John Humphrey Noyes: *Male Continence, op. cit.,* pp. 12-16.
[2] Benjamin B. Warfield: *Noyes and His Bible Communists,* Bibliotheca Sacra, April, 1921, p. 181.
[3] Edward Carpenter: *Love's Coming of Age.*

as a pioneer in a forbidden field. He was the Margaret Sanger of the nineteenth century—and yet more than that, because he believed not only in limiting childbirth, but also in a form of sexual communism which Margaret Sanger, with her middle-class idealism, could never have envisaged.

Noyes was one of those great, childlike geniuses, with a touch of the pathologic about him; he could be sophomoric as well as profound, gay as well as solemn, tantalizing as well as terrific. He was a paradox from every angle. No one really understood him, and ofttimes it is doubtful if he understood himself. He was driven by social instinct as well as individual intelligence, and when he was sure of himself, he would fight heaven and earth in order to carry out what he wished—as he did upon numerous occasions.

Although Noyes's theory of male continence never became widely popular outside of his Oneida group, it remained a matter of discussion for years and decades afterward, and sexologists like Havelock Ellis expatiated upon its virtues, and lauded it as a unique and striking discovery. Noyes's concern with it, as we have seen, was to free women from the bondage of pregnancy; he wanted to make women equal to men in the sex act. If women could feel sure they would not become pregnant every time they had sexual relations, they would be able to view sex as an ecstatic instead of an ominous experience. With his own Oneida flock, Noyes had no difficulty applying his theory. Women greeted it with enthusiasm and pursued it with joy. In the outside world, on the contrary, it was seldom practiced.

Important as male continence was in the Noyes curriculum, it was the sexual communism which it made physically and psychologically possible that caused most of the hostility from which Oneida eventually suffered. Noyes's aspiration was that there should be no private property in sex, that no one man should cling to any one woman, that no one should claim children as his own, that all men should be prospective husbands of all women, and all children the scions of all the men and women in the community. Only in this way could the private-property aspect of the family be eliminated; only in this way could every man love every child, and not feel a particular concern only for his own; if one child became ill, every man and woman in the community became concerned, and not just the immediate mother and father. This was like Socrates' concept of sociality in which everyone felt for everyone else, one for all and all for one. If one has a sore thumb, said Socrates, the whole body feels the hurt; so likewise, if one member of a society is suffering, every other member must share in his misery until it is abated.

It took considerable time before Noyes arrived at this conviction. It took even longer before he evolved it into a social philosophy. It sprang originally from his vision of heavenly love, but it derived its practical direction from personal experience. In his quest for fundamentals, he found sex a difficult enemy to encounter. He never mastered it. His belief in sexual communism, it must not be forgotten, was conceived long before he ever practiced it. For years he was a strict and solemn monogamist. He was led to practice his own ideas only after he found himself entangled in a sexual problem of his own.

And of all people, it was with Mary Craigin, concerning whose sexual involvement with Abram Smith he had acted as an arbiter in the past, that he became implicated. Mary was not what might be called a brilliant or intelligent woman, nor for that matter a home-maker, but she had, extending from head to toe, a sexual apparatus, which, like that of a firefly, fascinated everyone within sight. Men seldom love women for their brains; they love them because they are lovely, because they are seductive, because they are fireflies, because they illuminate and quicken the impulse of their lives. Noyes was not dissimilar in that respect. Women's brains interested him little. He considered them inferior to men and never hesitated to conceal the fact. His interest in women, as in Mary Craigin, was emotional, inspirational, sexual.

John Noyes and Mary Craigin, walking alone upon numerous occasions, discovered themselves attracted toward each other, and Noyes, being awkward at such matters, didn't know what to do about it. Mary, with her previous experience, was less troubled and distressed about the situation. After continued association, they found themselves so drawn to each other that sexual intimacy became inevitable. Mary didn't mind and was in favor of such intimacy. But Noyes's conscience was troubled. He didn't know what to do. Above all, he didn't want to do what was wrong. Yet something had to be done.

So, as customary and characteristic, he decided upon a conference. He called together his wife Harriet, and Mary's husband George, and Mary, in order to discuss the situation. Urging calmness and considerateness as necessary virtues, he described exactly what had occurred. Harriet Noyes and George Craigin listened with marked and painful astonishment; it seemed even more incredible to Harriet than to George. Although John Noyes had voiced such sentiments before, neither of them believed that he, their inviolate leader, would or could ever practice them. John Noyes, as usual, triumphed. Both Harriet and George agreed that he should take Mary as his new wife. They both spoke with admiration of his refusal to have sex relations with Mary until after he had discussed the matter with them.

If this did not mark an important point of departure in the sexual history of the United States, it certainly did in the history of the Oneida Community.

What John Noyes and Mary Craigin began, very rapidly developed into a community custom. The multiplication of marriages increased through the years, but never in an undisciplined or uninspired manner. Like the Mormons, the Oneidists did not believe in romance: kissing, caressing, embracing were tabu. They were frowned upon as the dark devices of Satan. When a man and a woman were attracted to each other, it had to be because of the will of God; otherwise the attraction was false, fugitive. In the deepest sense, all such relations were viewed more as heavenly than earthly ventures.

It is interesting to note some of the results of this unusually complex marital system with its revolutionary challenge to the old *mores.* Nothing like this had been attempted in centuries. It represented inbreeding and incest in a most intimate form, and strikingly enough, the results were contrary to those predicted by eugenists. In a scientific study made of the experiment, Anita N. McGee came to the conclusion that it was remarkably succesful. Here is what she has to say about it:

"Certain results of this experiment . . . probably the most systematic and extensive of modern times and civilised peoples, are displayed by the children born under its conditions. . . .

"Speaking only of the elder children, now twenty-two years old and under, the pride taken by the experimenters . . . is certainly warranted. The boys are tall—several over six feet—broad-shouldered and finely proportioned; the girls are robust and well-built. The present occupations of the older youths are interesting in connection with the fact that with the exception of the Noyes family and half a dozen lawyers, doctors and clergymen, the Oneida Community was composed of farmers and mechanics, and that the mothers generally belonged to the classes employed in manual labor. Of the oldest sixteen boys, ten are in business, chiefly employed as clerks, foremen, etc., in manufactories of the joint-stock company. The eleventh is a musician of repute, another a medical student, one has passed through college and is studying law, one is a college senior and one is entering college after winning state and local scholarships. . . . Finally, the sixteenth boy is a mechanic, the only one engaged in manual labor. Of the six girls between eighteen and twenty-two years, three are especially intellectual. It is also interesting to observe that the fathers (including

Noyes himself) were as a rule the intellectual superiors of
their mates, and inquiry develops the fact known in the
community that in these cases the children are markedly
superior to the maternal stock.

"As an index of the calibre of the offspring of stirpiculture, it may be mentioned that a favorite amusement
is found in a debating society of three girls and four of the
boys, which meets during the summer when all are at
home." [1]

Had the colony lasted over a century, it would be most interesting to see what would have developed with the younger
generations. It might have altered the whole character of
eugenic theory.

Noyes had been early convinced that disease was a fiction,
and that what man calls disease is only a result of sexual mal-
adjustment and malnutrition. If men and women could make
love to each other whenever God inspired them, regardless of
convention or custom, illness, Noyes believed, would vanish like
a vapor from the face of the earth. Noyes would have no
traffic with medicine or medical men; he viewed the latter as
magicians of darkness, and shut the gates of his colony against
them. But the conquest of disease was but part of Noyes's
program; it was the conquest of death that he was most interested in, and he believed that death, with the aid of Christ,
could be abolished. Though he never said it, it is reasonable
to believe that he entertained, deep in his heart, the hope that
some day, like Christ, he would be able to bring the dead back
into life. He had already achieved various faith cures, had
succeeded in freeing Mrs. Hall from her paralysis and restored
her ability to walk. These achievements had made him known
as a faith-healer in many parts of the state.

In this, as in all other things, Noyes was trying to strike at
fundamentals. However fantastic his theories might be, they
were always involved with the roots of things. His com-

[1] Anita Newcomb McGee: "An Experiment in Human Stirpiculture,"
from *The American Anthropolgist,* October, 1891, pp. 324, 325.

munism was thoroughgoing, more consistently thoroughgoing than that practiced by any other communist colony in the country. When he brought God into his calculations, it was always as a prime-mover in the cause of events—a force, a drive, a cosmic urge. Otherwise, he was practical as an engineer.

Noyes not only wanted woman to have equal rights with man in the economic and erotic spheres, but he also wanted to adopt all the methods and techniques which would help her achieve such equality. He objected to woman's dress because it was "immodest." It tended to set her off from man, convert her into a sexual being instead of a being who had sex, and he insisted that women should dress as much like men as possible. "When the distinction of the sexes is reduced to the bounds of nature and decency, by the removal of the shame partition," Noyes wrote, "and woman becomes what she ought to be, a female man (like the Son in the Godhead), a dress will be adopted that will be at the same time the most simple and the most beautiful; and it will be the same, or nearly the same, for both sexes. The dress of children—frock and pantalets—is in good taste. . . . This or something like it will be the uniform of vital society." Following the George Sand tradition, Noyes was even in favor of the bobbed-hair technique. It made the sexes more alike and at the same time made both of them look younger, fresher, and more dynamic. The sexual element would be diminished, the spiritual exalted.

It might be a little unfair to Noyes to say that he hid his sexual appetencies beneath spiritual aspirations, and yet at the same time there can be little doubt that the sexual factor was dominant, however, unconsciously, in many of his decisions. He was a powerfully-sexed man, and though he was unaware of it, his sexual drive functioned decisively in his behavior. Without it he probably would never have been led to the conclusions which he arrived at, decided upon, and consummated.

His communism was not of the Stalinist variety popular today in Soviet Russia; it was a God-like communism, not a godless one. "I would regret it," wrote Noyes's son, Pierrepont Noyes, "if the Oneida Community were to be confused with that modern 'communism' which denies God and makes material consideration paramount. The community adopted communism only that the members might live the unselfish lives ordained by Jesus Christ. This communism was non-political and non-contentious. My father aimed at a system under which the individual would forget self and strive for the happiness of all. It was thus he interpreted the spirit of the Primitive Christian Church." [1]

Noyes's son goes on to describe the life the colony lived, and many of his observations are extremely valuable today. "A review of my early psychology confirms a suspicion I have long entertained," he wrote, "that the desire for exclusive ownership of things is not a primal human instinct. Unquestionably acquisitiveness bulks large in the life of today. It is reckoned one of the important forces behind progress and a necessary support for civilized society. And yet, may it not be itself a product of our particular form of civilization? Did primeval man have anything he called his own except food which he devoured as fast as he could?"

The son goes on to describe how successfully the community managed to "exorcise" the spirit of acquisitiveness from its midst. "We were keen," he wrote, "for our favorite sleds, but it never occurred, to me at least, that I could possess a sled to the exclusion of the other boys. So it was with all Children's House property." When Pierrepont Noyes went away on a visit he never wore his *own* suit, but one of the community's "best suits."

The same tradition prevailed among the adults. As his father advised, the women dressed in the simplest costumes possible, short dresses, pantalets, bobbed hair, anything and

[1] Pierrepont Noyes: *op. cit.,* p. 125.

282 WHERE ANGELS DARED TO TREAD

everything which made them look as much as possible like men. They were all one in their social philosophy.

There was one contradiction, however, which Pierrepont Noyes reports, and that is that in their games they encouraged the competitive instead of the co-operative spirit. This is most interesting, especially in the light of the experience in Soviet Russia, where they tried co-operative games for a considerable time, and then reverted to competitive ones. The younger Noyes poses the question well when he says, "All of which suggests a novel question: Why did not our elders take measures against the competitive spirit? Why did they not seek a substitute for that anti-social, or at least anti-communistic element in their training of future communists? Neither Papa Kelly nor Mr. Clarence ever frowned on competitive games. They taught us such. Ball games, foot races, all kinds of athletic contests were encouraged, not to mention spelling bees, cards and dominoes.

"Those Perfectionists adopted communism of property to eliminate material self-seeking; they dressed in simple clothes, tabooed jewelry, and the women cut their hair short to eliminate vanity; they arranged that every member should take his or her turn at the humblest kind of labor to eliminate the selfishness of pride and power; they abolished marriage to do away with selfishness in love. Why, then, did their carefully worked-out program for bringing up Perfectionist children permit them, at the character-forming age, to cultivate such an egocentric passion as personal rivalry?

"Lenin, who was, I think, much like my father in carrying theory recklessly to its logical results in practice, struggled to prevent the competitive spirit from getting a start. He exhorted youth to play games for health and refreshment, but forbade a competitive spirit.

"When I visited Moscow a few years ago, my Russian friend and guide took me to inspect a great institution where thousands of young men and women were being trained as teachers. We visited the gymnasium. There I saw some fine-looking fellows playing basketball and as I watched them I tried unsuccessfully to persuade myself that their savage struggles were engaged in and the goals 'shot' without any feeling of personal rivalry."

In the Children's House itself, such competitive doctrine was not taught. There they were instructed in "selflessness" and they believed that "only bad boys, outside boys, attacked each other; we felt superior to outside boys. We rather pitied them. We knew that 'out in the world' things were different, but in that world were Sodom and Gomorrah." The children were free from parental dotage or sadism; no one "hovered" over them, hampered them; they had more freedom than any other children of their day. One of the reasons was, as Pierrepont Noyes writes, that "none of those fathers and mothers of the Children's House had, I am convinced, any great affection for us individually." Affection they had in abundance, but it was social rather than individualistic affection.

No other communist colony was so perfect in conception and design as Oneida, and yet Oneida, like the other colonies, slid backward, trembled on the horizon, wobbled, swerved, declined, and finally gave up the ghost of its idealism, and became a capitalist enterprise undistinguished from the rest of the country. Instead of idealists, the Oneidists became materialists, and the manufacture of silverware became their life-saving industry. Before this debacle occurred, outside pressures had made it necessary for them to abandon, at least officially, their complex marriage pattern. The surrounding country and the nation as a whole had risen up, in spiritual arms at least, against the Oneida way of life. After all, men and women who were lucky enough to find one husband and one wife were bound to be jealous of those who discovered several. Though an ancient virtue, jealousy still retains its potency.

From a sociological point of view, it is most important to note that after the Oneida group was forced to forsake its marital pattern—the Mormons put up a much better fight for their belief in polygamy as a Biblical custom—the whole colony dissolved. What was left of it was more reminiscent than real. When the colony decided to become monogamous, each man claiming his own wife—one must not forget that Noyes himself had said that "love is something to give, not to claim"—its economics changed with its sex. Private property invaded every sphere. The young people decided to become monogamists—which is a youthful tendency—and, besides, the outside world had made such a deep impression upon them, and the dream of Adam was still close to their hearts; it was not long before the "complex marriage" system of John Noyes fell into desuetude.

Noyes himself had always resented such terms as "free love" or "promiscuity," because he was opposed to such concepts or practices. Noyes had been perfectly willing that women who had passed menopause, should initiate youths into the sexual act, because he believed such procedure significant. He wanted sex reduced to its minimum. Like Christ, he insisted that a man who lusted after a woman in his mind, was as guilty of adultery as one who had physical relations with her. He wanted neither man nor woman to succumb to physical desire, which he considered a low, animal impulse; sexual intimacy which did not bring soul and soul into intimacy was sacrilegious. Sex was a sacrament, in Noyes's opinion, and anything which threatened to desecrate that sacrament was wicked. No wonder that Noyes declared that "amativeness, the lion of the tribe of human passions, is conquered and civilized among us."

Interestingly enough, Noyes did not believe in the equality of men and women. In answer to the query as to whether the Oneidists believed in such equality, the following reply is revealing:

"No, we do not believe even in the equality of men, but we do believe that every man, woman and child should be surrounded by circumstances favoring the best development of heart, mind, and body, and that no one should be excluded on account of age, sex or color from engaging in any occupation for which he or she is adapted by nature or culture." [1] When they were asked whether they belonged to the Republican or the Democratic Party, their answer was typical:

"To neither; we are Theocrats."

When asked to explain their religious doctrines, they declared:

"Yes, our people generally believe in the Bible as 'the text-book of the Spirit of Truth,' and as a record of 'supernatural facts and sensible communications from God'; that God is a dual being—Father and Son; that 'evil comes from the Devil as good comes from God'; that God was in no sense the author of evil; that a 'dispensation of grace commenced at the manifestation of Christ entirely different from the preceding dispensation'; that salvation from sin is 'the special promise and gift of the new dispensation,' and is apprehended by faith in the resurrection of Christ; that Christ came the second time and established his everlasting kingdom according to promise, within one generation of his first coming; that we are now living in the 'dispensation of the fullness of times,' and that the final judgment is approaching; that 'the divine obligation to specially observe one day of the week passed away with the first or Jewish dispensation'; as also many other external observances; that the baptism of the Holy Spirit is the only baptism recognized in the new dispensation; that personal communication with Christ is a privilege of the Gospel, and when this communication is perfected it will ensure salvation from all evil, including disease and death, etc. But the doctrine regarded as most essential to Communism is that of salvation from sin through Christ."

[1] *Handbook of the Oneida Community*, 1871, p. 29.

In terms of social principles, as we have seen, no "claim of individual property" of any kind, in thing or person, was recognized. Nevertheless, as Noyes insisted, the Oneidists had "no affiliation with those commonly termed Free Lovers, because their principles and practices seem to us to tend toward anarchy. Our Communities are *families*, as distinctly bounded and separated from promiscuous society as ordinary households. . . . Community of property extends just as far as freedom of love." [1]

When the colony began to disintegrate as a communist enterprise, many of the children found themselves attacked as "bastards," and even though Mrs. Noyes declared that "we consider you children more legitimate than any in the world," it did not take the sting away. "I also remember," wrote Pierrepont Noyes, "that when we heard of a birth of a child, the question, 'Who was its father?' seemed of more interest than formerly when we had thought fathers were appointed." [2]

Not much later, John Humphrey Noyes, broken by attacks from within as well as without, wrote his famous letter, proposing the end of the "complex-marriage" system—a system which had proved astonishingly successful for over two generations. His proposal was accepted, with only one negative vote, on August 28, 1879, and monogamy became the new marital pattern. Oneidists now changed their habits, most of the men marrying the mothers of their children, as far as they knew them, and the community became the same as all others in its sexual aspects. Children were now turned over to their parents, and the Children's House, though it was allowed to continue, lost much of its former influence.

Following the sexual change came the economic one. In June, 1880, it was decided that since "family selfishness . . . destroyed the spirit of self-abnegation so essential for communal living," communism in enterprise would have to be

---

[1] Hinds: *American Communities*, p. 127.
[2] Pierrepont Noyes: *op. cit.*, pp. 149, 150.

replaced by capitalism—and it was. From that time on, Oneida became inordinately capitalistic—so capitalistic that it became "difficult to borrow a hammer." Pierrpont Noyes later added that he often heard "old members say laughingly that when they borrowed a pin, they felt in duty bound to return it."

It was heartbreaking to old Noyes, as well as to the rest of his family, to witness this dissolution of their ideals. All that they had stood for and believed in was destroyed. During the days when the "provisional government" of the colony was being organized, Noyes was away from the colony, hiding from the authorities. It was the Towner influence which triumphed over that of Noyes. Towner was in favor of a private-property regime, in terms of economics as well as sex. Silver manufacture, which had been the colony's main industry, continued, but under private auspices, as did all other economic endeavors. For years Oneida silverware maintained a high price in the market. Private individuals reaped profits from it, but the workers in the factories had little share in them. All industry was operated from a ruthless capitalistic point of view. The Oneida Community now became the Oneida Community, Limited.

And no longer did any dream of socialism remain within it.

CHAPTER XVII

Modern Times

ANARCHISM IN PRACTICE

"Man seeks freedom as the magnet seeks the pole or water its level and society can have no peace until every member is really free."

JOSIAH WARREN

"Owen begat New Harmony; New Harmony (by re-action) begat Individual Sovereignty; Individual Sovereignty begat Modern Times; Modern Times was the mother of Free Love, the Grand Pantarchy and the American branch of French Positivism."

JOHN HUMPHREY NOYES

The last of the utopian colonies that really *counted* was Josiah Warren's creation: Modern Times. It was different from the other colonies in that it stressed an anarchistic instead of a communistic way of life. Labadie, Kelpius, Beissel, Rapp, Janson, believed in the subordination of the individual and of individualistic tendencies; Warren believed in the exaltation of the individual and of individualistic liberty. The communism of the religious colonies was thorough and complete. The individual had no existence outside the pattern of the community. He existed only to the extent that he was able to function as part of the whole. Otherwise he was a nonentity. In Warren's community, on the contrary, man existed only to the extent that he was free, individual, independent, separate from the commands and demands of the community.

Warren did not acquire his convictions by divine intuition.

He early became a member of Robert Owen's New Harmony colony, studied Owen's theories thoroughly, and became an apostle who was soon as erudite as his teacher. For two dark years, perilous with gloom and the final flicker of defeat, Warren held on, still hopeful that so great an experiment could be saved.[1] Long after most of Owen's followers had left him, Warren clung to the colony, eager to rescue it from decline and destruction. But no one could salvage an enterprise founded upon such shifting sands of dreamful aspiration. The structure of it was too shaky and unstable.

At the end of the eighteenth century, intellectuals became inventors, devised new machines and contraptions; it was almost part of the education of an extraordinary young man. Thomas Jefferson, Thomas Paine, Benjamin Franklin, just to take a few American names, were always fiddling around with new inventions: Franklin invented a new stove, studied light and electricity and the nature of lightning, Tom Paine invented a new form of bridge, and Jefferson had his hands involved in a dozen potential inventions. Warren belonged among them in his curious theories about so many things and so many matters. First of all, he was a musician; he had taught music for years, and was an accomplished orchestra leader. In Cincinnati, where he settled, he decided to become an orchestra leader, in which position he might have achieved distinction if not fame, but it was not long before his inventive genius claimed the major part of his time, and he was at work on a device for burning lard, which would provide a less costly light than that derived from tallow. He was so successful in this that he organized a manufacturing company in Cincinnati, and was soon, in terms of the times, a capitalist success. It was his discovery of a process by which sun-burnt bricks could be manufactured out of lime and gravel which proved of great advantage in building houses at a low price in his Modern Times community.

[1] William Bailie: *Josiah Warren*, 1906, p. 4.

ᵣas his success at lamp manufacture, however, which had
ᵢspired Warren with a desire to join Owen's colony,
ᵤ, ᵤe believed, his wealth could be shared by all. Warren
was one of the few men of his time, and of all time, who,
without religious millennialist delusions, believed that wealth
meant something significant when it was shared by many instead of by few. In New Harmony, Warren did more than
share his burden; his contributions helped lighten the burdens
of others.

The failure of New Harmony did not discourage Warren,
who was a Boston Puritan with a revolutionary flame in his
blood. He went on with renewed courage. But New Harmony's failure taught him a lesson. Twenty-nine years after
Owen's colony had vanished he wrote:

> "Many a time in the midst of them did I say to myself,
> Oh! if the world could only assemble on these hills
> around and look down upon us through these experiences,
> what lessons they would learn! There would be no more
> French revolutions, no more patent political governments,
> no more organizations, no more constitution-making,
> law-making nor human contrivances for the foundation
> of society . . . but they could not get our experience
> and so they have kept on organizing communities,
> phalansteries, political parties and national revolutions,
> only to fail, of course, as we did, and to destroy by de-
> grees the little hope that existed of making the world
> more fit to live in."

From that time on he decided to organize a new community,
one with a new purpose, a new ideal, a new aspiration. It was
to be anarchist instead of communist. The individual was to
be protected, not the group. Warren objected to the pontifical
influence of Owen, and the suppression of individuality which
existed in New Harmony. "Personal liberty," he said, "was
at a discount," and "incentive to sustain individual effort was
lacking." Individual freedom had to be, in his eyes, the cornerstone of progress. "Man seeks freedom as the magnet seeks

the pole or water its level," he wrote, "and society can have no peace until every member is really free." The individual, not society, must be sovereign.

Warren never went to the ultimate extreme that Max Stirner did in *The Ego and His Own,* wherein the latter maintained that the individual alone counted and nothing else. He knew better than that. He knew that the individual was a product of society, but he did not believe that because that was the case, the individual had to surrender to society all his rights. He had witnessed the decay of New Harmony, read of the disintegration of other utopian colonies, and concluded that what led them to ruin was their mistake in emphasis—they emphasized society instead of the individual. In that respect, Warren was the father of American anarchism, which was later to be led by such outstanding figures as Johann Most, Emma Goldman, Alexander Berkman, Tucker, and others. If his theoretical approach was not so profound as Kropotkin's, his conclusions were just as sound.

It was in Cincinnati, when he was not yet thirty, that he developed these new ideas. And it was in Cincinnati that he first tried out his experiment in his new conception of life. All he did was to open a country store, which he called the Equity Store; it was to be based upon the "Cost Principle," a principle which was to influence myriads of people before the century was over. Its operation was simple. All the purchaser had to pay for was the *time* occupied by the salesman in transmitting the goods to the customer, and it was for that reason that it early became known as the Time Store. Goods were marked at their cost price, plus overhead, which meant freightage, rent, and such inevitable incidentals. No profit was charged on anything. None was desired. All the purchaser had to do was to give a note, promising to pay back to the salesman, at that time Josiah Warren himself, the equivalent in labor that was required in servicing him. That and nothing more!

Warren's own description of his theory merits quoting:

"Cost . . . is the only rational ground of price even in the most complicated transactions; yet *value* is made almost entirely the governing principle in almost all the commerce of what is called civilized society.

"A man has a lawsuit pending, upon which hangs his property, his security, his personal liberty, or his life. The lawyer who undertakes his case may ask ten, twenty, fifty, five hundred, or five thousand dollars for a few hours' attendance or labor in the case. This law would be based chiefly on the *value* of his services to his client. Now there is nothing in this statement which *sounds* wrong, but it is because our ears are familiarized with wrong. . . . This is the first step in cannibalism. . . .

"Cost being made the limit of price thus works out the first proposition of our problem, the Equitable Reward of Labor

"With regard to security we see that in the wide range of the world's bloody history there is not any one horrid feature so frightful, so appalling as the recklessness, the cold-blooded indifference with which laws and governments have sacrificed persons and property in their wanton, their criminal or ignorant pursuit of some plan, passion or unsubstantial phantom of the imagination. Is it not time to seek *security* by some other means than by the workings of government! ! !

"While one's person, his time, his labor, his clothing, his lodging, the education and destinies of his children are all locked up in national, state, county, township or reform combinations, and all subject to be controlled by others who may differ from him, it is impossible for him to know security of person or property. The security of person and property requires exemption from the fear of encroachment from any quarter.

"It will be seen upon reflection that *value* being iniquitously made the basis of price produces all the ruinous fluctuations in trade, the uncertainty of business, the uncertainty of reward of industry . . . and trains us . . . mutually to encroach upon and invade each other.

"Liberty, then, is the sovereignty of the individual and

never shall man know liberty until each and every individual is acknowledged to be the only legitimate sovereign of his or her person, time and property, each living and acting at his own cost.

"You and I may associate together as the best of friends as long as our interests are not too closely connected; but let our domestic arrangements be too closely connected; let me become responsible for your debts, or let me by joining a society of which you are a member become responsible for your sentiments, and the discordant effects of too close connection will immediately appear.

"Harmonious society can be erected on no other ground than the strictest individuality of interests and responsibilities, nor can the liberty of mankind be restored upon any other principle or mode of action.

"When the washerwoman comes to set her price according to the cost or hardness of the labor compared with others, it is found that its price *exceeds* that of the ordinary labor of men. Of course the washerwoman must have more per hour than the vendor of house lots or the inventor of pills. To deny this is to deny the very foundation of the whole structure. We must admit the claims of the hardest labor to the highest reward or we deny our own rights . . . and throw everything back into confusion. . . .

"Let no one move to an Equity Village till he has thoroughly consulted the demand for his labor at that place and satisfied himself *individually* that he can sustain himself individually." [1]

At first the Warren store was a failure. No one came to buy things or even discuss rustic politics. Most people were suspicious of it and shunned it on principle. Finally, Josiah Warren had to persuade his brother to come to the store and make some purchases to convince the rest of the community that the enterprise was "on the level." It was not long before the store became crowded with customers. They clamored for goods, for nowhere else could they get them

[1] Josiah Warren: *Equitable Commerce*, 1852, pp. 43, 44, 48, 54, 55, 57, 82, 83.

at such a reasonable and cheap price. Thus it was that the equitable trading scheme of Josiah Warren became the basis of a new economy. It was co-operative without being coercive.

No other store was run with such efficiency. Warren had a genius for organization, and it displayed itself in his phenomenal endeavor. Every morning he recorded what goods he had and urged his customers to advise him as to what goods they wanted.

To begin his enterprise, Warren naturally had to have capital, and the ironic aspect of it all is that, an atheist at heart, Warren borrowed his money from a bank on a note which was endorsed by two solemn churchgoers. Both of the latter disagreed with Warren's religious views, but trusted his economic integrity. Warren was the kind of man who inspired trust and faith. One of the main reasons these churchmen undertook this obligation, was that they believed that Warren, though not a Christian by faith, was practicing Christianity in life. Richard Folger, a Methodist, and one of Warren's most ardent supporters, declared to his friends:

> "Well, brethren, people have been disputing for 1800 years about what is true Christianity. Now if you will go down to the corner of Fifth and Elm Streets, you will see it in operation for the first time in the world." [1]

Of such was the enthusiasm for Warren's colony made! An even better illustration is the following:

> "One day a friend came to the store and introduced a man . . . a stranger to the storekeeper. This man was to be turned out of his home and his furniture seized and sold . . . in default of the payment of $13.00 due for rent. . . . From the contingent fund of the store Warren readily agreed to lend the money. At the end of a fortnight the stranger came to Warren and declared, 'I will gladly pay you any premium you choose to ask.' 'You are a stranger,' replied the reformer, 'to the principle upon

[1] Bailie: *op. cit.,* p. 19.

which business is done here. I employed about five minutes in lending the money and shall employ about the same time in receiving it back. It was secured [by the friend] and there was no risk or loss. You have only to compensate me for my labor. If you could give me an equivalent in your own labor that would make it all right, but as you cannot do so, I will accept from you instead seven cents in money.' " [1]

So popular did Warren's store become, he was soon able to publish a weekly paper, *The Peaceful Revolutionist,* and not long after he closed the Time Store, having demonstrated to his own satisfaction the practicability of its principle. He and his followers then set out for Ohio, where they founded the colony which they called Equity. The Tuscarawas country in Ohio, where they settled, proved an unhappy region; it was infected with disease, in particular malaria, from which some of the colonists did not escape. Their next stopping place they called Modern Times, which proved to be their final venture.

When Modern Times was founded, its members sent the following announcement to the New York *Tribune,* which published it on April 4, 1853:

"A CARD—TO THE PUBLIC

"The undersigned are citizens of Modern Times, Long Island, two hours ride from New York upon the Long Island Railroad. We take this method of informing our fellow citizens who are desirous of bettering their condition in life by escaping from hostile competition and obtaining and retaining for themselves the full results of their own labor, that an opportunity is presented at this point such as we believe exists nowhere else. Several philanthropic gentlemen, having secured for the purpose between 700 and 800 acres of land at the center of Long Island, 'The Garden of New York,' invited the undersigned and others to commence a settlement upon it.

[1] *Ibid.,* p. 20.

"The object of the settlement is to furnish an opportunity to exchange labor equitably (bringing up the labor of women to the same prices as that of men, etc.) according to the plan expounded in the 'Science of Society,' by Stephen Pearl Andrews, and 'Equitable Commerce,' by Josiah Warren. . . . But no pledges are required and no understanding implied or expressed is had with the settlers that they are to live upon those principles or *in any given way*.

"The spring is now opening. . . . This domain is offered as no other lands upon which a town is to be built were ever offered; that is, without a dollar of profit . . . above their prime cost as wild lands. Hence a lot the size of an ordinary city lot such as is sold . . . from $50 to $500 is sold here to the settler at a price of between $1½ and $2. An entire acre costs about $22. The limit on each settler above which he cannot buy is three acres.

"There is no combination or association, but certain co-operative advantages offered which, as above stated, persons are free to accept or reject. The settlers on the ground all comfortably housed and beginning to establish various trades and branches of business are about 70. It is expected they will number hundreds before the fall. . . .

"We have not and no one has a dollar of pecuniary interest in spreading this information. . . . We request, therefore, that all editors and others who are interested in industrial reform assist us in making known the above facts.

"ROBERT GRAY, *late Congregational Pastor, Boonton, N. J.*
"WILLIAM METCALF
"B. F. BOWLES
"T. C. LELAND" [1]

Warren's project had early won an exponent in Stephen Pearl Andrews, who gave it a conspicuous place in his book, *The Science of Society*. Andrews was an erudite scholar,

---

[1] In Boston a Mr. Keith organized an Equity Store, based upon Warren's Cost Principle; it was most successful at first, but unfortunately burned down, and it was impossible thereafter to continue the enterprise.

sociologist, linguist, inventor of an international language, Alwato, and founder of a science called Universology.

Modern Times was often called a socialist community, but it differed sharply in intent from the socialism of the religious utopians. Its stress was upon individuality. The following words, culled from Stephen Pearl Andrews' book, alluded to above, are typical of this attitude:

"Man standing then at the head of the created universe is consequently the most complex creature in existence— every individual man or woman being a little world in himself or herself . . . hence the individualities of such a being are utterly immeasurable and every attempt to adjust the capacities, the adaptations, the wants or the responsibilities of one human being by the capacities, the adaptations, the wants or the responsibilities of another human being, except in the very broadest generalities, is unqualifiedly futile and hopeless. Hence every ecclesiastical, governmental or social institution which is based on the idea of demanding conformity or likeness in any thing has ever been and ever will be frustrated by the operation of this subtile, all-pervading principle of Individuality.

"When there remain positively no external restrictions, there will be positively no disturbance, provided always certain regulating principles of justice . . . are accepted and enter into the public mind, serving as substitutes for every species of repressive laws." [1]

Beneath, above, and beyond all this, was the principle of individuality which had played such a minor role in the other utopian colonies. "The first element of Equitable Commerce," declared Josiah Warren, describing the basic factor involved in the organization of his colony, was "the study of individuality, or the practice of mentally discriminating, dividing, separating, dissecting persons, things and events according to their individual peculiarities." [2] Warren made a fetish

[1] Stephen Pearl Andrews: *The Science of Society*, 1895, pp. 14, 15.
[2] Josiah Warren: *Equitable Commerce*, 1852, p. 15.

of individuality. He exalted it beyond everything else in the world. No man should look up to any other man; every man was his own judge, his own monitor. For that reason he hated government, even democratic government. "Governments," he argued, "have spread wholesale destruction, famine and misery all over the earth where peace and security might otherwise have prevailed. They have shed more blood, committed more murders, tortures and crimes in struggles against each other for the privilege of governing than society would or could have suffered in the absence of all government whatever."

Unlike all his utopian contemporaries, he believed in preserving instead of destroying competition as an economic principle. "While free competition," he maintained, "will lead to the adoption of the Cost principle, the Cost principle itself will inevitably bring about co-operation and mutual aid." [1]

Those were days when men believed that their "home was their castle" and they were willing to fight to protect any violation or invasion of it. They believed in the defense of what they called their own, however humble; the religious utopians never entertained such a conception. They believed that everything belonged to God, which meant to the society in which they lived, which was dedicated to the will of God; Warren would tolerate no such notion. God did not enter into his scheme of things. He wanted everything for man.

When Thomas Paine and Thomas Jefferson (and we should not forget Benjamin Franklin) said they believed in the "rights of man," what they meant was that they believed in a man's right to freedom, liberty, and independence from all outside authority: church, judiciary, or state. They were not ideas which they had invented. They were part of the intellectual atmosphere of the time. The French Revolution of 1789 had made them popular, and they spread over all Europe and into the remote Americas. In the United States, how-

[1] Bailie: *op. cit.*, p. 105.

ever, they had a chance to fructify and multiply more than in any other nation. Geography favored them. The Industrial Revolution had not yet developed into the monstrous machine it was later to become. America, in those days, was still an agrarian nation, and it remained so until almost the end of the century. If a man had a farm of his own, however small, and a gun to protect it, he possessed independence and individuality. He was a man in his own right, a true democrat, the kind of man Thomas Paine, Thomas Jefferson, Benjamin Franklin, and Josiah Warren might well extol.

Warren differed from the others only in that he believed in the Cost Principle, and the ultimate abolition of competition. The others believed in competition, and considered it a healthy form of enterprise. Warren believed, as do all anarchists, that the best way to destroy capitalism would be to avoid totalitarianism, which is what we have today in Germany, Italy, Soviet Russia, and other parts of Europe; he believed capitalism would destroy itself if the Cost Principle was put into action.

Although Warren loved the poor far more than the rich, he never entertained the hatred for the latter that people like Marx and Lenin, Kropotkin and Malatesta did. His attitude was gentler if less dynamic. In a letter penned a year before his death, he wrote:

> "I have said repeatedly that wholesale denunciation of ordinary business men as 'thieves and robbers' because they live on profits is first of all untrue; because these words, according to prevailing usage, apply only to those who know and profess themselves to be thieves and robbers. It is also untrue in another respect. Men may live on profits of their business and yet not get a tenth part of an Equitable compensation for their time and trouble. It is also philosophically wrong to punish people for being what their birth, training and surroundings make them. And this hostile attitude toward them is unnecessary, offensive and insulting, and tends to repel many

of the best of men and to array them against us: when if
we could get their attention long enough to be understood, they might gladly assist in the saving revolution
required. Therefore these wild denunciations are unjust,
suicidal, 'absurd and ridiculous.'

"It is absurd to 'demand the entire abolition of profits'
unless you explain your 'idea' of what constitutes profits.
If you mean the gains over and above compensation for
services (and I cannot think you mean anything else) you
place yourself in a dilemma; because (where common
money is taken for services) you never can tell *how much*
of it constitutes an Equitable compensation:—and there
is no yardstick, no common understanding to measure by,
and you expose yourself and the holy cause of Labor to
ridicule by any such announcements.

"In the holy word Freedom we encounter the anxious
world's greatest problem, one which waits for solution in
a definition acceptable to all, but the defects of abstract
language have baffled all attempts to furnish one. Almost
with fear and trembling I ventured years ago to offer one
on condition that I should preserve my freedom to change
it whenever 'increasing knowledge' should show its defects; and I gave the 'Sovereignty of every individual over
his or her own Person, Time, Property and Responsibilities,' and I here add Reputation." [1]

In addition to his theories, with many of which orthodox
anarchists would have disagreed, Warren was a superlatively
practical man. Like Napoleon, he not only knew how to lead,
he also knew how to follow. He was not only a general, but
also a private. He knew how to plan a store, organize a
colony, clear forests, construct houses, design streets, plan
industries, teach, work with tools, create. More than that,
he believed that girls and women had as much right to learn
trades, study arts, become economically independent, as men,
and this was a most progressive idea. Few of the utopian
colonies shared it.

Like all anarchists, Warren had unique ideas about mar-

[1] Quoted from Bailie: *op. cit.*, pp. 127-129.

riage, though he did not put many of them into print or try
to coerce the outside public to accept them. Whatever was
good, in his opinion, had to come from the voluntary decision
of individuals. To try to force them to accept it was the
worst of all evils.

How timely that sounds now with totalitarianism spreading
over the world, forcing, driving everyone to accept whatever
the totalitarian rulers desire or demand. Warren would have
fought them with all the power at his command, with no compromise, no quarter. And so it was with his ideas toward
marriage. He was not so extreme as William Godwin, Mary
Wollstonecraft, or even George Sand, Engels, or Bebel. He
realized that the marital concept needed revision. "It was
evident," he wrote, "that there was something frightfully
wrong somewhere; but what it was I did not see." He became
convinced, finally, contrary to the beliefs of most anarchists
and radicals of that day, that with "the sudden and total abolition of all Marriage customs and habits, without replacing
them with some definite regulating, preserving thought and
arrangement, our social condition would be worse, if possible,
than it is now."

Stephen Pearl Andrews, in a contribution rejected by the
New York *Tribune,* had expressed the sentiments of the
colony when he wrote "our whole existing marital system is
a house of bondage and the slaughterhouse of the female sex." [1]
In fact, Andrews did more than anyone else to articulate Warren's convictions on the subject, certainly far more than
Warren:

> "Mr. Greeley denounces me as favoring impurity and
> adultery. If by adultery is meant a breach of a legal bond,
> binding a man and woman between whom there are re-
> pugnance and disgust instead of attraction and love to live
> together in the marital embrace, then there may be some

[1] Stephen Pearl Andrews: *Love, Marriage, and Divorce,* p. 19. (A
pamphlet.)

302   WHERE ANGELS DARED TO TREAD

grounds for the charge; but if as I choose to define it, adultery means a sexual union induced by any other motive however amiable or justifiable in itself than that of mutual love, which by nature prompts the amative conjunction of the sexes, materially and spiritually, then do I oppose and inveigh against, and then does Mr. Greeley defend and uphold adultery. As to purity, I have no idea whatever that Mr. Greeley knows, owing to the prevailing influence of authority or legislation, what purity is.

"Sexual purity I will say is that kind of relation whatever it be between the sexes which contributes in the highest degree to their mutual health and happiness, taking into account the remote as well as the immediate results.

"It does not seem that the system in vogue by which the husband and father earns all the money and doles it out in charitable pittances to wife or daughters, who are kept as helpless dependents in ignorance of business and the responsibilities of life, has achieved any decided title to our exalted admiration." [1]

These doctrines were not new at the time, but they sounded a revolutionary challenge which will keep them eternally new, whenever uttered. Stephen Pearl Andrews in his *Science of Society,* and Josiah Warren in his *Equitable Commerce,* defended this anarchist theory of society, which both of them considered new, and it was new for America. It had been advanced with variations, in the old world, by numerous individuals, each of whom was dedicated to some special phase of it: Kropotkin, Stirner, Malatesta, Bianqui, and many others. In our own day, in this country, Johann Most, Emma Goldman, Alexander Berkman, and Benjamin Tucker carried on the torch which these earlier leaders had lighted. Although Warren stemmed from this tradition, he did not belong to it completely. He shared none of the revolutionary ideas of Bianqui, who was more of a twentieth-century Bolshevist than anarchist, and was entirely out of sympathy with the latter's conception of how to seize power. Power was the last thing Warren

[1] *Ibid.,* pp. 6-19.

desired. Power was an evil, something to be fought, not sought. The terroristic conceptions of Goldman and Berkman would have appalled him. He believed, as we have already seen, and as Most, Goldman, and Berkman did not, that capitalists as well as workers and farmers could be converted to his point of view. He did not consider capitalists demons, or workers angels; both were products of their environment. He saw both capitalists and workers as victims of circumstance, though he was one of the first to admit that workers were exploited by capitalists, wherefore the organization of his first community store.

Warren's anarchism was what many today might call philosophical anarchism, except that he translated it into actual practice. He believed in community living, minority independence, individualistic liberty. He believed also that the people, the masses, inherently believed in these things. Politicians of radical cast, both significant and insignificant, have believed in the masses, but their actions very often contradicted their convictions. Lenin and Trotsky, for example, two of the greatest radical leaders of our time, had implicit faith in the masses, but at the same time organized a society in which the masses had little, if any, control over their destiny. The masses were controlled from the top, by a party which set itself up as a supreme authority, the spearhead of progress, the main purpose of which was to educate them into a new way of life.

Warren, on the other hand, never believed in such procedure. He believed that power and authority should derive from below, not from above. In that regard he was far more proletarian than the professional proletarians.

The most influential apostle he acquired was Stephen Pearl Andrews, to whom we have referred before. Andrews wrote ably and extensively about the project, and his words were read with respect by most Bostonians, in fact by most New Englanders. Warren, for a time, as a result of Andrews' refined enthusiasm, became as interesting and noted a personality as Ripley. He was invited into the quiet, solemn parlors of the elite, and urged to discuss his ideas gently and suavely, in keeping with the austere atmosphere of the day. It was not long before he began to make an impression upon even the Boston Brahmins. Not being a demagogue, and practically never raising his voice beyond its normal subdued pitch, Warren was able to win over many of the sternest and most skeptical of the autumnal Puritans. His greatest strength was in his restraint, which was more convincing than eloquence in argument.

What injured, and finally undermined Warren's ideal was inherent in its substance. Anarchism carries within it the great hope and dream of the race; its bankruptcy results from the fact that the race is not ready for it. Great anarchists are among the noblest people in the world, but lesser ones are often the most ignoble—a condition not peculiar to anarchism but to all movements, conservative and liberal as well as radical and utopian. People crept into the Warren movement who were petty, selfish, visionless. They shared little of Warren's dream. Many were worse than those who corrupted Owen's colony and stole from it the last filament of economic faith out of which it had been born.

In addition, cranks with weird notions of how to conduct a perfect universe, dreamers whose dreams were nightmares, nineteenth-century Cagliostros with theories of animal and human as well as metallic conversion, astrologists who were no more than scratchers at the skies, evangelists who saw God in every niche of landscape, fanatics who believed that clothes were an anachronism, polygamy a virtue, and food a vice— all these, and more, became part of Warren's venture, or an extension of it, and hastened its end.

The main opposition to the colony from the outside was due to its supposedly dangerous ideas about food and sex. Several persons, it was claimed, died because they attempted to

live on fantastic diets: nuts, fruits, beans. Articles were
written in various papers, condemning the group for such
practices, and urging the abolition of the colony. When
some of these late members began advocating polygamy, the
storm of opposition thundered far and wide. Andrews himself attacked the institution of marriage as a social evil, and
spoke bluntly of the crimes committed in its name, one of the
worst of which was prostitution, a profession that, in his
opinion, grew out of the hypocritical morality bred by the
monogamous restrictions of the prevailing *mores*. So violent
did this controversy become, a debate was waged about it in
the New York *Tribune,* where Andrews defended his views,
and Horace Greeley and Henry James attacked him with their
characteristic superciliousness and arrogance.[1] New England
could tolerate reformers, even rebels, as history has shown,
but their recalcitrancy had to be confined to political and
economic realms. Marriage was something different; it was
more sacred, even though its canons were even worse dese-
crated; no criticism of it was permissible.

In the Modern Times community, however, marriage as well
as every other institution was constantly subjected to critical
scrutiny. Although it never ventured so far into multiple
marriage as Oneida, many of its members were advocates of
doctrines which were no less unconventional or challenging.
Nevertheless, it never needed, any more than did the other
utopian colonies, a jail or a police force to preserve law and
order; it never had mayors, secretaries, comptrollers, or any
other bureaucrats. Dr. Thomas Low Nichols, who lived in
the Modern Times community, has described it excellently:

> "Disciples came from New York and even from Bos-
> ton. . . . There were no churches, no magistrates.
> Everyone did what was right in his own eyes. The
> women wore bloomers or donned the entire male cos-

[1] Richmond Laurin Hawkins: *Positivism in the United States,* 1938,
p. 117.

tume. . . . As the sovereignty of the individual was opposed to all artificial social or legal restraints, marriages were abolished and families arranged themselves according to the law of attraction. Those lived together who chose to do so, and people parted without giving any trouble to the courts of common pleas. The right of the law either to unite or separate was denied and free love was placed in the same category with all other freedom. A man might have one wife or ten or more if he could take upon himself the proper cost or burthen, and the same freedom was asserted to women." [1]

In further connection with their marital attitudes, one member of the community put it succinctly when he said, "Folks ask no questions in regard to [marriage] among us. We, or at least some of us, don't believe in life partnerships when the parties can't live happily. Every person here is supposed to know his or her own interest best. We don't interfere; there is no eavesdropping or prying behind the curtain. . . . All laws tending to restrict liberty . . . are founded on error and should not be regarded." [2]

Marriage, then, was a matter of individual determination; it began and ended whenever the respective parties so decided. In that same connection the following excerpt from a newspaper clipping is distinctly revealing:

"We are not Fourierites. We do not believe in association. We are not communists; we are not Mormons; we are not non-resistants. . . . We are Protestants; we are liberals. . . . We protest against all laws which interfere with individual rights. . . . We believe in perfect liberty of will and action—hence we are liberals. We have not compacts with each other save the compact of individual happiness, and we hold that every man and every woman has a perfect and inalienable right to do and perform . . . as he or she may choose now and hereafter." [3]

[1] Quoted from Hawkins: *op. cit.*, p. 118.
[2] Bailie: *op. cit.*, pp. 61, 62.
[3] Hawkins: *op. cit.*, p. 119.

Although the Warrenites never called themselves anarchists, all this represented a strikingly unambiguous expression of anarchist philosophy. It was anarchism in one of its purest forms. Individual rights were exalted as sovereign and sacred. Individual happiness, not social happiness, was the shibboleth of success.

"Out of the indestructibility and inalienability of this Individuality grows the right to its exercise or the absolute sovereignty of every individual. Words are the principal means of our intellectual intercourse and they form the basis of our institutions, but . . . this subtle individuality sets at naught the profoundest thoughts and the most careful phraseology. There is no certainty of any written laws or rules or institutions or verbal precepts being understood in the same manner by any number of persons. . . . To require conformity in the appreciation of sentiments or in the interpretation of language or uniformity of thought, feeling or action where there is no natural coincidence is a fundamental error in human legislation—a madness that would be only equalled by requiring all to possess the same countenance or the same stature.

"After many years of patient watchfulness of the world's movements and of laborious experiments, we see in this Individuality the germ of a future so magnificent, so bright and dazzling, that the eye can scarcely look upon it. We see that as it is both inexpedient and impossible to overcome this Individuality, we must *conform our institutions to it!* . . . Institutions will be made for man, not man for institutions." [1]

No aspiration could be nobler than making institutions fit man's character instead of compelling man to fit the character of institutions. The difficulty was in the application of this doctrine on a widespread if not universal scale. Unlike most utopians, and most unlike demagogues, diplomats, and politicians, Warren believed that difference of opinion was a

[1] Josiah Warren: *op. cit.*, pp. 18, 19.

virtue instead of a vice. Note this interesting justification of his convictions:

> "It is when the voice or an instrument sounds *different* notes one after the other that we obtain melody; and it is only when *different* notes are sounded together that we produce *harmony*. . . . [The notes] never become combined. They never *unite* into *one* sound even in the most complicated nor in the most enchanting harmonious associations! If such were the result—if they were to lose their individualities in association and to unite into one sound, all musical harmony would be unknown or be suddenly swept from the earth as social harmony has been by the violations of the individualities of man." [1]

Warren went even further than that, and said that differences of opinion, which were born of the liberty to differ, effected harmony instead of discord. "Having liberty to differ," he said, "does not make us differ, but on the contrary, it is a common ground upon which all can meet . . . and is the first true step in social harmony. Giving full latitude to every experiment (at the cost of the experimenters) brings everything to a test and insures a harmonious conclusion. Among the multitude of untried routes, only one of which is right, the more liberty there is to differ and take different routes, the sooner will all come to a harmonious conclusion as to the right one . . . *Compulsion,* even upon the right road, will never be harmonious."

In short, Warren did not exalt difference in itself; he exalted it because he believed that it led to an ultimate similarity. Agreement between people: individuals, groups, masses, could only be achieved by ventilating their differences, not by suppressing them. When you suppressed them, disagreements increased instead of decreased. Chaos, not concert, resulted.

Modern Times failed because it could not harness its energies, raise sufficient capital to expand its project, or acquire

[1] *Ibid.,* p. 22.

sufficient men to carry out its labors. It succeeded for a time, despite the attacks made upon it by neighborhood hoodlums and urban Puritans; later, however, under pressure, it decided to change its name to Brentwood in order to escape some of the unhappy investigations and verbal attacks made upon it.

A letter, written by Edward D. Linton to A. C. Cuddon, an Englishman, describing the early days of the colony, is most informative:

"You have been here, Sir, and I ask you considering the natural obstacles to overcome, if you ever saw greater material success attained in so short a time by the same number of people without capital and with only their hands and brains to operate with, under all the disadvantages of habits formed by a false education and training . . . and as it regards individual and social happiness and the entire absence of vice and crime, I am confident this settlement cannot be equalled. This is emphatically the school of life. It is what has been learned here infinitely more than what has been done that constitutes what I consider the great success of the settlement.

"But if I ever live to see the practical realization of the principles or not here or elsewhere, I can never feel sufficiently grateful to the unostentatious man whose remarkable and peculiar constitution of mind enabled him to discover the most subtle and sublime truths ever made known to man for his self-government and the regulation of his intercourse with his neighbor. In my own person and in my own domestic affairs I have been incalculably benefitted." [1]

Cuddon himself, who visited and knew Modern Times more intimately than some of its own colonists, describes one aspect of it very well:

"Broad avenues, tree-shaded streets, pretty cottages, surrounded by strawberry-beds and well-tilled gardens, formed the outward appearance of Modern Times. The occupants were honest, industrious and had learned to

[1] Quoted from Bailie: *op. cit.*, pp. 65, 66.

mind their own business, while readily co-operating with their neighbors for mutual advantage. They were free from sectarian dissensions, courts of law, policemen, jails, rum shops, prostitutes and crime. No one acquired wealth save by his own industry."[1]

No wonder that Moncure D. Conway said that Modern Times was to be reached either "by railroad or rainbow." It was closer to the rainbow than to the railroad. It belonged to the rainbow division of humanity. It had the flash and flare, the dawning glory of newness, the magic and promise of man rising from the swamps to the heights of wonder. Man there was no longer to be man as he had been known before; he was to be clothed in new and more radiant garb; women were to luxuriate in a different world, in attire of strange and subtle fineness.

But all this was too beautiful to last, even as an aspiration. External as well as internal circumstances interfered. The economic panic and depression of 1857 undermined its early manufacturing enterprises, and the Civil War completed the task of annihilation. In that connection, it is interesting to observe that, whereas the panic of 1857 had discouraged utopian colonists, the panic of 1837 encouraged them to venture forth and found new colonies wherever they could carve out convenient spots in the wilderness, or discover free, or cheaply purchasable, timberless land. After the Civil War, with the spread of the railroads, over the entire nation, and the rise in land values, the organization of new utopian colonies became extremely difficult. From that time on we enter into the declining phase of utopianism in the United States.

[1] Quoted from Bailie: *op. cit.*, p. 67.

CHAPTER XVIII

Zion City

THE DOWIE PROJECT

Zion City was the last of the important religious utopias founded in this country. The only other that has gained wide renown is that of Father Divine, which is more of an enterprise than a community. Zion City was begun on a site of land adjacent to Chicago in 1893. Its founder, John Alexander Dowie, was an illegitimate descendant of Rapp, Beissel, and Janson; he had the same faith (perhaps more) in his powers that they did, but he lacked their overwhelming sincerity and unimpeachable honesty. He developed into a mountebank and charlatan, and represented in his own disintegration the disintegration of the whole utopian movement.

Like most of the other utopian leaders, he was born of poor parents, and had, in his youth, few advantages of environment. He describes his boyhood vividly in a letter:

"We were poor; I was often sick. . . . For some time before we left Edinburgh . . . I was quite unable to go to school, partly because of the condition of my clothes . . . and partly because I was still sick. I had a joyless childhood for the most part . . . and it was only my intense love for God and His work that gave me any joy. . . . Bitterly did I suffer from the consequences of the intemperance of some I dearly loved. This led me to sign the pledge when I was only six years old. I gave myself to God when a child, and although so poor and having so little opportunity for getting a really good education, I was diligent and obedient, and people kindly helped me, lending and giving me good books, which I read eagerly." [1]

[1] *Personal Letters of John Alexander Dowie*, 1912, p. 13. Compiled by Edna Sheldrake.

Poverty followed him for many years, and for a long time after he had escaped it, he was fearful of hearing the sound of its returning wings. His early economies were most pathetic, as the following letter to his parents reveals:

"September 25, 1872

"DEAR FATHER AND MOTHER:

"I enclose fourteen pounds, which is almost every penny I have, to meet bill due tomorrow.

"This comes very hard on me just now and causes me to be in debt for various small current accounts—store, butcher, blacksmith, etc., which brings a consciousness of 'owing' very worrying. Economical and careful as I am, this is one of the things which 'ought not so to be.' " [1]

Such experiences have varying effects upon different characters; most succumb and never revolt against them, but some revolt and become radicals, and others become unscrupulous exploiters. Ultimately Dowie became a combination of both of the latter. In the beginning, his idealism was soul-conscious as well as mouth-conscious. In October, 1877, he wrote to his wife, who had been complaining about his lack of financial success:

"You are looking at all my life and all my work and all my prospects from a radically wrong standpoint, viz., the mere standpoint of worldly success. That is a very good standpoint for worldlings, but it was left behind by me many years ago. . . . If I go back to that—then my whole life since has been a huge miserable failure. . . . If you want me to try a judicious mixture of serving God and Mammon—and I won't—I can't—I will serve God or Mammon—nay, I will serve God alone, though I be as poor as the Lord Jesus, who had no home. . . ." [2]

There can be little doubt but that his idealism in those years was unimpeachably genuine. He believed that one should serve God instead of Mammon, just as had Labadie, Kelpius, Rapp,

[1] *Ibid.*, p. 21.
[2] *Ibid.*, pp. 149, 150.

and Janson, and there was a fervor in his words which in time
was to become infectious. What corrupted him, as we shall
see, was success and power. People who have never known
power are seldom able to escape its destructive influence.
Dowie was one of those people.

When he was young and lacked power, he was able to
preserve his integrity but when he grew older and achieved
power, he became a different man. His vices soon outstripped
his virtues and in the man who became the founder and despot
of Zion City there remained only the shell of the being who
once preached that ministers should never accept a salary, but
work voluntarily in the vineyards of the Lord.

Like certain of the characters in Dreiser's novels of big
business who rose from poverty to the summits of success,
only to end in defeat, Dowie rose and fell—and never rose
again. His rise was even more meteoric than his fall. He
was unable to wear with grace the mantle of success and
power. If he had been a failure, he might never have been
heard of, but he most likely would have turned out to be a
simple, sincere, unselfish parson. He would have been honored
by his community but unknown beyond it; as it was, in the end
no community honored him, but the whole western world knew
of his existence. Like Oscar Wilde, he believed that there
"was one thing worse than being talked about and that was
not being talked about." He remains the founder of the
Billy Sunday tradition, and all the other tabernacle-rousers
who came after him were his spiritual children. More than
that, in his faith-healing theories, he not only anticipated but
also helped inspire Mary Baker Eddy's Christian Science idea
and movement.

II

Dowie had a curious mind; it was keen without being brilliant, piercing without being profound. It possessed that
pseudo-poetic, sub-rational, clairvoyant quality which has little

appeal to the intelligent, but great appeal for the unintelligent. It finally swept hordes into his camp, and he knew how to convert those hordes into disciplined followers.

As a boy Dowie envisioned himself as a leader and a prophet. When he discovered that his names John and Alexander meant "Grace of God" and "Helper of Men," he knew that God had already determined his destiny.[1] Later, he called himself "Elijah, the Restorer." He acquired his theological training in Edinburgh, going thence to Australia, where he became a Congregationalist minister. Soon after he became a social idealist, a temperance enthusiast, and an educational reformer. In all these fields, he proved a powerful influence. When he came to America a decade later, he organized "The Christian Catholic Church of Zion," which, following in the steps of the other religious utopians, he claimed to be founded upon the theocratic concept of primitive Christianity. God's ambassadors, not kings, queens, politicians, or statesmen, should be the rulers of men. It was this belief which inspired him to enter politics and to found the city of Zion.

Dowie's power, like Rapp's, was inherent in his personality. He was not a tall man, but his body seemed to rise beyond its natural height when he spoke; his words shot out with the velocity of bullets and he rose from the preacher to the commander. His sermons were rife with violent alarms and scabrous denunciations of the Devil, whom he considered a personal as well as religious enemy. He was not one of those wild-eyed hierophants who strut and bellow for hours, only to put their listeners to sleep. He believed in keeping his flock awake, and in taxing rather than in begging it for support. He was a direct man, whose speech was ofttimes violent and vituperative, but never equivocal. He made friends or enemies wherever he went, spoke, or lived; no one could feel indifferent or neutral about him.

Long before he founded Zion City, he had won dubious re-

[1] Rolvix Harlan: *John Alexander Dowie*, 1906, p. 28.

nown as a faith-healer. He called his work in this field
"Divine Healing," which he claimed to achieve largely as a
result of prayer. His own words describing his awakening, in
The Gospel of Divine Healing and How I Came to Preach It,
are striking:

". . . At noontide eighteen years ago I sat in my study
in the parsonage of the Congregational Church at Newton. . . . My heart was very heavy, for I had been visiting the sick and dying beds of more than thirty of my flock
and I had cast dust to its kindred dust into more than
forty graves within a few weeks. 'Where, O where was
He who used to heal His suffering children?' . . .

"There I sat with worry-bowed head for my afflicted
people until the bitter tears came to relieve my burning
heart. Then I prayed for some message from Him . . .
the Man of Sorrow and Sympathies. And then the words
of the Holy Spirit, inspired in Acts 10:38, stood before
me . . . revealing Satan as the defiler and Christ as the
healer. My tears were wiped away, my heart was strong,
I saw the way of healing. . . .

"A loud ring and several loud raps at the outer door,
a rush of feet, and then at my door two panting messengers, who said, 'Oh, come at once. Mary is dying.
Come and pray.' With just such a feeling as a shepherd
has who hears that his sheep are being torn from the fold
by a cruel wolf, I rushed from the house, ran hatless down
the street and entered the room of the dying maiden.
'O,' I thought, 'for some sharp sword of heavenly temper
keen to slay this cruel foe who is strangling that lovely
maiden like an invisible serpent. . . .'

"In a strange way it came to pass; I found the sword
I needed here in my hand, and in my hand I hold it still
and never will I lay it down. . . .

"And so we prayed . . . and lo, the maiden lay still in
sleep. . . . I saw that Christ had heard. . . .

"It is the Old Time Religion and no new gospel that
is preached. . . ."

What Dowie was doing was little more than the "laying on
of hands," a tradition which had once been the exclusive

prerogative of royalty. His cures were numerous but not invariable. It is hard to estimate the relative frequency of his victories and defeats; at all events his victories were numerous enough to win him an ever-mounting number of devotees, and to crowd an impressively large area behind his pulpit in Zion City with the crutches, braces, trusses, and other implements peculiar to the injured, as proof of his therapeutic power.

Few others of the religious utopians had claimed such healing powers; they believed more in the healing power of the millennium, in which all souls would be purified in the celestial crucible of God. Dowie believed in the here and now; he was not a millennialist. He wanted to save people for this world as well as for the next, which explains why so many individuals fell so quickly under his influence. It has been estimated that, in a decade, he treated eighteen thousand people, and contended that the vast majority were cured by his powers. His success was so marked that in 1895 he took his cause in his own hands, and severed his relations with the International Divine Healing Association, declaring at the same time that his followers should desert the organized churches, and join a new church which he was to found. For years, Dowie had to battle daily to protect the Christian Catholic Church which he established. He was attacked on every side, warrants were issued for him,[1] detectives were constantly on his trail, private enemies dogged his footsteps, but he went on somehow, if with a discouraged, yet never with a defeatist, spirit.

He had always a feeling of conquest, of glorious triumph, to uphold him. Until the day when he was struck down with a paralytic stroke, he persisted in his unmitigated and redoubtable fight against his adversaries and their unhallowed designs. Even after that he did not give up, but the effort was too much for a body so weary and worn with pain. He could hardly go

[1] Harlan: *op. cit.*, p. 34.

on with half a being and a maimed mind which was tortured with the agony of indubitable defeat, and dimmed with the dark clouds of despair.

If he surrendered quickly, and perhaps too quickly, he did it because he saw no chance of victory. Above everything else, however close Dowie felt himself to God or whatever gods there be, he never allowed divine elements to impede or impair mundane forces. He met opposition wherever he went, from the clergy as well as from laymen, but he never succumbed to it; he fought it unrelentingly from city to city, state to state, country to country. Even on his deathbed, he obstinately clung to his clairvoyant convictions.

Dowie was a faded theocrat, a religious anachronism, a twentieth-century Puritan who continued to exploit the tradition if not the spirit of his ancestors. Like the Puritans, he believed in theocratic government, and naturally preferred God to Mammon; but, unlike the Puritans, he thought Mammon could be bought off by compromise, and one could be a theocrat without being an ascetic. It was not that he preferred the fleshpots, but he liked to live well, in pleasant and charming, if not luxurious, surroundings, with all the modern conveniences of life at his disposal. This was his most vulnerable weakness, and his enemies inevitably attacked him for it as an opening shot. He was a theocrat in public, but a plutocrat in private.

He cited the Bible as the source of authority for the establishment of a theocracy. Ultimately, this led to the foundation on April 7, 1902, of the Theocratic Party, which was an outgrowth of the determination of the citizens of Zion City to reform American politics. This party was to include and absorb all churches. "The whole church," Dowie cried, "Presbyterian, Congregational, Baptist, Episcopal" was to unite behind it. Dowie was not modest about his claims. "I tell the church universal everywhere," he exclaimed, "you have to do what I tell you. Do you hear? You have to do what I tell you, because I am the Messenger of God's Covenant."

III

Such was the man who founded, built, and developed Zion City, one of the last of the religious utopias to be established in this country. Zion City, established on the outskirts of Chicago, became an international curiosity. People from all over the world came to visit it. They were concerned not only with its social-minded aims, but also with its healing facilities, embodied mainly in the person of Dowie himself. Dowie was not only a theocrat; he was *the* theocrat of the place. He dominated Zion City far more despotically than Rapp did Harmony; Beissel, Ephrata; or Janson, Bishop Hill. His word was law, and anyone who refused to accept it left the City; needless to say, few left it. They were all hypnotized by Dowie's personality.

Dowie set out to organize an ideal, utopian community. He spent numberless hours attacking alcohol and tobacco as the root and source of all evil. Speaking of tobacco, these words are typical of his vitriolic speech and violent personality:

"The majority of men in Chicago can be smelled several yards off. They stink of nicotine and tobacco and all kinds of medical muck. Ugh! you dirty dogs, who chew your tobacco and puff your smoke. The sun dries it up, that dirty catarrh and cancer in your throats, which you expectorate in the streets . . . and good women and some clean men are forced to breathe your disease-breeding filth. Ugh! you dirty dogs!

"Doctors as a profession are directly inspired by the devil. . . . Dr. Gray is one of the dirtiest spewing buzzards of this town. His mouth is a tobacco churn all day long. . . . He is a dirty stink-pot . . . and I will tell you more. He spends many of his Sundays riding the bicycle.

"From this time henceforth Dr. P. S. Henson, of the
First Baptist Church, stands before the world as a grin-
ning clown, a fool who is neither a theologian, a Christian,
nor a gentleman, but is an infernal liar. . . ." [1]

As is obvious, Dowie objected to more than tobacco and
alcohol. Even bicycle-riding was tabu. The stage was another
prime abomination. He was bitterly opposed to all stage
presentations, however simple and demure. Actors and actresses were emanations of evil, prancing conjurations of the
netherworld. He would have none of them in Zion City.
Nor would he have card-playing, dance halls, or even drug-
stores or physicians, whom he detested as frauds and fakirs,
medicine men, not medical men. Dowie himself, with his
healing technique, was, in his own eyes, the only true medical
man.

His loathing of alcohol was so fantastically exaggerated
that when his daughter died from injuries caused by the flames
from an alcohol lamp, he condemned her for using alcohol in
whatever form. At her burial, broken-hearted though he was,
he could not restrain himself from saying:

"She was a good girl, but she disobeyed me. I forbade the use of alcohol in any form. She violated my
command and she has been punished for it." [2]

His various publications, particularly *Leaves of Healing,*
had international circulation. For a time, Zion City became a
flourishing publishing center. Dowie was one of the most
independent editors that ever existed. To be sure, he had a
vast following; he claimed one hundred thousand, but other
estimates, which were much closer to the truth, put it at fifty
thousand. At all events, the number was large enough to

[1] James L. Dwyer: "Elijah the Third," *American Mercury,* July, 1927,
Vol. XI, No. 43, p. 292.
[2] I. K. Friedman: "John Alexander Dowie," *Everybody's Magazine,*
Nov., 1903, p. 571.

subsidize his publishing enterprises as well as his many other ventures. He not only alienated people who liked alcohol and tobacco, but also those who appreciated pork as a food. "I would just as soon preach to a goat," he wrote, "as to a man or woman full of pork. Stinking, foul, filthy thing! When you eat it you are putting within you the food that creates tuberculosis and trichinosis and cholera and cancer . . . a mass of scrofulous filth." [1] He was not less vigorous in his diatribes against people who played cards, were blasphemous, or used the mildest profanity. Such offenders were satanic in his opinion.

Zion City was organized for the Dowieites to isolate themselves from the world and found a haven, or heaven, as Dowie preferred to express it, where the members might prepare themselves for their great future. The outside world represented too great a temptation and snare, and, as Dowie said, "in order to make it easy to do right, Zion has to isolate her people entirely from the world and its ungodly occupations, both in business and in pleasure." But that was not enough for Dowie. He not only wanted his people to feel superior to the outside world, but he also wanted to rule it. "Zion will not withdraw from the world," he declared with characteristic vehemence, "but Zion aims to rule the world, and to compel the world, which is so largely now in rebellion, to submit to the love and the rule of God." [2]

Zion City had its farms as well as its factories, its grocery stores, as well as its meeting places in the schools, its bank, planing mill, brick yards, laundries, publishing houses, and hospices, but they were all owned by Dowie himself, who, as General Overseer, insisted that God wished it so. No oriental or occidental despot ever ruled his people with firmer authority. Ten per cent of everything that his followers earned, saved,

[1] *Leaves of Healing:* Vol. X, No. 26, p. 855.
[2] John J. Halsey: "Genesis of a Modern Prophet," *American Journal of Sociology,* Nov., 1903, p. 324.

or inherited, Dowie claimed as part of God's fund.[1] Part of this money was to be expended in the construction of a great temple, in imitation of the Temple of Solomon. But it was never built. Dowie became too interested in other plans and projects, especially in his determination to convert the heathen city of New York to Dowieism. In 1903, Dowie attempted his first great conversion. He and three thousand of his followers, traveling on chartered trains, dashed into New York, equipped to outfight the Devil and to lay him low. Numerous meetings were held, and a baptismal tank was constructed in Madison Square Garden, in which he hoped to douse countless thousands of converts. But the converts did not come in anything like the abundance that he had anticipated. His first visit to New York, initiated by a triumphal trip in an ornate barouche from Grand Central Station to the Murray Hill Hotel, a distance scarcely more than two hundred yards, ended in a fiasco. This second trip, God assured him would be a success. But God must have forgotten his promise, because it wasn't a success at all.

At his first meeting at Madison Square Garden, thousands came and thousands were turned away. It was like a vast circus projected into a religious atmosphere, with deacons for sky-jumpers and deaconesses for tightrope-walkers, and Dowie himself as the major magician. Dowie sanctified that atmosphere with words and tears and weird, abracadabral ejaculations. He had come equipped with all the devices necessary to transform an "inhuman hell," which is how he described New York, into a living heaven. He had his musicians, his commanders, and his elegantly clad choir, rehearsed and prepared for the theatricality of divine display. They were most impressive. Their appearance was excellent, their voices were good, and they put their hearts into what they sang. The result was superb. Dowie damned and double-damned the am-

[1] John Swain: "John Alexander Dowie," *Century Magazine*, Vol. LXIV, No. 6, Oct., 1902, p. 933.

bassadors of hell, who had ruined our civilization, and destroyed its Christian foundation. No invective was too sulphurous for him. He was opposed to all profanity in Zion City, but on the platform from which he preached, he never hesitated to use profanity in his condemnation of things and people he hated. And in his speeches or sermons, the man would snarl, preach, sneer and snigger as well as coddle and pamper his prospective converts. He was a composite of contradictions, a curious compound of the sublime and the sophomoric, of pure and impure, spiritual and sensual. He was at one and the same time kind and cruel, gentle and fierce, calm and clamorous.

In Madison Square Garden, he flung at his enemies oaths which stung with scorn and contempt; he cried and shouted upon the platform, gesticulated like an actor, writhed, leaped, smashed vases, crushed flowers, threatened to jump from the rostrum to the floor, and break to pieces anyone who did not believe in his holy mission.

This was not a new spectacle. Back in the old days, he had threatened his critics with death and eternal suffering in the furnaces of Satan. "I have lived," he wrote, "to see every one of my enemies who fought me in 1895 dead or driven out of their places. Where is Joseph Medill, editor of the *Tribune*? He is dead. . . . Washington Hessing, editor of the *Staats-Zeitung* cursed me. . . . He is dead. Hutton and Scott, of the Chicago *Herald,* where are they? They are dead. Where are Joseph Dunlop and the *Dispatch*? Did I not prophesy that the paper would die and rot and be buried, and wasn't my prophecy fulfilled?" [1]

All this time, however, he pronounced their deaths before they had died, predicted their sufferings, agonies, and final crucifixion of spirit as well as body. Many who had come to hear him resented his aspersions, and could not tolerate his vicious manner of attack. He was almost a fiend when he

[1] Quote taken from Dwyer: *op. cit.,* p. 296.

dwelt upon such matters. Jonathan Edwards' pictures of what sinners would suffer in hell, or even the horrific conjurations of Dante in his *Inferno,* were mild compared with the monstrous harbingers and threats which Dowie invented. His followers were constantly torn between jitters and tears, victims of them both.

Despite Dowie's second failure in New York, and it certainly was that, if any estimate of converts was to be compiled or influence over the community was to be recorded, Zion City continued to survive. This expedition to New York, to cure a combination of the Sodom and Gomorrah of the time, had cost the Zionites over $300,000,[1] and Dowie, realizing that he had not succeeded, decided to make a trip around the world to convert the heathen. The trip was no more of a success than his invasion of New York, but the places he ventured into were more remote and obscure, and he had little difficulty in convincing his followers that the cause had been advanced.

To meet the expenses involved he had to increase the taxes of his Zion City colony, and to demand that every Zionite deposit his extra funds in the City's bank. His followers, in customary style, responded—whereupon Dowie set out upon new missionary projects, especially to Mexico, where he hoped to establish a "Zion Paradise Plantation." But these projects were no more successful, except at times in a faith-healing sense, than his New York incursions.

In the meanwhile, however, his educational ventures in Zion City proceeded at a happy pace; he had established preparatory and junior schools, and then also a college, all modeled upon the Zion City religious pattern. Dowie, it is needless to say, prescribed all that they taught, and saw to it that nothing other than sound Dowieism was introduced into any of the courses.

Every Dowieite was a sharer in the Zion City enterprise; but Dowie really owned it all, and dictated what the people

[1] *Dictionary of American Biography,* Vol. V, p. 413.

should do with their suppositious property. In the beginning, Dowie organized the Zion Land and Investment Association; his capital came from his votaries, but his votaries had little or nothing to say about what happened to it. Dowie assumed complete authority in that matter, and kept no records. Within the short span of a year, Dowie had the Shiloh Park site, where Zion City was founded, converted from a barren place into a flourishing one. As soon as it became an active community, Dowie had the City incorporated, and demanded all the rights, freedoms, and protections granted every other city in Illinois. "The City," Dowie stated, "is governed municipally according to the law of the State of Illinois and of the United States of America," and then added with characteristic bluntness and candor, "but I may as well tell you, the people would not vote a ticket if I did not approve it."

In short, he was dictator as well as prophet, despot as well as theocrat, egomaniac as well as humanitarian. Even when he proposed the reorganization of the country in a theocratic instead of a democratic direction, he insisted, in the platform of the Theocratic Party which he created, that it should all be done "in the manner provided by the laws of the United States." He did not believe in defying the authorities, at least not until he could defy them with success.

After his second New York fiasco, he ventured into various countries, all with the same aim. In Mexico, where he tried to organize the "Zion Paradise Plantation," he was at the point of transforming his dream into reality, when he was stricken with an apoplectic stroke from which he never recovered. Once handicapped beyond repair, with his faith-healing impotent in the face of such a disaster, his Zionites deserted him, overthrew his authority, expelled him from the Zion Church, and accused him of a host of charges, of most of which he was innocent. They even attacked him as a polygamist and political vampire. In his crippled state, his struggles against his enemies were feeble and futile. He died before he could make any headway in his campaign for the restoration of Zion City to its original design.

It was a sad fate for a man who aspired to so much and, in the end, achieved so little. He was not a writer of consequence, who could delude himself into believing that his fame would live on in his books, nor a painter whose canvases he might hope would capture the eyes of posterity. His strength had lain in his personality, his voice, his gestures, his healing technique, but above all in his colony, his city, Zion City, the city where Christian co-operation should flourish and flower. As a young man, he had been more skeptical than credulous; as an old man, he became more credulous and less skeptical. Back in 1882, he had written his wife a letter from the Victoria Coffee House, in which his dubieties were interestingly voiced:

"BELOVED WIFE:
"O, it has been a sorry time for me since I last saw your face. Alone in this great cold city, I have spent some of the most sorrowful hours of my life. . . . Fears for the future of this uncertain life, doubts as to the past, questionings . . . strugglings with the dire realities of the present . . . my growing shabbiness and ofttimes positive hunger—all these and more have been my companions day and night for months." [1]

As he succeeded, his faith increased, and though three years later he wrote, in another letter, concerning a younger daughter's death, that he hoped he would die soon, his earlier skepticism had disappeared. Even on his deathbed, his belief in himself, God, and paradise remained steadfast.

In his mind's eye, he could see the five hundred robed singers, children leading the procession, and old men with silky silver hair following at the end—he could see them not only as human beings, but as angels marching through the

[1] *Personal Letters*, p. 309.

gates of paradise. Then there were the deacons clad in black, and the Zion Guard, all mingling as in a magic mosaic—all this he saw, lived through again, watched himself stand with clairvoyant power behind the pulpit, heard his voice ring round the tabernacle, and knew that Zion City, which had been taken from him, was the true Zion. He was no longer the General Overseer, but the Eternal Overseer.

He was too weak in his last days to realize that his Zionite children had repudiated him, discarded him with the dust. He knew that his best friends had turned against him, denied him even as Jesus had been denied by Peter, spat upon him, stolen his authority as well as his property. Wilbur Glenn Voliva, who succeeded Dowie as General Overseer, had been Dowie's closest friend; but when the chance of deposing the paralyzed old man occurred, Voliva was the first to drive a dagger into his moribund frame. He led the rebellion against him, decried him in the highways and byways of the city, exposed his financial obliquities, which were numerous, and, in effigy, burned him in the market place.[1]

Whether Dowie was sincere or insincere, a fanatic or a fakir, a dreamer or an imposter, will never be known. Undoubtedly he was a good deal of them all. That he was an autocrat rather than a democrat, he himself declared. He preferred describing himself as a theocrat. He wanted to be a king, but a benevolent one. He wanted power, but he wanted to use it wisely. When he founded Zion College, in 1899, it was not for reasons of this world, but the next—"to prepare the workers," as he wrote, "for service in the Master's kingdom." However much he demanded of this world in flesh, and with his boats, his estates, his phaetons and buggies, his fine dogs, his numerous servants, he demanded a lot, he demanded more

---

[1] An interesting picture of Dowie is to be found in Gilbert Seldes's *Stammering Century*, p. 204. For a sharp, critical attack on Dowie, see James M. Buckley's article, "Dowie Analyzed and Classified," *Century Magazine*, Vol. LXIV, No. 6, Oct., 1902.

of the world beyond, where all demands would cease, dreams would become realities, and realities would become dreams.

Zion City lived on a little longer after Dowie's death, but it would have lived much longer had Dowie lived and governed it.

CHAPTER XIX

Father Divine

BLACK KINGDOM COME

"Last night I shook hands with God and watched him eat. He seemed quite human . . . in the way he handled his knife and fork, and I might have thought him just a man had it not been for the buxom woman at my side who kept shouting, 'Father Divine, he God. God Almighty, he never born. He never die. God Almighty. Oh, my God, my God.' And five hundred others, black, brown, and white, echoed her words in a tireless, monotonous chant for three solid hours."

FRANK S. MEAD, *Christian Century*

It is doubtful whether Father Divine, whose cultural erudition is scarcely profound, ever heard of Dowie or read any of his publications, and yet both developed a spiritual salutation that was surprisingly and arrestingly similar. Father Divine's famous greeting is "Peace, it's wonderful," and in every Divine restaurant the waitresses and the hostess will greet their customers with the one word, "Peace," uttered with a sibilant softness. Dowie, decades earlier, had begun the greeting of "Peace to thee," with the response "Peace to thee be multiplied," and every Dowieite repeated it dozens of times day after day—just as the Divineites repeat their "Peace, it's wonderful" with equal repetitiveness.

The Negroes in America have always been captivated by religion. But they have always been individual and unique in their utilization of its potentialities. All that is original in Negro religion can be traced to the economic institution of

328

slavery and its influence upon the Negro spirit. The Negro lived in America as a slave for over two hundred and forty years. He was forced by the system of slavery into habits of life and forms of behavior that drove him inevitably in the direction of emotional escape and religious delirium. Existence offered him nothing to hope for but endless labor and pain. Life was a continuous crucifixion. The earth became a place of evil. As a member of a downtrodden and suppressed race, he had nothing to discover within himself that insured emancipation or escape. His revolts had all proved ineffectual. Inevitably he turned toward the white man for the materials of his "underdog" logic. He accepted and absorbed the ideas of the ruling class, as do most subordinate groups, until they became a part of his reactions. The white man's paradise suddenly became a consuming aspiration. He grew enamored of it as a holy vision. His belief in it became a ferocious faith. Its other-worldly aspect only lent it a richer enchantment. There were no realistic categories to thwart or limit its undimensioned beauty and magnificence. The scarcities of this world had no meaning in the infinite plentitude of the next. Gold could be had for the asking, and everything was as a dream would have it in some land beyond the sun.

It was as an expression of this consecrated other-worldly ardor that the Negro spirituals came into being and grew into form. There is more, far more, than the ordinary Christian zeal embodied in them. These spirituals are not mere religious hymns written or recited to sweeten the service or improve the ritual. They are the aching, poignant cry of an entire people. Jesus to the Negro is no simple religious saviour, worshiped on Sundays and forgotten during the week. He is the incarnation of the suffering soul of a race.

Father Divine has carried on that tradition, except that his stress is more upon God than Christ. He supplies his followers with that spiritual sustenance which they crave. His enemies call him a fakir, but so also are many other Negro parsons and many white ones, too. As many of the earlier utopians, he envisions himself as an ambassador of God. No, more, as God himself, emulating Janson in that regard. In that respect, Janson preferred to be known as Christ rather than God, but Father Divine would accept no secondary role. He refused to be the Son of God; he had to be God himself.

Earlier Negro leaders have believed God was black, and conjured up a whole hierarchy of sable cherubim and seraphim, but few, if any, ever envisioned themselves as the Creator Himself. Marcus Garvey had made a "racket" out of pampering the hope on the part of many religious Negroes that God was black, but he had never dared substitute himself for God. He had his black God, black Jesus, and black Virgin Mary; he had his black angels, black apostles, black saints. In more mundane fields, he had his Black Star Steamship Line, in contrast to the White Star Line, and he had his dream of Liberia as the New Canaan to which he was going to take the Negro people en masse, in ships captained and manned by black men, with black funnels, black smokestacks, and black flags flying in the breeze. Garvey, however, was not so clever as Divine; he made bad investments, chose untrustworthy associates, and finally was arrested and imprisoned. With his imprisonment, all his fantastic dreams of a new Liberia faded, and when he got out of prison and died, not so very long ago, the public had almost forgotten him.

Not so Father Divine. He will never let you forget him. He is one of the greatest publicity men of our time. He never ventures into anything in a small way and he never lets himself be "caught" in a big way, as Garvey did. He knows how to take as well as give, and also how to take away again, and yet make those happy from whom he has "taken." There have been dissensions in Father Divine's group, but they have not been numerous. The vast majority of his followers are so devoted to him, so convinced that he is God, that all thought of dissension is alien to their minds.

The Divine colony, if it may be called such, numbers over the world somewhere between 15,000,000 to 20,000,000 members.[1] Its constituents are white and yellow as well as black, for as his movement developed into a world-wide affair, few races or colors failed to be influenced by it and people from the Orient as well as the Occident joined it. In many groups it has more white than black members. It has regular busses which run from Los Angeles to New York, carrying white and black angels who are on their way to see their God in his Harlem haven—which Divine himself calls his Divine Peace Mission. Devotees from many parts of the world have come to visit him and worship at his feet, and gaze enraptured at the photograph of him, beneath which are the challenging words: "Father Divine is God."

Father Divine's colony, or what is now almost a colonial system, is very different from other utopian colonies we have discussed. His movement has spread around the world by spiritual osmosis; in no country has he set up missionary organizations, or tried to formalize or denominationalize his doctrine; he is violently opposed to theology, and believes that all that people need to know to be pure, to become angels, is that he is God, and his magic phrase, "Peace, brother—it is wonderful." In economics, too, his procedure is dissimilar. All angels who enter his fold must surrender all their earthly possessions, their wealth in whatever form: cash, real estate, stocks, bonds, insurance policies, even their furniture and surplus clothes, because none of this will be needed in the Kingdom of God established by Father Divine. Those who work for outside employers contribute their tithe or more to the support of the kingdom. In return, they are all guaranteed security for life against any adversity. They will always have shelter, abundance of food, and medical care; besides they will have all the joyous advantages of living in the Kingdom

[1] Will Irwin: *Liberty*, pp. 12, 13.

of God, singing, chanting, dancing, and living constantly in the presence and within the sight of the Creator.

This is not the communism of Rapp, Beissel, Kelpius, or even that of the early Mormons, but it is a twentieth-century blurred carbon copy of it. Although Father Divine is not so ascetic as most of these earlier leaders and prophets, he is far superior to Dowie in his way of life. He has none of the private country houses, yachts, fast horses, and hunting dogs that the founder of Zion City possessed; it is true that he possesses several expensive cars, but only one of them is for his personal use, that he also has an airplane in which he flies like God over his children at their parades and picnics and other public functions, but the rest of his life does not seem to be reprehensively luxurious. He lives and dresses unpretentiously, eats the same food as his angels, and aside from proclaiming himself God, carries himself without ostentation or arrogance. Like so many of the other religious utopians, he is opposed to smoking and drinking, and in favor of celibacy; but like the Shakers he is also in favor of dancing and entertainment and all the spiritual joys which he believes are the privilege of the heavenly host.

II

Important as it is to bear in mind that the Divine movement gained its main impetus in New York City during the depression of the early thirties—Divine came to Harlem in 1932—it is scarcely less important to trace the career of this strange, weird little man, who has changed the lives of so many millions. It is easy for intellectuals who make a fetish of rationality to dismiss him as a lunatic, which in part he perhaps is, but it is his kind of lunacy, embodied in higher but more sinister form in a person like Hitler, that has so often influenced a considerable part of the world. Being a Negro,

Divine could never become in a white-dominated world the political force that Hitler is; his followers, however, are no less devoted to him than the Nazis are to their Fuehrer. Divine is God, Hitler is the Fuehrer; both recognize their destiny. Divine dominates by a heavenly power that lives in him, Hitler by the heavenly powers conjured up by the astrologers. In short, dissimilar though the two men are in most respects, they are the same in one, namely, in the source of their power, which is mass hypnotism. And that mass hypnotism is possible only because they both believe they are men of destiny; to believe that, one has to be abnormal, irrational, and perilously mystical. But it is such men in times of crisis that wrest power from the shrewd and cunning statesmen and diplomats, because they can hypnotize the masses—their very incoherency and illogicality is their strength instead of their weakness.

Divine started off even more humbly than Hitler; he was no house-painter, but an unskilled worker who undertook every possible odd-and-end job that would provide him with food and shelter. In those days his name was George Baker, at least that was his name when he lived in Baltimore.

From Baltimore, where, inspired by a Negro Holy Roller who called himself Father Jehovia, Baker began to think of himself as God, he went to the South; there he was arrested in Valdosta, Georgia, and declared insane. Driven from the South, he wormed his way by devious detours into what was for him the strange, wicked city of New York. En route, stopping at villages, hamlets, and nondescript places, he gathered together a handful of disciples, all of whom were convinced that he, and he only, was God. Baker himself, not yet known as Father Divine, had become more convinced than ever that he was no mortal man, had never been born from human flesh, but was a supernatural creation, God incarnate. But a number of years had to elapse before he could impress this upon multitudes. His stay in New York this time was relatively brief.[1] He established his first heaven in Manhattan, but soon moved it to Brooklyn, and then to Sayville, Long Island. He was now no longer known as George Baker, but as Reverend Divine. He managed to find jobs for his angels in various places near Sayville, and news of this spread far and wide and within a short time his followers multiplied by the scores. After becoming an angel their worries ceased. They achieved *security*, which provides another reason why Divine's success was so expeditious. His feasts became famous throughout the countryside and the angels, unaccustomed to such delicious food, screamed out their appreciation in wild, reverberating hallelujahs, followed by preaching, haranguing, dancing, tomtom stamping of feet, and other hysterics. The neighbors naturally protested, Divine was arrested, and tried in Mineola for violating the peace; he was fined five hundred dollars and sentenced to a year in jail. But Justice Smith, who convicted Divine, died several days later, and the Divine-ites declared it a miracle. Father Divine was truly God if he could kill his enemies with a word or a wish. Later, Divine was acquitted in a higher court, and from that time on his stock as God soared to fantastic heights.[2]

It was time now to return to New York, as Christ to Jerusalem. From then on his followers multiplied by myriads, and he had constantly to buy new places in which to house and feed them. Before long there were more than two score of heavens in operation and Divine stores of almost every variety were opened up: groceries, barber shops, eating houses, clothing shops, pressing establishments, and whatnot. A virtual colony had been formed. None of the angels were paid for their work except in terms of the gratuities at the various

---

[1] For a good deal of the information concerning this part of Divine's life, I am indebted to an article of Jack Alexander, "All Father's Chillun Got Heavens," which appeared in the *Saturday Evening Post*, Nov. 18, 1939.

[2] For an extended account of this most interesting episode, see John Hoshor's striking book: *God in a Rolls Royce*, pp. 70-84.

heavens. All worked as one, white, brown, and black. Divine believes "there are no races, but only one race, the human race." Consequently, white women and black women, brown women and white women, black men and white men, brown men and black men, sleep together in the same beds, sit beside each other as they eat, and sing, dance, and worship side by side.

So fabulously successful has the venture become, Divine at length found it possible to move part of his flock to a thirty-four acre piece of territory in upper New York, facing the Franklin D. Roosevelt estate. This became "The Promised Land." Since its original purchase, it has been expanded into a two-thousand-acre affair, where Divine's followers live a co-operative life, each a contributor to a communal enterprise. The land is owned in common by the angels, who contribute all they produce to the common hoard and then divide it equally, or as need demands, among themselves. They owe no mortgages, ask for no credit, pay no installments. They are as free as the Mormons were, of all such economic obligations and encumbrances. In fact, in more ways than one, Divine's concept of The Promised Land resembles Joseph Smith's and Brigham Young's vision of The United Order. The Mormons, to be sure, had a higher and finer grade of humanity with which to work, and there can be little doubt that Divine will never be able to achieve as great a success. After all, the vast majority of Divine's followers are failures, defectives, incorrigibles, derelicts, and even criminals. As it is, he has accomplished miracles with numbers of them, given purpose to their once hopeless lives, transformed the personalities of many, made honest, upright people out of chicken thieves, gamblers, prostitutes, and even felons. Divine is a kind of poor man's Buchmann. He uses the same form of confessional approach to his followers that Buchmann does; the main difference is that Buchmann's converts are fairly well-to-do if not rich people, and, therefore, are more restrained and refined in the manner of their confessions than Divine's proselytes, who spring largely from the poor and illiterate sections of humanity. With both groups, however, the confessional is exploited as a form of catharsis.

Death Hath No Sting

A unique part of Divine's teaching is that he and his angels, and all that become his angels, are immortal. Death and disease have no existence for them. They are above them. If one follows his teachings, learns to think as he does, live as he does, eat as he does, eternal life is his for the asking. Divine is God, and he has decreed it. It is only when an angel falters or stumbles, and succumbs to Luciferian temptations,that sickness can overtake him and death ensue. After all, they are living in a new world: 1940—1940 A.D.F.D. (Anno Domini Father Divine)—and that world is governed by different laws from the one in which ordinary mortals exist.

Divine himself believes that he was born centuries ago, perhaps at the beginning of the world, the maker of the world. In the following speech, printed in his paper, *The New Day*, he stresses the fact that, as God, he has concealed himself in many religions, and has only lately allowed himself to be truly revealed:

"Here we all are again! We are pleased to be just as we are, the same as we have been. Aren't you glad? I have reason at this instance to say . . . there are visiting friends with us. Those who wish to speak are welcome to do so. Feel free to move and be moved volitionally if you wish to and be governed and guided intuitively. By so doing, you will not feel cramped, but you will feel inspired no doubt, for this is the place of inspiration; this is the place of the resurrection of the dead. I have always striven to avoid publicity until ill-famed publicity forced the positive out in opposition and as a rebuttal to the negative. . . . Feeling I desired not that man should observe ME as a person, I strove persistently to prohibit any in-

dividual from observing ME personally; hence I desired
to hide Myself in different religions, in different teachings and Representatives of the people. But finding there
was no place wherein I could hide, I was obliged to be
revealed." [1]

Another quirk of his is to speak of himself as the Fundamental, and in the following letter to Mr. C. W. Thomas, of
Vancouver, in which Divine discusses the matter of sex, his
stress upon the Fundamental is most interesting:

"*Mr. C. W. Thomas*
"*840 Gore Avenue*
"*Van Couver, B. C., Canada*

"MY DEAR MR. THOMAS,

"I am writing in response to yours of the 1st, and wish
to advise concerning the matter in question, those who I
find slightly indulgent in such attracting their minds and
attentions even to corresponding distantly with the opposite sex (men and women) that which is commonly known
as distantly and modestly with the opposite sex, they are
not of ME for God has requested each and every individual's mind and attention, their life and devotion, their
ideas and opinons all to be concentrated on the Fundamental. . . ." [2]

In even the simplest matters, his God-intoxicated megalomania reveals itself. The following letter, written to a social
worker in connection with getting a job for a certain Mr.
Banner, is typical:

"Your letter of the 16th at hand, to which I wish to
say I will be glad to help Mr. Banner to secure a position,
and will appreciate you or he sending ME information
as to the kind of work he is capable and competent in
doing.
"With sincere wishes to you and to all who may be
concerned, this leaves ME desiring each and all to be the

[1] *The New Day*, Vol. II, No. 17, April 28, 1938, A.D.F.D.
[2] *The New Day*, May 11, 1938, A.D.F.D., p. 50.

same,—as I AM Eternally Well, Healthy, Joyful, Peaceful, Lively, Loving, Successful, Prosperous and Happy in Spirit, Body and Mind and in every organ, muscle, sinew, vein and bone and even in every atom, fibre and cell of MY bodily Form.

"Respectfully and Sincere, I am

"(Signed) REV. M. J. DIVINE

"(*Better known as FATHER DI-VINE the Creator and Establisher of Righteousness, Truth and Justice among all mankind.*)"

All the angels and the "children" who are members of the movement, but who have not yet become angels, believe in Divine as much as Divine does in himself. Mr. Mead gives a vivid picture of how the Divineites act and also of this squat, little man, whose everlastingly restless, beady eyes are supposed to shine with a beatific radiance:

"Last night I shook hands with God and watched him eat. He seemed quite human . . . in the way he handled his knife and fork, and I might have thought him just a man had it not been for the buxom woman at my side who kept shouting, 'Father Divine, he God. God Almighty, he never born. He never die. God Almighty. Oh, my God, my God.' And five hundred others, black, brown and white, echoed her words in a tireless, monotonous chant for three solid hours, while they waited in the modest basement in Harlem for God to honor them with his presence. They screamed out their love of Father to the accompaniment of tunes borrowed brazenly from old gospel hymns and hot-stuff jazz. There were parodies on 'My Buddy,' 'The Music Goes Round and Round,' and 'I Surrender All.' They danced as they sang; some closed their eyes and swayed gently where they stood; some twisted their bodies and flung themselves all over the place with an African abandon. . . . They never wearied of it. They never slowed down. . . . A seventeen year old girl went swirling around the room with her eyes clamped shut, careening into tables and breaking chairs and smashing china and tumbling to the floor with a crash. . . . When they caught sight of Father coming down the basement stairs, they piled scream on scream: 'God. O God. Father. Father. Father.' " [1]

The following description, revealing another aspect of the Divine kingdom, is equally interesting:

"Thirty or thirty-five guests sat down to this feast. Verinda (a Negro maid who spent her two weeks vacation at Father Divine's place) noticed that all the silverware, glassware, china, and linen were perfectly matched in style and design. Her amazement increased when the viands appeared. Seated at the head of the table, Father blessed each dish by placing a fork or serving spoon in it. Meanwhile he made a rite of pouring the coffee and passing the cups. For quantity and quality of food, Verinda confessed later, she had never seen the equal. Heaping platters of chicken and ham were passed down the table; casseroles of beef stew, an endless procession of steaming vegetables — corn, tomatoes, mashed potatoes, rice, hominy, beans, peas, salads—cole slaw and lettuce. Then followed ice cream, and 'two enormous cakes, oval-shaped and as large in diameter as automobile tires, but higher,' pies and a whole cheese." [2]

Despite all this display of food, talk, dancing, soul-purging, feet-stamping, hallelujahing, hand-waving, God-crying, and what not, the Divine service, at mealtime or worshiptime, is a severely unornate and unextravagant affair. Divine hates the paraphernalia of ecclesiasticism: flaming robes, glittering diadems, dull black suits, sepulchral collars buttoned backward, incense-flingers, bell-tollers, artifically tutored choirs, paid soloists and quartets, because in his eyes all this is synthetic and not authentic, material and not spiritual. He believes in a simple, humble service, with no man-made additions or embel-

[1] Frank S. Mead: "God in Harlem," Christian Century, Aug. 26, 1936, p. 1133.
[2] Robert Allerton Parker: The Incredible Messiah.

lishments. He will have none of them. He wants his followers and converts to appear in their natural clothes and to speak as they are and not as they would like others to think they are. He will abide no form of fake, affectation, or artifice. Since he is God and is a simple man, he wants all his followers to be simple, plain, and unarrogant in bearing or posture.

These banquet festivals of Divine are very much like the love feasts of Beissel's Ephrata group. The food and drink is blessed, and those who partake of them are supposed to feel that same sense of spiritual intimacy and ecstasy that Christ's apostles did when they ate at the same table with the Master. Spiritual, not physical, love is exalted and after the food is consumed, that love radiates from the angels in an incandescent variety of forms. Some sing, some dance, some speak in strange, unborn tongues, and Divine himself, his enthusiasm mounting into hysteria, flings words about which ricochet up and down the vast hall like bullets of weird omen. At times, in his religious excitement, his English will become so distorted and agglutinative that it is scarcely more than mystical mumbo-jumbo. If his twisted, gnarled, and hunchbacked words conveyed communicable meaning, Divine would be regarded as the greatest neologist in the English language. For minutes at a time he will talk as if to himself, and his speech will become consummate incoherency.

An excellent example of his incoherence is to be found in this passage, culled from Divine's paper:

"As I say I have explained, I am re-saying it again— the Person may be a reality apparently the Person is the reflector of the Inspirator, but the Inspirator is the One who inspires through Whom your inspirations come. The Person will reflect in you and the Inspirator will demonstrate in you. You will observe the demonstration of the Impersonal, the Demonstrator and the Inspirator—the one who is inspiring you, reflecting and impressing in your personality and in your individuality and in the personality and individualities of others. But you must not bind yourself from your thoughts to the mortal versionated point of view as you might observe it; for this is the reflection merely as a sketch and a reflection of the Impersonal reflecting something to the Person, for the Person cannot observe it saving that it is expressed in individualities, personalities, and persons." [1]

A MODERNIST IN WORDS

But his followers are not concerned with meaning, coherence, or intelligibility—rather with their opposites; and Father Divine is no amateur in satisfying them on that score. Speech, Divine believes, is an emanation of the soul, subject to no laws of man, and certainly not to those of grammarians and lexicologists. Without knowing it, he is, in language at least, akin to the expressionist, cubist, and vorticist schools of art, and of the Dadaist school of writing, all of whose disciples believe that what is most important is that the individual *express* himself regardless of whether he communicates himself to others. They developed an artistic and verbal jabberwockie, which became so unintelligible and untranslatable that not even Divine could surpass it. Like Divine, they believed in acetylinizing the unconscious, and then excavating it to the surface, where all its curious cracks and crevices, its illogical indentations and fissured contours could be converted into art. The conscious mind was too commonplace to interest them. It was the backwash of the obvious. Without possessing their esthetic and psychological erudition, Divine likewise believes in the same thing, the superiority of the inner or unconscious mind, and his appeal is to that rather than to the conscious mind, where man is a slave to temptation and evil. The kingdom of heaven living in every human creature is in that subconscious mind, where it is emancipated from all the corruptions of civilization.

[1] *The New Day*, May 12, 1938, p. 25.

Divine a Freudian

Without knowing it, and certainly without having read Freud, Divine is more than a little of a Freudian in his concern with the subconscious mentality. He himself, as God, is the great Censor, as Freud liked to describe the inhibiting force in the mind, which prevents the subconscious from expressing itself as an independent reality. Only in sleep, Freud contended, did the censor relax his asphyxiating grip upon the subconscious mind, which then manifested its character in dreams. Father Divine, as the great Censor, knows how and when to relax and release the subconscious minds of his followers, and, utilizing his hypnotic technique, frees their unconscious minds and spurs them to speech and sacrifice. His confessionals are famous for their revelations. Divine constantly insists upon his angels relaxing their "conscious mentality" and opening the windows of their "higher intuition" (subconscious mind), so that the winds of heaven can sweep in. Men who have been killers, felons of divers varieties, gangsters, kidnapers, pimps, petty thieves, jail-breakers; women who have been baby-snatchers, burglars, house-crooks, professional prostitutes, disease-ridden street-walkers—all have confessed their sins, and many of them, at Father Divine's behest, have given themselves up to the police, confessed their crime to the judge, accepted imprisonment without a murmur, and ended their stay with their Father's words: "Peace, it's wonderful."

Divine has always kept in touch with these followers, sending them gifts and letters from time to time, and getting their relatives to see them, or at least write to them and mail or bring them presents, too, if possible. Few if any of these followers have ever deserted the faith. Not all the suffering of prison could conquer their souls. And when they return, regardless of how many years have elapsed, it is as purged creatures; and they take their seats among the rest of the heavenly hierarchy, face to face with God.

III

Like all the utopian movements, the Divine contingent has recorded its miracles, embroidered its legends, hallowed its songs, exalted its myths. Above the chair in which Divine sits is the simple word "God," and in the minds of the angels and children that word stands out as an eternal symbol. These followers are no longer earthy bipeds, victims of the mundane laws of gravity, or subject to the evils of disease and death; they are heavenly creatures who are one with God, walk upon carpets framed with clouds, and float among skies ethereal and limitless. When Divine tells them that "it is a privilege to live in the ACTUAL PRESENCE OF GOD," they cry back in unison, "Father Divine is God." They are not millennialists, as were most of the German utopian colonists, because they believe the millennium has already come in the body and spirit of Father Divine, and that heaven is here and now and not hereafter—for, as Father Divine says, there is no hereafter.

Divine's movement, it is reasonable to predict, will not come to an end because of financial bankruptcy, as so many of the earlier utopian colonies did, but through the death of Divine himself. The death of Divine would rob the movement of all meaning and significance; death does not exist for the Divineists and if their God should die, never to rise again, the movement itself could not survive it; it would become a dead thing, and its ashes would be swept away by the evil winds of distress and disaster.

CHAPTER XX

Epilogue

The history of these utopian colonies, extending from that of Labadie's to Divine's, reads like the odyssey of an ancient people. Despite their advanced conception of a co-operative society, they were far more ancient than modern in their religious perspective. They wanted to go backward, not forward, in their struggle for perfection. The vast majority of them were, as we have seen, Christian in outlook; they yearned to go back to Christ, return to primitive Christianity, to the simple communal life of the apostles; they loathed the Churchianity that conquered at the council of Nicaea, loathed its bureaucratic controls, and all the red tape designed to impede contact with Jesus. These utopians were religous democrats, whereas the leaders of the organized Church were clerical autocrats. Like the early, primitive Christians, most of the religious utopians were millennialists, more concerned with preparing themselves for the next world than for this. They did their work efficiently enough, but their eyes were on God rather than the soil. They watched the skies for signs of Christ's return, and by calculations more weird than hieroglyphics, established in many cases dates for the happy event. No wonder that they were so democratic, so contemptuous of class distinctions, so free of economic and social prejudices.

After all, Christ was one of the world's first democrats. He it was who said that God was concerned with every hair upon every being's head, regardless of whether he was king or slave, rich or poor, Jew or Gentile, Greek or barbarian. This was strange doctrine in the world of those days. The Egyptians, the Babylonians, the Assyrians, the Hyksos, the Ethiopians, the Greeks and Romans, believed in no such fantastic, revolutionary creed. They did not believe, even in their religions, in the equality of men, but in their inequality.

In the conflict between the Christian attitude and the pagan, the presence of social struggle is immediately patent. The contrast between the attitudes and personalities of Petronius and Paul brings it out in sharp relief. Christianity was the religion, in the beginning, of the oppressed masses, the swarming multitudes for whom the enchantment of another world became a magnetic incentive. It was the religion of the underdog. Its wild manias, its asceticisms, its burning denunciations of the flesh and the devil, were the contributions of the Pauline creed. They captured the emotions of the masses as completely as the slogans of Lenin captured the Russian masses in 1917. Paul, a reactionary in earthly vision was, nevertheless, in his ability to meet the demands of the millions, the Lenin of his day. Petronius, on the other hand, an exemplar of the best in the upper-class culture of his period, disdained the Pauline ideas as the obscene salvos of the mob. Petronius was a pagan. He viewed Christianity with the incurious contempt of the intellectual. It was a religion for plebeians and slaves. Why should any man advocate asceticism when the world offered him wealth? Why should he seek pain when life offered him the pleasant anodynes of beauty and loveliness? In this contrast between Paul and Petronius we find the contrast not of two men, but of two cultures, of two philosophies, arising from two different sides of the social struggle of their era.

In later centuries when Christianity had become the religion of the ruling classes, it changed like a chameleon. As the conditions of life altered, the seemingly inexorable basis of its philosophy had to be modified. That has been the vast contradiction involved in the history of the Christian Church. Beginning as a religion of the lower classes, it has become bureaucratic, and has stultified its meaning by trying to reconcile its upper-class practices with its lower-class convictions.

Ever since, Christianity has been divided into two mainstreams: the democratic and the bureaucratic. The utopian groups, in Europe as well as in America, have belonged to the democratic stream, whereas the organized denominations have belonged to the bureaucratic. The democratic element represented the poorer element, the insecure; the bureaucratic element the wealthier, the secure. The economic conditions of society during the times of Christ were terrifyingly desperate. Life could offer neither palliative nor aspiration. And men of the lower classes, slaves and freedmen, perforce, turned to another world with the gesture of a falling warrior. It was their only escape. It fed them with a promise of paradise, an other-worldly utopia. A spiritual mania was created. It swept from city to city, and province to province, winging itself upon the wild enthusiasms of men and women suddenly seized by the mad prophecies of a delirious dream. Persecution only made it thrive the more. At length, straggling members of the upper classes, sick with the decay of their own life, came within its spell. The end of the world was at hand. A new world, fresh with eternal peace, was about to dawn. It was a world beyond the skies, a paradise of light. Men believed these things. They became part of their life. They were willing to die for them. "Everything for the new world," became their cry. This world was of but a moment; but that world was of eternity. Martyrdom became an obsession. The lion's roar could not frighten souls dedicated to the destruction of the flesh.

It was these men who believed in the return of Christ, in the imminence of the millennium. It was these men in Europe who carried down through the centuries the democratic tradition, and later transported it to America. Among its leaders were John Ball, the revolutionary English cleric, Thomas Munzer, the challenger of Luther, Johann Huss, who gave his life that his doctrine might live; and among the groups who suffered in order that that tradition might not die were the Waldensians, the Albigensians, the Taborites, the Huterites, the Labadists, the Quakers, the Levellers, the Diggers, Harrison's Fifth Monarchy Men, the Pilgrims, and many others. With the exception of a few colonies, America was born of this democratic religious tradition.

These utopian colonists, however, went further than the denominational democrats, because they believed in adopting the apostolic way of life, and living collectively instead of individualistically; the latter believed that the apostolic way of life was impracticable in the existing world, and that one had to live individualistically in order to survive and succeed.

II

Peculiarly enough, as we have observed, primitive Christianity was profoundly concerned with the problems of sex and celibacy. Perpetuating that tradition, almost all the religious utopian colonists exalted celibacy as an ideal. Sex became in their eyes a sin. As millennialists they condemned it. Sex perpetuated this world—it was, therefore, a device of evil. Castration sects sprang up. Men made themselves into eunuchs for Christ's sake. Men must consecrate themselves to the hereafter, and not to what is. Sex was an intrusion in a world that was about to end. And so continence became a virtue, and celibacy was exalted into a way of life. Sex was unclean in its worldliness. It lacked the purity of a heavenly vision. It was a joy of the body instead of the soul. The body now was an unclean sheath that enclosed an immortal soul. The body was to be despised, the soul cherished. The body died, but the soul lived on forever. Nakedness, because it emphasized the body and magnified its temptations, became sinful, and sexual intercourse, because it fed upon the body for its ecstasy and tended to reproduce its forms, was scorned as a craving born of the evil of the flesh. The saintly would never surrender to it. Even those, as Paul said, who could not constrain themselves, must never come to look upon their act as sweet and sinless.

The condemnations of sex, and the exaltation of celibacy, which so many of the religious utopians in America advocated, derived from that early Christian tradition.

III

It is a common belief among most social and historical thinkers in this country that the individualistic nature of American enterprise was an inevitable outgrowth of the expansive nature of the American environment with its elastic frontiers and inexhaustible resources. In contradiction to that hypothesis, it is illuminating to note that the Pilgrims, who were not communists at all, adopted a communal way of life in the beginning, because they believed they could survive more successfully that way. They forsook it only after they had paid back most of the debts they had contracted and found themselves safely ensconced in the arms of prosperity.[1]

Certain of the communist colonies in the new world, especially the non-millennialist ones, were founded by groups which were not communist in the old. Like the Pilgrims, they adopted a communist form of life in America because they found it more advantageous than an individualistic one. Incredible as it may seem to many, almost all these colonies prospered so long as they practiced what they preached. They failed when certain individuals violated their principles of economic faith, or when the younger generation no longer wished to perpetuate the traditions of the old. In short, it was not their communism which failed, but corrupting elements within the groups which vitiated their communist resolve.

It should not be forgotten, however, that such success was

[1] Bradford: *History of the Plymouth Plantation* (1606-1646), p. 65.

acquired at a spiritually exorbitant price. All individuals had to sacrifice themselves to the cause, dedicate themselves to the apostolic ideal. Their individualities were immolated upon the altar of group success. They ceased to be individuals, became parts of a social organization. They were willing to resign individual desires for the greater good of the social whole. Without such sacrifices, none of the religious communist colonies would or could have succeeded. Their temporary triumphs were dependent upon their vision; few of them ever deserted it. When they did, they failed—as all things do when vision dies.

The economic colonies, on the other hand, possessed the same vision but did not possess the same resolution. They sought utopia but too many of their followers were not utopian. They did not have the faith to continue the struggle when it became too bitter and severe. They believed in immediate and not in protracted prosperity. Most of them failed in days when they could have succeeded. The majority of them were born when America was still a predominantly agrarian country and their agrarian utopias could have fumbled their way toward economic security. A few of them did, but too many did not.

They were all, however, motivated by high ideals. They sought a better way of life for humanity as well as themselves. Practically everyone who came to settle in this country did so in order to find a better way of life but more for themselves than for humanity. The utopians wanted a new world which would be truly new, and they thought if they organized communities which were successful, the whole country in time would copy them. They were devoured, however, as the land about them congested into an industrial octopus.

Though they have died, their dream lives on. It can never die any more than the Christ myth of equality can ever die. Churches may abuse it, clergymen exploit it, but, in the end, humanity will exalt it.

Man can achieve a co-operative commonwealth in our industrial society, but he cannot do it in terms of an agrarian or theocratic utopia. It must be through an industrial democracy which would make democracy whole, include everyone in it without restriction or discrimination as to race, color, or creed.

APPENDIX

Unfortunately, it is impossible to include in this book a discussion of all the utopian colonies established in this country. There were, all told, over two hundred of them. What I have done has been to select from the multitude those which I consider the more important, the more significant, and the more exciting. The colonies which I have discussed in detail are not in all cases the most significant in terms of economic success, but they are, I believe, the most significant in terms of social direction.

This appendix is devoted to a brief discussion of other colonies which were important, but which I feel do not deserve the entire space of a chapter. Of all the strange, curious, fantastic, and optimistic colonies founded here, those which challenged most attention were the Fourieristic. It is hard to say how many colonies of different origin deserve mention. I cannot deal with all of them, but in these final notes I shall concern myself, for the sake of those scholastically interested in the subject, with a few details about a small number of the others.

Most important of all are the Icarian colonies, which were not Fourieristic. They were really all one colony but the vicissitudes of circumstance separated them and, for that reason, they could very well be classified as separate. We shall not do so, however, because our concern is mainly with the ideas and ideals of Etienne Cabet, the founder of all the Icarian groups in the new as well as the old world. He conceived of their structure and significance in terms of their socialistic contribution to cultural life. Icaria, as Charles Gray wrote, was "at one time . . . probably the greatest socialistic enterprise

351

the world has ever seen, numbering its enthusiastic admirers
and supporters by the thousands. At no period of its life in
America did Icaria boast so large a membership as many other
socialistic communities . . . indeed the zenith of its prosperity
seems to have been reached before the Icarians departed from
France." [1]

The Icarian ventures were all inspired by the compulsive and
spiritually coercive doctrines of Etienne Cabet. From a Marxian point of view he belonged among the utopian socialists.
His original ideas sprang from the left-wing section of the
French Revolution. His leading inspirations were Babeuf
and Robert Owen, the latter of whom most likely fortified his
dream of the possibility of realizing his vision of society in the
new world. This quotation from Cabet's own writing is unforgettably typical of the man and also of his social concept:

"Let us replace the old world by a new one, the reign of
wickedness and Satan by the reign of goodness and God;
let us replace darkness by light, injustice by justice, domination and slavery by emancipation and freedom. Let us
substitute the well-being of all for the excessive opulence
of a privileged minority who possess almost all the wealth
without working. Let us replace the old religion—a mixture of superstition, intolerance, and fanaticism—by a
reasonable religion that shall lead men to love and help
each other. Let us replace individual ownership, the
source of all abuses, by social, communal, undivided
ownership, which has none of the disadvantages of the
other kind and is infinitely more productive of utility for
all. In short, the old form of society is based upon individualism: let us base the new form upon communist
fraternity, equality, and liberty."

Like so many utopians, especially those of a Gallic character,
Cabet lived closer to fiction than to fact. The very way in
which he planned his communities confirms the truth of that
conclusion. His first expedition was catastrophically un-

[1] Charles Gray: *Annals of Iowa*, Vol. VI, No. 2, 1903, p. 107.

happy. Although he considered it a scientifically organized expedition with very little likelihood of failure, nothing that it attempted succeeded. First of all, Cabet himself did not accompany the party; he remained in France, where he hoped to schedule future expeditions and gain additional advantages for this one. The expedition left Havre in February, 1848, and arrived forty-five days later in New Orleans, where it learned of the revolution which had occurred in France. Although most of the members now felt that they had made a mistake in leaving France, since Icaria might have been constructed in their native country instead of in a strange new world, they were willing to continue their pilgrimage to Cabet's Promised Land, far into the interior of Louisiana. Men and women died of sundry diseases, food was insufficient, the waters about were polluted with germs, and misery spread like the wings of some strange bird across the face of the country. Finally, a decimated group, they began to quarrel with one another. Even when the second group arrived, there was little chance of peace; wherever failure descends, peace vanishes. And so it was not long before the two groups began their weary trek back to New Orleans, where after considerable anxiety and delay their leader, Cabet, put in appearance, only to be shocked at what little remained of his original cohorts.[1] He must have felt somewhat like Napoleon when he saw what was left of his soldiers after the bridge of Beresina had sunk beneath them and left only the fragments of what had been the Grand Army of France. Cabet could not believe what he saw. It broke his heart and almost shattered his dream.

But Cabet, though ultimately a failure in his colonial utopias, did not know what failure was in these middle-aged days of his life. It was only later, when the dusk of life was coming on, and one failure mounted upon another, that he realized

[1] For part of this specific information in this immediate connection, I am indebted to Charles Gide's *Communist and Co-operative Colonies,* pp. 132-137.

that his work had been built upon sands more footless than the wind.   Before he recognized that failure, however, he led his first followers into Texas, where Robert Owen advised him to retreat, but his luck there was no better than that of his votaries in Louisiana.

Cabet's colonies were founded upon his dream of utopia, similar to many of the other dreams of utopia conceived and invented by different humanitarians.   Cabet wanted people, or let us say his devotees, to sacrifice their individual interests for the common whole.   His vision of utopia was first expressed in his novel, *Voyage en Icarie*, which ran riotous with romance, and which changed the hearts and minds of myriads. In it he voiced his protest against the society of his time, the impediments which held it down, the manacles which enslaved it.   He wanted a new, a free society which had no such impediments or fetters.   He desired a utopian, a communist society. All this he expressed in his novel, or romance, or call it what you will.   The followers who flocked to him were not dissimilar from those who gathered into the religious camps which flared up like small fires over the American landscape, glowing for a time, glimmering, smoldering, and slowly, ever so slowly, going out.

His vision of the new world, especially the North American aspect of it, was as romantic as that of a religious prophet. People in other countries became fascinated by it, and some tried to construct blurred carbon copies of it.   In England there was Ebenezer Howard, who built his city of Letchworth upon the Icarian communist model.   Cabet's vision, however, was not confined to towns or cities, but was as infinite as the American horizon.   He expected, ultimately, to conquer the new continent with his ideas.

The organization of the Icarian societies was not greatly different from the other utopian groups.   In Cabet's communities there was, as he himself said, "no opulence, but also no poverty . . . neither rich nor poor, neither rulers nor ruled,

no anxiety or worry, no crime or police, and no trials or tribu-
nals. . . . The work is organized, free, unpaid, with no money
and no other compulsion than the sense of duty to the
community. We enjoy the produce in common, according to
the needs of each on the principle of fraternity and equality,
with no special privileges for anyone." [1]

Curiously enough, his leading colony was founded in the
city of Nauvoo, which the Mormons had been forced to desert
when their enemies threatened to annihilate them; if he and
his followers did not make of Nauvoo what the Mormons did,
they converted it, at least for a time, into a living and pleasant
place. After Cabet returned to France, however, to meet a
charge of fraud, which a few of his dissentient followers had
filed against him, differences and disagreements among the
colonists multiplied; when Cabet returned, acquitted of the
charge, he found a far less united group. Secession set in,
Cabet was defeated at an election, and forced out of his position of control in the colony. Then the strife became violent;
force was resorted to and the chaos which resulted undermined
the vitality of the enterprise. Even Cabet himself was guilty
of a large measure of chicanery in his vain attempt to hold
power in the colony. Finally Cabet and his minority left
Nauvoo, perforce, and went to St. Louis, where Cabet in 1856
died of an apoplectic stroke. His death was a severe blow
to his followers; in France the majority party, which remained
in Nauvoo, was condemned as a menace and blamed for Cabet's
untimely death. Fury mounted into frenzy, and one votary,
a German named Fritz Bauer, killed himself out of sheer
despair.[2] The Nauvoo group, though weakened by the schism,
managed to continue until 1860, at which time it moved to
Iowa, where it was able to survive for over a decade; later
the youths, revolting against their elders, founded still another

[1] Quotation from Cabet, excerpted from Gide, *op. cit.*, p. 138.
[2] Albert Shaw: *Icaria, A Chapter in the History of Communism*, 1884,
p. 67.

colony called "Icarian Hope." After this colony failed, there
was still one more Icarian venture attempted and that was
entitled, "New Icaria." All told, the Icarian groups lasted
from 1848 to 1898.[1]

As a final word about the early Icarian communities, it
should be said that, unlike most of the utopian colonies, marriage was extolled by them and celibacy condemned. The
sentiments expressed by one of their leaders are typical of the
attitude of the Icarians in general:

> "Marriage is obligatory here; that is to say, celibacy
> is considered an anomalous condition, contrary to nature,
> save when the number of members is so limited as to pre-
> vent the celibates, men and women, from readily finding
> suitable mates."[2]

The North American Phalanx

Of all the Fourieristic colonies, the North American Phalanx was the most widely celebrated and the most successful.
Brook Farm, of course, was more internationally known, but
it adopted Fourierism, as we have seen, toward the end rather
than at the beginning of its career. The North American
Phalanx was more Fourieristic than Brook Farm or most, if
not all, the Fourier colonies founded in the United States. It
had also the advantage of being the last of the Fourier colonies
which made it possible for it to profit from the defects of the
earlier groups. Sylvania, which was the first of the phalanxes,
and the special favorite of Greeley, achieved no such longevity.
Sylvania began with one hundred and fifty people, but
dwindled rapidly. Even the Wisconsin Phalanx, which was
one of the most interesting, could not compete in importance
with the North American.

The North American Phalanx, was one of Brisbane's creations; it was established in 1843 and lasted more than a decade.

---

[1] Gide: *op. cit.*, p. 149.
[2] Hinds: *op. cit.*, p. 73.

Its roots were American, even though its ideas were European. The very name of the colony is suggestive of its continental aspiration. It included all North America within its perspective. It was a macrocosmic, not a microcosmic, enterprise. If it failed to realize the magnitude and magnificence of its concepts, it was not because the latter were lacking in vision or dream. They believed that all North America could be modeled in its image.

Noyes called this colony "the test experiment on which Fourierism practically staked its all in this country." [1] Greeley invested heavily in it and others contributed their share. The founders were as optimistic as those who created Brook Farm. Like some of the other colonies, it suffered from religious conflict, from inadequacy of rewards, and various forms of material destruction.[2] Its original leaders, however, Albert Brisbane, Horace Greeley, Osborn, McDaniel, Edward Giley, J. T. Smith, and Frederick Grain, did not early lose faith in their experiment. The place in which the colony was settled was Redbank, New Jersey, and there it was that all these apostles of a Fourieristic world devoted their best energies to create a true utopia.[3]

Charles Sears, one of the founders of the North American Phalanx, described the organization of the colony as follows:

"Among those who, after following Brisbane's expositions, became interested in the idea of social progress, were a few persons from New York, Troy, Catskill and Albany, who from reading an interchange of views were induced to unite in an organization for the purpose of deliberately and methodically investigating the doctrines of Fourier's social reform, as expounded by Albert Brisbane. . . . These persons in April, 1843, organized themselves into the Albany Branch of the North American Phalanx, opened a correspondence with Brisbane, Greeley,

[1] Noyes: *op. cit.*, p. 449.
[2] Hinds: *op. cit.*, p. 248.
[3] Charles Sears: *The North American Phalanx*, 1886, p. 4.

Channing, Ripley and others. During the summer a commission was appointed (Brisbane and Allan Warden) to explore the country, particularly near New York and Philadelphia, for a suitable site. . . . A site was selected in Monmouth County, about forty miles south of New York City, and on August 13th, 1843 . . . the North American Phalanx was organized by adopting a constitution and subscribing to a covenant to invest in capital stock. The number of subscribers to the stock was disappointingly few, only ten qualifying, with an aggregate subscription of $8,000. This by common consent was the absolute minimum of men and means." [1]

Sears also tells of the opposition which the enterprise met with from the neighbors in the community and from the press. Its members were denounced as madmen, idiots, and even felons. The productivity of its mills, however, manufacturing in such prodigality rye, wheat, flour, cornmeal, and hominy, convinced the public that there must be some sense to the phalanx plan. Its followers as well as its leaders knew what they were about; they worked with co-operative intelligence and not by the individualistic trial-and-error approach. It was not long, consequently, before the farmers in the surrounding countryside came to envy as well as scorn the Redbankers. As in the case of Brook Farm, a vast fire caused the dissolution of the enterprise. [2]

The number of Fourieristic phalanxes established in America is hard to calculate. [3] The Skaneateles Community, to which we have already alluded, was one of the phalanxes, although for a considerable time it repudiated any relationship

---

[1] Quotation taken from Norma Lippincott Swann: "The North American Phalanx," *Monmouth County Historical Association Bulletin,* Vol. I, No. 1, May, 1935, p. 49.

[2] Sears, *op. cit.,* p. 16.

[3] The man who has made the most thorough study of Fourieristic doctrine in terms of its American Phalanxes and colonies is Arthur Eugene Bestor, Jr., of Columbia University. I am deeply indebted to Mr. Bestor for the generous privilege which he extended me of reading his study of the Fourier colonies in manuscript form. It is to be called *American Phalanxes,* and will be published within the next year.

with Fourier. Its survival was brief. The New York *Tribune* complimented their efforts in 1845:

> "They have bought a large farm and partly paid for it, giving a mortgage for the balance due. But our existing laws do not allow them to hold their property as a Community, so that they lie at the mercy of every unprincipled sharper who can get possession of any part of their goods, and have thus lost a considerable portion of their slender means—at one time by a great sacrifice narrowly escaping utter ruin. They laid their case before the last legislature and asked a charter to enable them to hold and protect their property, but the cry of 'Infidel,' 'Fanny Wright,' &c., was raised against them, and their prayer was rejected. . . . Now all they ask ought to be given them by the general laws of the State." [1]

There was the Sodus Bay venture, which began in the spring of 1844 and excited the interest of so many of the utopians of that time. Religious differences, according to Charles A. Dana and A. J. MacDonald, were the tragic factors which disrupted the community. Dana declared that:

> "Religious differences, pressed in an intolerant manner on both sides, had at the time of our visit, produced entire uncertainty as to future operations, and carried disorder to its height." [2]

Then there was the Bloomfield Union Association, which was a derivative from the Sodus Bay enterprise. Both were Rochester creations, with the bad conditions of 1843 providing their best inspiration. Rochester was a leading milling center, but it could not survive the depression of 1837, and many of the people in the vicinity were attracted by the possibilities of Fourieristic co-operation. Theron C. Leland, Benjamin Fish, and Edwin A. Stillman, the last of whom was an engineer and the most practical of the three, were the leaders of the enterprise.

[1] *Ibid.*, p. 279.
[2] *Ibid.*, p. 220.

To recount the history of all the other Fourier ventures in a volume which aims at interpretation rather than at recitation, is needless.   Suffice it to say that, despite their eager hopes and valiant efforts, all these colonies failed.   But it was not because they were lacking in enthusiasm or faith or vision of the dream of a greater race, which has charged men through the ages, but because the industrial age overtook them and rendered their dream a futility.   In the late years of the century these colonies had little to draw from for their sustenance.   The railroads, business advance, technological progress, rendered their existence impossible.   They were part of an agrarian but not of an industrial age.   They could survive in a barter or even a small business economy, but not in a big business era.

Nevertheless, in general they were happy enterprises.   The people who founded them believed in expression rather than repression, in joy rather than in pain.   "I have often heard strangers remark upon the cheerfulness and elasticity of spirit which struck them on visiting our little association at Brook Farm," wrote Ripley after his visit to the North American Phalanx, "and here I found the same thing so strongly displayed that in conversing with our new friends it seemed as if they were the same I had left at home [in Brook Farm]."   As Constance Rourke noted, in her description of the North American Phalanx, "labor . . . had a classic air; about the workers hung something simple, merry, secure." [1]   Fredrika Bremer, who visited the colony in person, observed that "music as yet in the Phalanstery is merely a babe in swaddling clothes, as they regard their work as play." [2]

II

In addition to the Fourier colonies there were scores of other co-operative colonies.   (Of course, as in the Northwest, California, and elsewhere, even today there are numerous con-

[1] Constance Rourke: *Trumpets of Jubilee,* 1927, p. 276.
[2] Fredrika Bremer: *Homes in the New World.* 1853, Vol. I, p. 82.

sumer co-operatives that are remarkably successful, but this book is not concerned with them because they are not interested in communal living or spiritual reform.) [1] Many of the communal colonies not mentioned hitherto were interesting, one in this way, one in that, but not exciting or important enough to deserve more than brief consideraticn. There were the Dukhobors (often spelt Doukhobours), who came to the new world after being persecuted for over a century in Russia; they settled in Canada and established co-operative communities there which continue to thrive.[2] Like many of the other communities described, they scheduled their lives in accordance with their social ideal. They believe that love is the great need of the world, love of everything: humans, animals, insects. J. S. Dunn describes an interesting experience with them in that connection:

"I had a demonstration of the repugnance the Doukohbours have for killing anything. I saw a nest of tent caterpillars sunning themselves on the limb of an apple tree, and called to two of the [Doukhobour] youths with

[1] For the reader interested in this phase of co-operative endeavor, see Harlan Randall's *Consumers Co-operative Adventures Case Studies*, and Charles Gide's *Consumers Co-operative Societies*. There is, for example, the Co-operative League of the United States (Randall: pp. 349, 350), with branches in New York, Chicago, Minneapolis, Los Angeles, Berkeley, California, Amarillo, Texas, Kansas City, Missouri, Columbus, Ohio, Seattle, Washington, Springfield, Massachusetts, Lansing, Michigan, St. Paul, Minnesota, and numerous other cities. In addition, there are Recreation Co-operatives, Life Association Co-operatives, Fire Insurance Co-operatives, Housing Co-operatives. "The Consumers Co-operative Movement," Mr. Randall says, "represents one form of economic democracy." Better still, in illustrating the function of these co-operatives, is his description of Cloquet Co-operative Society. "Its purpose," he writes, "is to supply its members with food, clothing, fuel and other necessities as economically as possible." (*Ibid.*, pp. 79, 80.)

[2] The most recent and one of the most revealing books about the Dukhobors is J. F. C. Wright's *Slava Bohu*, 1940, which describes their essential principle, quoting a Dukhobor: "All ownership of property should be abolished, and no one must exploit the labor of another on the land. There should be no rent, no taxes." Later the same Dukhobor says: "We are the ringing bells, the scouts on the hilltops, clearing the way for freedom." (P. 326.)

me to get something to kill them; the boys looked but would not act, so I went after the pests. . . . The boys could not look . . . and turned away in mute but horrified protest." [1]

The Dukhobors are remarkable gardeners, gifted craftsmen, and skilled mechanics. Like the Mennonites and Amish who settled in the United States, they are opposed to alcohol and tobacco, and are determined pacifists. In addition, there are the House of David enthusiasts, who settled in Benton Harbor, Michigan, and who cling still to the millennialist creed. They believe, like the old Millerites, that they shall never experience death because God will come down like Elijah in a cloud of fire and chariot them to heaven. Despite that belief, and also the fact that they wear beards which grow reprehensibly long and fiercely frizzled at the edges, they are best known to the American public for their baseball team. Like so many millennialist colonies, they are primitive Christians and advocate "an apostolic commonwealth wherein all labor is for the common good." [2]

Among other communal settlements still extant is Commonwealth College, which is well-known to the radical movement in this country. W. E. Zeuch was the experimental and progressive academician who organized the Commonwealth College and Academy in California as part of the Llano Colony, of which mention will be made later. Mena, Arkansas, is its present home, and to it flock at divers intervals political radicals of various descriptions, some to visit, some to lecture, some to live. One of its most progressive leaders was Lucien Koch, who is no longer connected with it. Many of its students have become active and influential in the labor movement and sometimes in radical political parties. For a time it suffered from domination by the American Communist Party, but

---

[1] Quotation excerpted from Ernest S. Wooster: *Communities of the Past and Present*, 1924, p. 111.

[2] *Ibid.*, p. 116.

today it has largely escaped that virus. In order to survive, it has fought off with inspiring courage Vigilantes, Ku Kluxers, and other reactionary elements. Unfortunately, it has never been successful, as so many of the other communal projects were, as an economic project.[1]

Then, too, there were strange fellows walking up and down the skyline, hitch-hikers from eternity, who were founding new groups and colonies here and there on virgin soil. One of the most arresting of these was Andreas Bernardus Smolniker, a professor and author, and the founder of the Peace Union Settlement,[2] who declared that he was the "Ambassador Extraordinary of Christ and Apostle of Peace." In addition, there were Swedenborgians, who believed they saw the spirit of Jesus walking upon the hills at dusk in the form of their leader, and who, when they became dominant in a colony as in the Leraysville Phalanx, converted it into a garden of goodness. There was Equality, a community founded by Socialists which failed because the members did not understand what socialism meant in practice. Adonai-Shomo was a co-operative community established by some of the followers of Janson, the Swedish Christ, which lasted several decades, despite internal dissension that finally undermined it. Howland, the founder, believed, like Janson, that he would never die and when he did, it disillusioned his followers, who could no longer feel that eternal life was their heritage.

Other communities worthy of notation were the Ruskin Commonwealth, which grew out of the literary efforts of J. A. Wayland's paper, "The Coming Nation," Fairhope,[3] a still extant Single Tax settlement on Mobile Bay, Alabama, founded upon the doctrines of Henry George that "all men

[1] For details concerning its economic deficits, see *Monthly Labor Review*, U. S. Department of Labor, Vol. XXXII, No. 5, May, 1931.
[2] Rev. Alex. Kent: *Co-operative Communities in the United States*. Bulletin of the Dept. of Labor, No. 35, July 1901, 604.
[3] "The Single Tax Colony on Mobile Bay (1894-1904)," A Town Tract, 3.

have equal right to the use of the earth," Arden,[1] a Delaware
venture, built upon a guild program which has turned out
to be a tiny petty-bourgeois escape from Philadelphia, and The
Woman's Commonwealth organized in Belton, Texas,[2] in the
last quarter of the nineteenth century. The Woman's Commonwealth was unique in that it was an exclusively feminine
project; the members left their husbands, first organized a
boarding house which soon led to the establishment of a successful hotel, and finally in Waco they established a colony
which became a marked success. They later moved to Mount
Pleasant in the District of Columbia in 1898, and all told they
existed for over thirty years. They were a celibate group but
very tolerant of other amenities of life.

Best known, perhaps, of the twentieth-century communal
communities was Llano,[3] recently deceased. Llano, officially
known as the Llano Co-operative Colony, was founded by Job
Harriman, who was a leader in labor and socialist politics.
Harriman, in brief space, described vividly why he founded
Llano:

> "I was so impressed with the fact that the [Socialist]
> movement must have an economic foundation that I
> turned my attention to the study of means by which we
> could lay some such foundation, even though it be a small
> one as well as an experimental one. After two or three
> years I decided to try to establish a co-operative colony.
> This was undertaken in Los Angeles County, Cali-
> fornia . . . about 45 miles from Los Angeles due
> north. . . .
> "To accomplish this purpose I proposed to organize a
> joint-stock company, in which each member would pur-
> chase 2,000 shares, paying for the 1,000 in cash or prop-
> erty, and paying for the other 1,000 shares by labor. The
> reason for this was to give each an equal voting power.

[1] "Arden: A Social Experiment," *American City, Town and Country.*
Ed. July, 1916 gives an interesting picture of the early days of Arden—
especially see pp. 23-26.
[2] Kent: *op. cit.*. 602.
[3] *Ibid.*, 602, 603.

We provided that each member of the colony who was engaged in the work of the colony . . . should receive $4.00 a day. It was understood that those working in the colony should equally receive only as much as was necessary to feed and clothe them and $1.00 a day as payment on their stock after their other thousand shares should be paid for, and the balance was to accumulate as credit until the net returns from the colony should be sufficient to pay them.

"This would lay an economic foundation, as it seemed, of equal ownership and pay. We established at the first a social system which was free alike to all . . . whether it was dancing, moving pictures or what not.

"These three elements then—equal ownership, equal wage and equal social opportunities—were the fundamental principles of the colony.

"Having been a Socialist for 23 years and a believer in economic determinism and in the Marx philosophy of surplus value as determined by the social labor power necessary to produce products, and the belief in the materialistic conception of life, I assumed that if a co-operative colony could be established in which an environment were created that would afford each individual an equal advantage, then they would . . . react harmoniously to this environment and the extreme selfishness and greed . . . would be done away with. . . ."[1]

In the Louisiana settlement, which the Llano-ites established, everything went well until Job Harriman had to return to California and McCorkle became secretary and ran the community well-nigh into ruin. McCorkle was inefficient and, what was still worse, he was unco-operative. But somehow the colony managed, however unprogressively, to struggle on. Bob Brown, who lived there with his wife for ten months, describes it graphically:

"We were in the two hotel rooms on the ground floor. . . . The rooms were barely furnished like those of all hotels in this section of the sulky South, but the beds

[1] Wooster: *op. cit.,* p. 119.

were more comfortable than the average, sheets clean, and no Gideon Bible, thank God!

"We got up to breakfast with everybody when the big bell clanged, sharp and long at six o'clock. We lined up with a blue-nosed, shuffling lot, mostly old men. . . . A sweet faced old lady, Mother Wright, wiped the breakfast trays and handed them out to breakfasters as they passed—service as efficient as in a New York cafeteria. But the trays were battered and old, of tin soldered in spots. . . . It was pretty gloomy, that first breakfast of horse-bean coffee, corn bread and some kind of inedible mush, with only a driblet of milk and frugally measured-out sugar.

"To see Llano at its worst, get up in time to breakfast at the hotel. No more than a third of the colonists do. . . . These early breakfasters turned out to be the shock troops of co-operation. . . . Quite obviously there was nothing very cushy in this community of workers. . . ."[1]

Inefficiency continued to gnaw at the roots of the colony, and by November, 1937, developments had already taken on a sad shape. The end followed close after. Brown called it "a sinister Southern failure."[2] The finale, with its group splits, financial bankruptcy, and personal quarrels, was, alas, all too similar to that of many twentieth-century co-operative colonies. The time for agrarian utopias was over. The new century, with its new techniques, was in too solid a conspiracy against them.

[1] Bob Brown: *Can We Co-operate?* 1940, pp. 31-33.
[2] *Ibid.*, p. 226.

Acknowledgments

Grateful acknowledgment is made to the following publishers for permission to reprint material which is in copyright or of which they are the authorized publisher: *The American Mercury, The American Socialist,* Brigham Young University, Catholic University of America Press, *The Christian Century,* The Chronicle Company, Doubleday, Doran & Company, Inc., Gelber & Lilienthal, Farrar & Rinehart, Harper & Brothers, Houghton Mifflin Company, Indiana Historical Society, Johns Hopkins Press, Little, Brown and Company, Longmans, Green & Co., Inc., The Macmillan Company, *The New Day,* G. P. Putnam's Sons, Swarthmore College, W. G. Voliva, Zion City, Ill., *Western Pennsylvania Historical Magazine.*

INDEX

INDEX

Acrelius Israel, describes Ephratian service, 65-66
Adams, Maude, 153
Adonai-Shomo, 363
Advertiser (Buffalo), 213
Albigenses, the, 15
Alcott, Anna, quoted, 242, 246
Alcott, Bronson, interest in Brook Farm, 201, 210
    criticized by Hecker, 236
    founds Fruitlands, 236
    early life of, 237, 240
    beliefs and philosophy of, 237, 241-242, 243-245, 246
    characteristics of 237-239, 240
    role in American education, 239, 240, 241
    criticized and admired, 240-241
    Fruitlands unsuccessful, 246, 250-253
    life at Fruitlands, 247, 248-249
    returns to family, 251-252
    compared with Noyes, 261
Alcott, Mrs. Bronson, worries about husband, 247
    joined by Alcott, 251-252
Alcott, Louisa, Diary of, 242
    writes of father, 251-252
Alcott House, 246
Alwato, international language, 297
Amana, *see* Chapter VIII
Amanites, founding of colony, 111-112
    ceremonies of, 112
    beliefs of, 112, 114, 115
    hymns of, 113, 114
    sturdiness of, 114
    present-day colony, 115-116
"Amelia Palace," 165
Amish, 362
Andrews, Stephen Pearl, and Modern Times, 296-297
    and anarchist theory, 300-302, 303-305, 307-308
    defends views of Modern Times, 301-302
Andros, Governor, opposes Labadists, 28

Arden venture, 364
Atlantic, 69
Aurora, 69
Aurora, Oregon, 93, 94
Aurora colony established, 93-94
    Wolff leads caravan to, 94-95
    dissolved, 95-96
Avard, Dr., 161
Avenging Angels, 162

Babeuf, 352
Baker, George, 333-334. *See also* Father Divine
Baldwin, Peter, 221
Ball, John, 19, 255, 346
Ballou, Adin, describes Owen, 182
    interested in Brook Farm, 210
    corresponds with Ripley, 213
    ideals and convictions, 225-230, 232-233
    describes origin of Hopedale colony, 226
    organizes Hopedale, 231-232
    disagrees with Collins, 232
    a forceful character, 234, 235
Baltimore, Lord, 29
Banner, Mr., 337-338
Barclay, Robert, 40
Battle Axe and Weapons of War, The, 268
Battle Axe letter, 268-270
Battle of Crooked River, 139
Bayard, Petrus, 30
Beissel, Conrad, influence by Labadists, 40
    founds Ephrata, 54-56
    in Dunkard community, 55
    hymnologist and author, 56, 57, 67
    charges against, 57-58
    stresses unattractiveness and discomfort, 63-64
    (as Father Friedsam) described, 66
Bellamy, Edward, visits Mormons, 152
    writings of, 152
Bellers, John, 180

371

INDEX

Ostinelli, Frances, 203
Owen, Robert, beliefs and ideals,
    178-179, 180, 181-183, 190-193,
    194-195, 218
  background of, 179-180
  founds New Harmony colony, 181
  and "Boatload of Knowledge," 184
  one of first prohibitionists, 194
  believes in equality of sexes, 194
  failure of colony, 195-196
  and Brook Farm, 217-218
  criticized by Ballou, 229-230
  influences on Cabet, 352
Owen, Robert Dale, tries to carry
    on father's work, 195
  introduces advance divorce laws,
    195

Paine, Thomas, 289
  religious concepts of, 189-190
  and "rights of man," 298-299
Palmyra, New York, 128, 129
Parker, Theodore, 201, 223
Parsons, Anna, 221
Passavant, Rev. William, describes
    Rappite colony, 81
Patterson, Samuel, 79
Paul, 345
Peabody, Elizabeth, 199-200, 205
Peaceful Revolutionist, The, 295
Peace Union Settlement, 363
Pears, Thomas, 184
Pears, Mrs. Thomas, describes New
    Harmony, 184
Peasants' War, 20-21
Penn, William, writes of Labadists,
    38-39
  fails to convert Labadists, 39-40
  denounced by Kelpius, 50-51
Perfectionist, The, 265-266
Pestalozzi, Johann, 185
Petronius, 345
Phillipsburg, Pennsylvania, 84
Plato, 207, 243, 245
Plotinus, 207, 243, 245
Pompanazzi, Pietro, 188
Poor Konrad movement, 20
Powell, Commissioner, 164
Practical Christian, The, 230
Pratt, Minot, 220
Pratt, Orson, 156
Present, The, 211
Proclus, 242
"Promised Land, The," 335
Putney, Vermont, 258, 259

Putney colony, organization of, 259,
    262-263
  life in, 263-265
  aims and ambitions of, 267
Putney Corporation of Perfection-
    ists, 259

Quakers, attacked by Labadists, 37-
    38
  join Camisards, 98
  treated Indians well, 256

Rapp, Frederick, quoted, 73, 79
  letter of, 76-77
  important to colony, 77
Rapp, George, founds colony in
    Penn., 69-70
  beliefs of, 70-71, 74-76, 78, 82
  migrates to Indiana, 70
  moves colony to Economy, Penn.,
    70
  compared with Bimeler, 72
  communistic views, 78
  fear of steam engine, 81-82
Rappites, founding of, 69-70
  beliefs and practices of, 70-71, 78-
    79, 84-85
  life of, 73-74, 80-82
  and Rapp's conceptions, 74-76
  communism among, 78-80
  and Count Leon, 82-84
Redbank, New Jersey, 357
Reformation, the, 20
Revocation of Edict of Nantes, 97
Richards, Dr., 142
Richelieu, Cardinal, defends Laba-
    die, 21, 22
Rigdon, Sidney, becomes Mormon,
    137
  persecution of, 137, 138
  mobbed, 138
  becomes vice-president candidate
    for Mormons, 140
  accepts polygamy, 158
Ripley, George, beliefs of, 198, 200-
    201, 215-216
  founds Brook Farm, 199-200
  at Brook Farm, 203
  advanced school of, 204-205
  financial difficulties of, 210, 223
  and Fourierism, 211-218
  maintains religious independence,
    224
  writes about North American
    Phalanx, 360
Ripley, Sophia, 223-224, 253